Time in a Bottle

Historic Halifax Harbour From the Bottom Up

Bob Chaulk

Pottersfield Press, Lawrencetown Beach, Nova Scotia, Canada

National Library of Canada Cataloguing in Publication

Chaulk, Robert

Time in a bottle: historic Halifax harbour from the bottom up / Robert Chaulk.

Includes bibliographical references.
ISBN 1-895900-51-4
1. Halifax Harbour (N.S.) — History. 2. Scuba diving — Nova Scotia — Halifax Harbour. I. Title.
FC2346.55.C44 2002   971.6'225   C2002-903588-0
F1039.5.H17C49 2002

Book cover design by Dalhousie Graphics

Back cover photograph by Dana Sheppard

Pottersfield Press acknowledges the ongoing support of the Nova Scotia Department of Tourism and Culture, Cultural Affairs Division. We acknowledge the support of the Canada Council for the Arts which last year invested $19.1 million in writing and publishing throughout Canada. We also acknowledge the finanacial support of the Government of Canada through the Book Publishing Industry Development Program for our publishing activities.

Pottersfield Press
83 Leslie Road
East Lawrencetown, Nova Scotia, Canada B2Z 1P8
Web site: www.pottersfieldpress.com
To order, phone 1-800-NIMBUS9 (1-800-646-2879)
Printed in Canada

 Canada Council for the Arts / Conseil des Arts du Canada

To my wife, Sandra,
and
my sons, Christopher and Jeremy.

Acknowledgements

I wish to acknowledge the assistance of those who aided in the effort to make this book possible. Peter Fanning and Ruth Chaulk gave me sound advice at the beginning and got me off to a good start. Lise Duggan put in many faithful hours of critiquing and taught me to assume nothing about my readers. Christopher and Sandra Chaulk edited and critiqued the final work. I want to especially acknowledge Greg Cochkanoff, for his ongong advice and assistance, ready willingness to share his vast knowledge of the subject and access to his files; and Dana Sheppard, for arranging so many great dives, especially at the Dockyard, and for sharing my desire and willingness to dive anywhere, at any time, under virtually any conditions.

The voyage to Halifax was made in twenty-six days – a very good passage. On Tuesday, September 25th, 1849, at 3 a.m. we saw Sambro Light bearing northwest by west, distant fourteen miles. We took in the mainsail, backed the yards, and got a sounding. At 4 a.m. we took on a Halifax pilot, and at ten o'clock anchored off Halifax town in eight fathoms of water, north of George's Island. Old Halifax never gave me the same thrill, before nor since. I wanted to go right ashore, but it was not until the following afternoon that we could haul into the wharf. We cleared up the docks in a hurry, and again and at last I stood upon the land that I was born in.

Benjamin Doane,
Nova Scotia whaling captain

Table of Contents

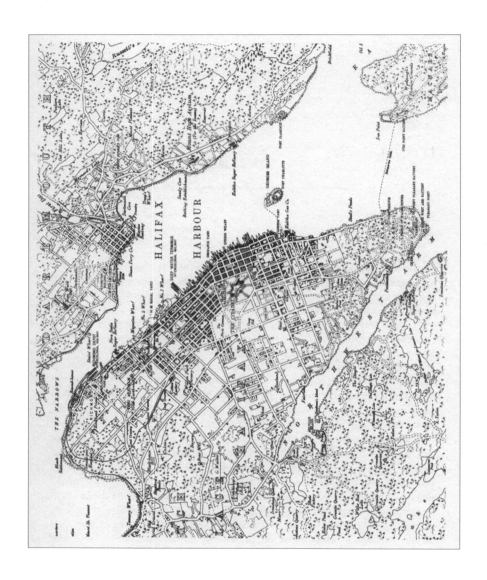

Map of Halifax Harbour. (Public Archives of Nova Scotia)

Introduction

One day late in September of 1746, the French warship *Northumberland* sailed into the great harbour of Chebucto, known today as Halifax Harbour. She was the flagship to the largest fleet of ships that had ever crossed the Atlantic Ocean. It had been a fearsome voyage of three months across the Atlantic from France, and most of the fleet had become separated from the flagship. When they left France, the sailors and soldiers had been expecting a short voyage across the English Channel to assist the Scots in their historic struggle against the English, but the fleet was ordered to the Western Ocean instead and on to the wilds of North America. The year before, the French had lost their big fortress at Louisbourg, Nova Scotia, to the British, and they intended to get it back. They were to rendezvous at Chebucto with other French ships and harass the British colonies. As the big ship-of-the-line passed between what today are called McNab's Island and Point Pleasant, the Duc d'Anville, the Admiral of the fleet, hurried to finish his evening meal.

The ship's captain, Duperrier, was in command on the bridge but the Duke wanted to get on deck to survey the harbour as they passed. He didn't entirely trust the captured English pilot who was guiding them into this unfamiliar place. His personal steward quickly cleared the table and removed the leftovers, including the six empty bottles from which the officers had just enjoyed the best French wine. As he always did, the steward threw the waste over the rail and into the water on the leeward side of the ship.

Most of it dispersed on the surface, providing an evening repast for a group of gulls. One of the short, long-necked bottles struck the side of the ship and shattered, but the others soon filled with water and sank to the bottom. Two broke on impact thirty metres below. Of the three remaining, one lasted over a century, until a fisherman's anchor struck it one day in 1859. Another had been perched on bedrock and, for a century and a half, it endured until a hurricane struck the harbour in 1892 and finished it off. Only one remained. As time passed, the sole survivor's dark green colour became partially obscured by pink and yellow coral, which grew on its upper side as it lay on the gravel. For more than 250 years, it got swept by the currents, nudged occasionally by a crab, sometimes sprouting growth, sometimes clean, always witnessing the great movement of men and ships coming and going in this great and historic harbour.

Many years later, as a high school visitor in 1967, I sat and took in the commanding view from the Citadel that for two hundred years had dared an aggressor to try and enter this important naval base. Off to the left in the distance stood a half-built suspension bridge, hanging in the air as if controlled by a puppeteer above the clouds. To the right were the horizon and the distant shores of Africa. Straight below lay the main harbour, which has hosted huge fleets of war, humble fishing boats, the private yachts of kings and emperors, and the grandest and greatest ships afloat. Having played a part in an untold number of lives and having left its imprint on the millions who have been upon its waters, the harbour holds a unique place in the history of Canada.

The French sailors who congregated in Chebucto that autumn in 1746 were probably the first large group of people to visit the harbour. They were certainly the first large group of Europeans to do so. While they did not settle there — nor did they have any desire even to be there, given their circumstances — their presence in North America led to the British decision to colonize the harbour that was to become so significant in the history of Canada and in the winning of two world wars.

Diving Halifax

Halifax Harbour is a special place. Its geography and history make it unique in Canada. It is more than a body of water that floats ships and requires bridges that cause traffic bottlenecks. It is a place of beauty that its residents love and appreciate. In their more pensive times, many are drawn to the shores of this large and historic body of water to let it speak to them – of soldiers going to war, of refugees seeking asylum, of immigrants searching for a new life, of seafarers escaping the wilds of the North Atlantic. They walk, jog, bicycle, drive and picnic on its shores; they scream across its waters on jet skis or sail languidly on a late summer's evening. They ride to and from work on its ferries.

And a very small group explores under its waters. Like all seaports, Halifax needs commercial divers to keep things working underwater, but this harbour is different from other large seaports. Because it is so big and so deep and its geography so varied, Halifax Harbour has attracted a small and dedicated group of recreational divers. The harbour speaks to us in another way.

I became interested in the harbour the first time I saw it on a summer's day in 1967. And though I lived in many places, I knew that one day I would move to Halifax and get acquainted with this veritable inland sea. It seems to have an endless store of things to discover. My patient wife has learned that all roads do not lead to Rome; they have a remarkable habit of leading to the waterfront. She long ago lost count of the number of ships she has watched coming into the docks or steaming through the Narrows, and listens with good humour to the latest revelation about the first ferries on the harbour or the tugs that operated at the turn of the century. And no matter when we visit the waterfront we are never alone. Go to the many parks and access points to the harbour, and you will find cars with people in them, sipping a coffee from a nearby donut shop, and looking out across the waters; walkers scavenging on the beaches and ship-watchers with binoculars and cameras. And there are always people standing and just staring down into the water, as if they expected something to materialize.

The waters of this spacious harbour, on the surface and below the waves, have many stories to tell. Learning about the harbour's surroundings is a straightforward undertaking in historical research, but investigating the bottom of the harbour is a complex and time-consuming process. You can do it remotely, through the use of sensing equipment and cameras, or you can go there – using scuba equipment. This takes much longer, and is more involved, but it is far more exciting and rewarding.

I was a teenager when I took my first dive in a shallow lake in 1968, using borrowed equipment. Even though the water was only about six feet deep, I took great pleasure in cheating my own physical limitations and I felt that in some way I was getting away with something as I invaded this new world. The sun shone through the water and it was like flying over a garden. I was exhilarated, as the regulator seemed to force the air into my lungs when I went to the bottom of the lake. The weeds parted gently to make room for this important visitor who had mastered their world, and curious little trout stared with bulging eyes a few inches in front of my mask. There was life everywhere in this new and very different realm.

Not long after I had taken up scuba diving in the mid-1980s, an experienced harbour diver and a fellow history enthusiast, Greg Cochkanoff, talked me into trying out the harbour. Since then I have done hundreds of dives with Greg, Dana Sheppard and other members of the Aqualantics Dive Club. We have spent some exciting Saturday mornings and Sunday afternoons diving – in the bone-chilling November rain, in snowstorms in

February, in minus 30 degree Celsius temperatures in January and in plus 30°C in August. We have recovered anchors, tools and even the harbour pilot's eyeglasses, and have shocked or fascinated hundreds of bystanders as we have come from or gone into the waters off downtown Halifax.

I popped up among the ice floes on a winter's day to see a startled woman wrapped in her winter coat staring down from the dock in disbelief. "Are you cold?" she peeped from under her fur-lined hood. "I'm probably a lot warmer than you are!" I replied, as I bobbed about in my neoprene drysuit. Underneath, I was cozy, wearing a shirt, sweater, jogging suit, and three pairs of wool socks.

Like other sports, scuba diving attracts all kinds of people. Greg is high energy, methodical and detail-oriented, while Dana is calm, deliberate, and blessed with extremely steady nerves. Both are excellent divers and good companions. They are also rather talkative individuals – as I can be – and we have developed some interesting ways to communicate with one another underwater. There are standard international hand signals used by scuba divers for basic communications, but we often talk to one another when we are diving. It isn't easy and it requires a lot of air to project sounds through water, but I can hear Greg yell from at least six metres away. And we have other hand signals that have evolved out of necessity, as we comment on the quality of the bottom, the sounds we hear, the presence of boats above us, and so on.

Harbour Activity

If you set out to identify the major uses for Halifax Harbour, you could probably put them under one of four categories: harvesting the sea, naval activity, commercial shipping, and recreation.

Even before the towns of Halifax and Dartmouth grew up on the shores of Chebucto Harbour, fishermen had visited for two and a half centuries. The time-honoured occupations that surround the harvesting of the ocean's bounty continued after the towns were founded and still continue. But Halifax was settled as a military post and intense naval activity has been carried out in the harbour ever since. The fishery and the navy require people, and people move about and need goods, so commercial shipping became a major activity as well. And finally, people also like to amuse themselves, so they have turned to the harbour for their major recreation, primarily in the form of boating. Rowers, sailors, and, in this century, power-boaters have become substantial users of the resource that is Halifax Harbour. There is plenty of evidence of all these activities on the harbour floor.

What Do You See Down There, Anyway?

Many times, I have been asked the question "You dive in the harbour? What do you see down there anyway?"

The answer is: everything. It's like visiting your own private museum.

If there is an object on the land, there is probably one like it somewhere on the bottom of this corner of the ocean. For at least three hundred years Halifax Harbour has been the depository of everything that humankind has manufactured, from bottles to bicycles, from crockery to cars, from tires to toilets. In the glory days of the big ocean liners, many lazy passengers, enjoying an evening cup of tea on the deck, threw their teacups overboard instead of returning them to the steward for washing. Things slipped off the decks of other boats, and thieves threw their booty off a dock after deciding it was of no saleable value. They still do.

Steamship line dishes recovered from Halifax Harbour. Photo by Greg Cochkanoff.

Tidy housewives of the past threw their household garbage into the harbour because neat people disposed of things, and what more convenient place than the ocean? It was easy, it was quick and it was gone – forever. Occasionally, a careless child rode a bicycle straight off the end of a dock. The rider managed to get to shore, but without the bike.

straight off the end of a dock. The rider managed to get to shore, but without the bike.

A father, frustrated by his children's squabbling over a toy, would threaten to throw it off the end of the wharf and finally, out of patience with the quarrelling, he would hurl it, supposedly out of existence, never to be seen again. Likewise the thief, after stealing a wallet and removing the cash, can easily dispose of the credit cards, identification and photographs in the water, for who will ever find them?

Unheeding sport fishermen who don't hold their spincasting rod tightly enough get to see it fly through the air, and the last sight they have of it is when it strikes the surface of the water on its way to the bottom – the one that got away. There are plenty of fishing rods in the harbour. Airplanes have crashed into the harbour and ships have sunk; and there they lie, silent witnesses to the vagaries of bad judgement, bad weather or just plain bad luck. To those of us fortunate enough to see them, they are locked in time, and we are taken back years or even centuries.

There is a story of a ship leaving Halifax transporting horses on its deck "turning turtle" and disgorging its startled cargo into the harbour. Inside the harbour, a huge part of the bottom of Bedford Basin is strewn with live ammunition from the 1945 explosion of the navy ordnance magazine. The bottom of the Northwest Arm is covered with the pop bottles from close to 150 years of picnicking, canoe regattas and sailing competitions – bottles that tell the history of soda pop manufacturing and bottling in one of Canada's oldest cities.

The big French armada that gathered in Bedford Basin in 1746 in preparation for an attack on Louisbourg left behind several ships, burned or scuttled because there was nobody to man them. The crews had died of disease and other causes while languishing in the vicinity of what is now Mount St. Vincent University.

In days gone by and for some people even today, throwing something overboard is like sending it to outer space. Nobody will ever see it again. It will cease to exist. What better place to dispense with those things that no longer serve us than to end their existence? To people in the nineteenth and much of the twentieth centuries, this was entirely reasonable. For, if they

15

A rare Quebec Steamship Company cup and saucer with clay pipe, bottles and a crock. Photo by Greg Cochkanoff.

buried it, it could be dug up again; if they burned it, they had ashes; but if they threw it into the ocean, it was as though it had never existed.

The bottom of Halifax Harbour is strewn with the castoffs of twenty generations of citizens, navies, armies, steamship lines and railways. Some of it is buried under three metres of mud while other items lie exposed in rock outcroppings or on the beach, barely under the surface. On the few remaining beaches of Halifax Harbour, at low tide you can pick up broken bottles going back 150 years or more. Occasionally, if you search carefully, you can pick up an intact find – your own little piece of history! As the saying goes, one person's junk is another person's treasure.

When I first visited the bottom of the harbour, it became clear to me that there is a preponderance of certain objects, and after a while I have come to realize that some things remain for the long term while others go away quickly. If it can float and a seagull can swallow it, or a fish can eat it or a crab can cart it off, an item has a short life in the ocean. Otherwise, there it sits until it decomposes. Things like wooden wharves, ships, barges, and iron objects such as anchors eventually fade away. Rubber, plastic, concrete, ceramic, brass, glass, and stainless steel are there for the long term.

On a dive in 1992, we found a wooden boat of perhaps nine metres sitting upright on the bottom of the harbour, completely intact. I went looking for it five years later and it was virtually gone; all that remained were the engine, the keel . . . and the paint. The wood had been devoured by the teredo – or shipworms – which bore into ships and wharves and devour the wood. They did not like the paint, so it remained on a cardboard-thin layer of wood spread about the surrounding area. In 1999, a new dock was constructed at the site and the boat's remains ended up under a thousand tons of rock.

From time to time, a diver can find little bits of very thin copper, almost like paper. For a time, sailing ships were clad in copper sheathing to protect them from teredos. The Royal Navy started using it at around the same time as the founding of Halifax. The first such ship to be clad in copper was HMS *Dolphin*, which at one time was commanded by the grandfather of the famous English poet, Lord Byron. His grandfather, who was also Lord Byron, visited Nova Scotia in 1760, when he came to oversee the destruction of the French fortress of Louisbourg, which the British had captured in 1758.

There are lumps of coal strewn around the harbour bottom, most of it lost by accident, no doubt, for it was valuable when it was the main source of energy in society, providing heat for buildings, fuel for cooking, energy for industry, and as the mainstay of transportation, it drove the steam engines of ships and trains. And there is the by-product of burning coal: tons of ash dumped by design out of the boilers of countless ships and trains, and industrial and household stoves.

Some Halifax and Dartmouth golfers see the harbour as an ideal driving range and have deposited thousands of golf balls from the convenience of their backyards. On a good day, if you're in the right place, you can pick up a bucketful. One day, I found another kind of ball, a bowling ball, lying in twenty-five metres of water and hundreds of metres from shore. I have wondered for years how a bowling ball found its way out into the middle of the harbour. There are well-worn bricks from buildings that existed near the waterfront and have been torn down or destroyed. As always, the quickest way to dispose of the debris has been to plough it into the harbour.

Bottles and Tires

The most abundant things that have lingered are bottles and tires. The tires must have come from the hundreds that are used as fenders to keep boats and ships from bumping against wharves. They are used, that is, until they come loose and fall into the water where they float for a while and eventually sink. There are thousands on the harbour's bottom. In some locations, you can take in fifteen or twenty at a glance. No doubt, others must have been dumped from barges as a convenient way to dispose of them.

And there are countless numbers of bottles. They are spread from Mc-Nab's Island to Bedford. Wine, beer, milk, and pop bottles bear the names of the bottlers in raised lettering. There are preserving jars, medicine bottles from early Halifax druggists, and crockery bottles for wine, beer, rum, ginger beer, boot polish, ink, and glue. There is also domestic china, virtually all of it broken and discarded with the household trash, in the same way that the bottles found their way to the bottom, and, of course, there is china from ships and boats that have frequented the harbour.

Occasionally a doll has made me nearly jump out of my skin as it stared up from the murk – for that split second I thought I was seeing the body of a baby. Greg saw a hand sticking up out of the mud one day, reminding him of a horror movie scene where the hand reaches up from the grave. He gingerly touched it, gave it a tug and pulled up the arm of a mannequin – the plastic models used in stores to display clothes.

Personal items abound in places and often add a certain eeriness to the dive. Plastic and rubber gloves decompose slowly, and have a very human dimension to them as they lie like an upturned hand trying to be noticed and to communicate. A boot here or there always makes me think of a person struggling in some way and ultimately losing the battle. They all leave me wondering if their owner might be close by, having succumbed to the fatally cold water that envelops me just millimetres from my skin. Such sightings at times will cause an extra shiver to pass through my body.

When a war is over and there are enough explosives left to destroy a nation, what do you do with them? Dump them into the ocean, of course. Shiploads of ammunition left Halifax Harbour in the years after World War II and were dumped overboard in 180 metres of water sixty or so kilometres out to sea. Author Jack Zinck, describing HMCS *Middlesex*, writes flatly,

"For awhile she was used as a ship for dumping ammunition off Halifax Harbour during 1946."

The Beleaguered Ocean

There is an old love song with the title "You always hurt the one you love." It speaks of one of the paradoxes of the human condition that even though we don't mean to, we often take for granted those people and things that we hold most dear. The very people who have loved the ocean for centuries have been its worst abusers, thinking that its bounty was limitless and that its capacity for regeneration would never die.

Like a loyal and dutiful wife who has served her unappreciative husband for twenty-five years and one day declares "Enough!" leaving the befuddled man exclaiming that he has never understood women, so our ocean – which we have so poorly understood – has had enough. And like the confused husband, we too have shown a despicable lack of understanding, thinking we could exploit the ocean's riches and in return she would willingly accept our waste.

She is finally speaking up and we are only now beginning to appreciate the extent of the abuse she has endured. We are wringing our hands over the state of the world's oceans, but it did not happen overnight. For too long, our attitude has been to take what we want, as much as we want, when we want – and to throw back into the ocean what we don't want, whether it originated there or not.

The effects of this abuse are clearly evident in many parts of Halifax Harbour. We cannot turn back the clock, so the best that we can do is stop the abuse and learn from the past, by not repeating the mistakes. Ironically though, the results of this abuse make for some interesting diving and provide an opportunity to study what is already there.

The World Next Door

On a dreary day in November, the harbour seems to be lifeless. Slate-grey water lies under a brooding sky, and small waves shudder across the surface, moved along by a blustery and raw easterly wind. There are no pleasure boats, no youngsters learning to sail, no kayakers, no speedboats or jet skis — just the lonely ferry, going back and forth on its imaginary treadmill. On such days, most Haligonians see the harbour only as the place that sends in those cold, wet winds and fog. It is barely noticed, just another part of the landscape and an impediment to getting about.

Lifeless though it may appear from an office tower or a car crossing the bridge, or from its shores, the harbour surface hides a world that is very much alive. Here, as on the land, is a space where creatures come into existence, struggle to survive and ultimately take their place in the food chain, consuming and being consumed. Here microscopic organisms doggedly reduce wood and iron to unrecognizable lumps and the world's largest creatures come, stay awhile and move on.

Different parts of the harbour support different kinds of life. On the deep slopes of the Bedford Basin below the Bedford Highway, scallops grow to a size that would astonish the average consumer. The bite-sized scallops in the grocery store are perhaps a sixth the size of some that inhabit the harbour. Long-legged snow crabs sit motionless, like foot-long spiders, twenty-five metres below the bridges. Anywhere in the harbour, large lobsters inhabit their dens burrowed snugly below rocks. And crabs, mussels, and other ordinary shellfish exist throughout the harbour, growing to uncommonly large sizes.

They all get big because they have virtually no enemies in these secluded waters. There are few fishermen, at least not in the inner harbour, and even though seals sometimes slither about the outer harbour, few venture down the Narrows and into the Basin. One of the few found its way into a parking lot in January of 2002. Four of us came back from a dive one Saturday morning and as we stepped out of the boat and headed to our cars, our way was blocked by a speckled white and grey seal. We took some pictures and tried to feed him a fish. He wasn't interested. I guess he felt that he didn't need our help to catch his lunch, given the banquet awaiting him when he slipped back into the water. Flounder, perch, sculpins and other bottom dwellers abound in the harbour, especially in summer and fall.

They leave the harbour during the cold months of January to May but this fellow looked like he was getting plenty to eat.

The liveliest months for wildlife are from July to November, when large creatures such as porpoise and whales follow the herring that inhabit Nova Scotia waters. Both herring and mackerel come in large schools in and out of the harbour and, like the hangers-on that trailed behind Napoleon's armies as they tracked around Europe, a variety of followers – from fishing boats to whales – rely on them for their livelihood. The large mammals are in and out of the harbour, feeding on the plentiful fish at their leisure. They, in turn, are followed by curious tourists wielding cameras and binoculars. On more than one occasion in summer, meetings in downtown office buildings get interrupted by the spectacle of whales breaching below the office windows.

One Sunday morning in April 1998, I was walking alongside the Northwest Arm and looking at its waters from the Jubilee Road boat ramp when a loon popped to the surface three metres from me. Knowing that loons come in pairs, I waited motionless and, sure enough, up came its mate, even closer. In the same area, on a winter's afternoon, in full view of houses, apartment buildings and businesses, I watched an eagle eating its prey on the ice, less than a stone's throw away. I was reminded again of my good fortune to live in an urban area where I can take a walk within the city and see creatures that most Canadians consider the epitome of the wild.

On many occasions, while walking along the busy thoroughfare of Quinpool Road, I have seen osprey dive into the waters of the Arm and come up with a large fish. On another peaceful morning I rowed to my boat, which was anchored in the Arm, and my heart leapt to my throat when I climbed aboard and found myself nose to nose with an otter. He got a bigger fright and made a quick exit over the side. A few years later, an unabashed otter sashayed across a busy street in front of me on its way back to the Arm. On other occasions, late at night or in the early morning, I have also seen raccoons, muskrats, ferrets, a fox and, early one morning when it was barely light, a coyote.

Most of us see the ocean as a two-dimensional place. It has a surface that we can see but it limits our perceptions and leaves us with an impoverished view of the real thing. We know the third dimension, depth, exists but we must often access it as blind people, groping around in it, or inserting a line, hook, net or rake and hoping to come up with something. As children, walking knee-deep in it, we were vigilant and fearful that a crab would nip our toes. (I wonder if any toe has ever been nipped by a crab.) Entering the third dimension has been complex, tedious and expensive, and has produced its share of tragic consequences.

The Mysterious Ocean

In one of the oldest pieces of literature written, the sea is a mysterious and forbidding place. We read the familiar words known to generations of sailors: "Those who go down to the sea in ships, who do business in great waters; they have seen the works of the Lord, and His wonders in the deep. For He spoke and raised up a stormy wind, which lifted up the waves of the sea. They rose up to the heavens, they went down to the depths; their soul melted away in their misery."

Like the Biblical writer, many in the past have learned that the ocean is to be feared, for even though it gave us food, transportation and recreation, it has also taken fathers and sons by the thousands and left widows and orphans in almost every little coastal village.

We don't trust what we don't understand and we have never understood the ocean, with its capricious ways, one day tranquil enough to cradle a kayak and another day wild enough to snatch a ship. To many who stare into its black depths, it presents an expanse seemingly without end, like the universe itself, and has engendered feelings of fear and suspicion. When I was a boy, there were places in the ocean that had "no bottom!" Down there were mysteries defying knowledge and anything entering that interminable space would cease to be.

The idea of entering this mysterious world that can be so brutal often leaves people puzzled. Many a scuba diver has heard the familiar challenge "Why do you want to go down *there?*" Not from tourists who have seen the blue Caribbean or from residents of large inland cities do such perplexed queries come, but from the men who have made their living off the sea and have seen the cruel north Atlantic at its worst. Descended from generations of people who have lived in houses literally clinging to the rocks, scratching a living from the sea and dying penniless, such people see no pleasure in descending into a world where they were never meant to go.

The diver makes a naturally suspicious target, for if you couldn't trust the ocean, how could you trust somebody who plays in its depths, in some inexplicable way cavorting with the monsters that exist therein? Boaters watch with consternation as we swim under their boats riding at anchor, not realizing that we are ten or more metres below the surface. In the same way, many a lobster fisherman concludes that we really have only one reason to engage in such an activity – to scoop up the lobsters that he must work so hard to catch in his traps to feed his family. And there we are, robbing him!

Layers of Water

The biggest puzzle, even for other divers, is why anybody would possibly want to go into the so-called polluted waters of Halifax Harbour. On the evening news they receive a steady diet of the squabbling over who will pay to clean it up, and conclude that it must be frightful, with the noxious products of industry, shipping and shipbuilding, the naval base, oil refineries, and a multiplicity of other sources.

Like all things viewed from the surface, the harbour is completely different when seen from within. The waters are far cleaner than most people realize and the pollutants that enter the harbour are contained in "fresh" water (as opposed to salt water) which floats above salt water, meaning that a diver is unaffected while below the surface. Because most of the pollution lies on the surface, it looks all the worse to a person walking along the waterfront and adds to the perplexity of those who don't dive.

In fact, the water has perceptible layers that a diver can differentiate by temperature and clarity. The transition zone where a temperature change occurs is called a thermocline. In summer, the sun heats the surface of the water to a depth of a few metres. There is a noticeable temperature change at three metres or so. On an 18-metre (60-foot) dive there may be several thermoclines. In the harbour there are days when the underwater visibility may be quite poor, but a descent of nine metres or more will pass you through a thermocline and into much colder water with vastly superior visibility.

The most significant and striking example of this phenomenon occurs when diving in the tidal regions of deeper rivers. The waters of many Nova Scotia rivers are amber in colour, because of tannin contained in the waters they carry. Diving in this water can be like diving in cold tea because the visibility is so poor that you literally cannot see as far as you can reach. But at the mouth of the rivers, salt water comes in with the tides. The dark, fresh water flows on top of the clear, salt water and, if you can dive at the right time and in the right place, before the waters mix, you are in for a special treat.

It requires steady nerves to go down through the top layer of dark water, but when you come to the salt-water layer, the effect is marvelous. You feel like somebody has removed a blindfold as you hit the clear water, but another surprise awaits you. With the dark water above, the sun shines through what amounts to an amber filter, subduing the light and producing a rich and peculiar ambiance. It is unlike anything that I have experienced in my years of diving.

The Day Greg Found the Money

Greg is very observant, whether he is walking down the street or scouring the bottom of the ocean. He also has a knack for finding money. He is forever picking up nickels, dimes and quarters. On a dive in one of the Dartmouth lakes he came up to me underwater and flashed a five-dollar bill he had just found. He carefully dried it when he got out and bought himself lunch the next day. On another day, as we had lunch at an outdoor restaurant on the Halifax waterfront, he sadly pointed to a $20 bill floating past our dock, just out of reach.

After years of diving with Greg, I've become used to seeing him come out of the water with unusual booty. On another dive near downtown Dartmouth, he came out with an armload of flat pieces of brass. By arranging the pieces like a puzzle, we found it to be a cross. After asking around, Greg discovered that Grace United Church in Dartmouth had been vandalized twelve years earlier. Among the things stolen was a cross from the wall, where it had hung for the previous seventeen years. The delighted congregation had it cleaned and returned to its place.

Gold and silver coins from the SS *Atlantic*. From the collection of Greg Cochkanoff.

On other occasions, harbour divers have found briefcases, purses, and all manner of wallets. We suspect that wallets found in the harbour were stolen, the cash removed and the evidence tossed overboard. Usually there is no identification because it has decomposed, but on occasion there are credit cards, which do last a long time. On those occasions when we have tracked down the owners, the credit cards have long since been cancelled or have expired.

Greg's tenacity paid off on a dive in May, 1997, near the Dartmouth waterfront. I barely noticed as he fished yet another wallet out of his "goodie bag" after we had stepped out of the water and onto the beach. He was, as usual, brimming with boyish enthusiasm and wondering what jackpot he might have struck. The thing was in dismal shape, almost rotted to nothing and barely recognizable as a wallet. But it contained a lump of black material that looked like it might have been paper many years before. It was stuck into a mass and was difficult to distinguish from the blackened leather that held it. But he took it home and I scoffed.

Later that evening he phoned to give me his prognosis. There were no cards that could be read, so he couldn't identify the owner. But in the process of peeling apart the wallet he thought he saw fragments of paper money. He was certain he had found a wad of older Canadian dollar bills about a quarter of an inch thick. Fearing the paper would disintegrate if handled, he placed it all in a tray of fresh water so it would not dry out, and called the Bank of Canada.

After several conversations with bank officials, he was instructed to send the black lump, sealed in a plastic bag with water, to a forensics lab associated with the Canadian Mint for identification. After several weeks of patiently waiting he received a call to come and collect his money. The lab had determined the black wad had once been a stack of bills, totalling at least $415, and the Bank of Canada was replacing them at face value. The next day he bought me lunch too.

The Harbour

Drive north, south, east or west from downtown Halifax and you will strike the ocean, in the form of the waterfront, Point Pleasant, the Northwest Arm or Bedford Basin. The harbour is inescapable. Few residents of a seaport have to contend with as much water and shoreline as do the people of Halifax, Bedford and Dartmouth. Most seaports consist of a harbour with the city surrounding it. Halifax, on the other hand, is a harbour that splits and fragments the areas where its people reside.

The city of Halifax exists because of its harbour, a harbour of which admirals dream. Deep, secluded, large, and easy to defend, it is a haven for those who know the way in and deadly for those who do not. The eastern gateway to mainland Canada, Halifax Harbour is a huge, northern, ice-free harbour, second only to Sydney, Australia, in size. If you leave the harbour by boat, from its northern extremity on the Bedford waterfront, cross the Bedford Basin, go through the Narrows, past the ports of Halifax and Dartmouth, past George's and McNab's Islands to the outer harbour terminated by Chebucto Head, you travel nearly thirty kilometres. At its deepest point, the Basin reaches seventy-one metres (230 feet) in depth. It is 4.3 kilometres wide and 7.3 kilometres from Bedford to the first bridge, the A. Murray MacKay, spanning the Narrows. This is the bridge that I had seen seemingly hanging in the air in 1967. It's another six kilometres from this bridge to George's Island and just under sixteen from there to Chebucto Head.

Geologists tell us that the Basin was once a fresh water lake and that the Narrows was a river, emptying into the ocean south of the MacDonald Bridge near downtown Halifax. This is an interesting theory, because there is a discernible underwater trench extending from the point where the Narrows and Basin meet and going south out the harbour, following the shoreline on the Halifax side and widening, as the mouth of a river widens, near George's Island. That trench is generally twenty to thirty metres deep.

The rest of the harbour, with the exception of the Basin, is less deep and can be surprisingly shallow in places. Ships must follow a well-defined track when entering or leaving the harbour. Big container ships bound for the Fairview Cove container terminal in the Basin come alarmingly close to the Halifax waterfront, not for the view but because that is the route of the deepest water. On first entering the harbour, they steer clear of McNab's Island, especially the outer part, for here lies the large and treacherous Thrumcap shoal, which reaches like a long snake out into the ocean and has snared many ships over the centuries. At low tide, three or more kilometres from shore, even a speedboat would strike bottom in what its unsuspecting driver would suppose to be the middle of nowhere.

Likewise, large vessels avoid Point Pleasant, for it continues out to sea close to a kilometre and only the smallest pleasure craft can float over what has the disarming name of the Pleasant Shoal. It was this shoal that deterred the first English colonists from settling at Point Pleasant, for there they started clearing land until they got a taste of the gales that strike this area, and they soon discovered just how shallow the water is far out from the shore.

Little wonder that Halifax has never been attacked from the sea, for the natural design of the harbour made it a fortress, easy to defend. While the entrance looks wide and open, it is full of unpleasant surprises, as the number of shipwrecks in the harbour approaches will attest. Seemingly far out to sea but uncomfortably close on a foggy night lurk many shoals with revealing names like Broad Breaker, Blind Sister and Mad Rock. Some have shipwrecks almost surrounding them, like trophies.

There are two other distinguishing features of the harbour. Guarding the entrance is the huge island named after Peter McNab, who was one of the first settlers there and whose grave is at the southern end of the island. Running parallel to the Narrows, on the other side of Halifax, is a very pleasant surprise – the Northwest Arm, a three-kilometre inlet of the sea that almost severs Halifax from the rest of mainland Nova Scotia. It is extremely well sheltered and breathtaking in beauty. If Nova Scotia is (as it claims to be) Canada's ocean playground, then the Northwest Arm is Halifax's ocean playground.

In light traffic, it takes an hour and a half to drive from the southern extremity of the Halifax side to the southern extremity of the Dartmouth side of the harbour, a distance of seventy kilometres, while the proverbial crow would need to fly only ten kilometres. It took me more than eighteen hours to walk the distance, mostly around the shore. Before the bridges were completed across the Narrows in the period 1955-1970, a young man wishing to visit his sweetheart on the other side could row or, if he really wanted to impress her, swim the 360 metres. The unattractive alternative would have been to drive almost twenty kilometres around the Basin.

This body of water is big, with a rough and intricate shoreline. It is deep and has an equally convoluted bottom. And it has a long and interesting past. I have spent more than fifteen years diving its waters, walking its shores, observing its vessel traffic, and studying its history. I don't think I'll ever exhaust the subject.

Duc d'Anville and
the Founding of Halifax

Historians generally agree that Halifax came about because of an event that happened in 1746, when Britain's old enemy, France, mounted a gigantic campaign against British North America. The leader of the campaign was Jean-Baptiste-Louis-Frederic de la Rochefoucauld de Roye, the 37-year-old Duc d'Anville. Even though most people of Halifax know Duc d'Anville as nothing more than the name of a Halifax school, to harbour divers his name holds a special allure. That is because he did something that is sure to attract divers – he left some ships on the bottom of the harbour. The number, location and condition of those ships at the time of their sinking has been speculated about for years.

There are several accounts of the sad tale of the d'Anville expedition and they differ slightly in their details, but the story goes like this. After the loss of Louisbourg to a British army out of Boston in the summer of 1745, the French decided to retaliate by sending a fleet to re-take the fortress, attack the English fortifications at Annapolis Royal and burn Boston and other English possessions. The news of the expedition spread terror throughout the British colonies in North America.

The fleet included 11 ships-of-the-line, 20 frigates and 34 transports and other vessels, manned by 6,790 officers and seamen. There were 3,150 veteran troops of the regiment of Ponthieu. The fleet included two-fifths of the available men-of-war of the French Navy. After countless delays in getting the ships assembled from several French ports and then being hemmed in by contrary winds for weeks, they left France in late June of 1746. From the start, there was discontentment among the veteran naval officers at having to serve under the young duke. Some thought they were heading to Britain to assist their allies, the Scots. But the Scots had lost the decisive Battle of Culloden in April and the fleet was at sea with only d'Anville knowing the nature of their orders. The crews were almost mutinous when he announced the destination, afraid of the long voyage and the wild coast of America. The officers knew it would be too late in the season to mount an effective attack by the time they got to Louisbourg. To complicate matters further, nobody was familiar with the rocky, fog-bound coast of Nova Scotia.

They had every reason to be afraid because the trip across turned into a nightmare. The winds that had prevented their departure now kept them from making headway. It took three weeks to get out of the Bay of Biscay. Some ships lagged behind so the faster ships had to shorten sail and wait for them. The fleet was becalmed for days in the longitude of the Azores. James Pritchard, in his book *Anatomy of a Naval Disaster*, writes: "Hard, foggy gales alternated with calms, leading to additional collisions and further distress. Sailors rowed across to disabled vessels and quickly effected repairs, but some ships had to be taken in tow and others were forced to turn back to France . . . During the evening of 3 July, *La Perle* received a smashing wave and was badly knocked about. The transport *Le Prudent* also reported difficulties and the same day *L'Ardent*'s longboat had to take off stores and provisions from a merchantman in distress. The next day *Le Mercure* took *La Marguerite* in tow, but not without accident. Approaching the small, Canadian-built schooner from windward, the much larger hospital ship collided, smashing the bowsprit and jib-boom. Frustration and demoralization grew under such trying conditions, as great ships-of-the-line spent much of their time hove to or bearing away, awaiting much slower merchantmen and attempting to keep the fleet together."

The conditions on board and the poor quality of the provisions led to sickness, which had been a problem even before they departed. One account calls it a pestilence, another calls it a plague, a third calls it typhus; whatever it was, it broke out on the ships and eventually killed 1,200 men. And there were storms to deal with. A lightning squall struck several ships. One ship was struck and six men killed, while a stores ship was burned and had to be abandoned. On the *Mars* of seventy guns, a box of musket and cannon cartridges blew up, killing ten and wounding twenty-one. (It is reasonable to assume that this is the ill-fated ship that wrecked at the harbour entrance in 1755, while sailing under British registry.)

By mid-September, after being at sea for almost three months, they were in the vicinity of Sable Island when, again, they got walloped by one of the storms that hit the East Coast during hurricane season. The fleet was battered and dispersed and part of it was lost. In the process, a transport collided with a ship-of-the-line and sank with all hands. Two ships were even driven to the West Indies by the wind. Another, the 64-gun *Ardent*, returned to France on September 15.

In company with the *Renomme* and one or more transports, Captain Duperrier finally managed to bring the flagship, *Northumberland*, into Chebucto. Admiral Conflans, with four ships from the West Indies squadron, had been waiting at Chebucto but had sailed for France a few days before d'Anville arrived. With a name like *Northumberland*, the flagship must have been English at one time. She, in fact, was an English prize that had been captured by Captains Serier and Conflans in 1744. During the second and final siege of Louisbourg in 1758, there is mention of a 70-gun ship called *Northumberland* fighting in the British fleet. It may have been a different ship or, more likely, the British had re-captured her. During this period of almost constant naval warfare, it was not uncommon for ships to change hands several times during their useful lifetimes.

During the rest of September, what was left of the fleet drifted in dribs and drabs into Chebucto Harbour. The frigates *L'Aurore* and *Castor* had sailed from France in April and arrived in Chebucto in early summer. They had spent the summer raiding English shipping and had taken a warship of ten guns, and at least eight vessels laden with cattle, fish and other dry provisions. They had also left before the arrival of the flagship containing d'Anville.

At 2 a.m. on the morning of September 27, d'Anville died of apoplexy, though some in the crew thought he had been poisoned. He was buried on the 28th on a small island in the harbour, known to have been George's Island. At 6 p.m. on the afternoon of the Duc's death, D'Estournel arrived with the rest of the fleet, including three ships-of-the-line. The French held a council of war on the *Trident*, with D'Estournel, now in command, proposing they return to Europe. The others disagreed, feeling duty bound to attack the English, at least at Annapolis Royal. As a consequence of being voted down and distraught that the expedition had failed, D'Estournel killed himself by falling on his sword. He was also buried on George's Island. His remains were afterwards removed to France.

What was left of the fleet, now under Jonquiere, remained at Chebucto well into October. They spent several weeks around Birch Cove on the western side of the Basin, receiving fresh supplies from Acadian farmers and trying to recuperate from the voyage. According to sworn reports from two English prisoners, at least 1,135 died of scurvy and dysentery during this period, out of a total of about 2,400 men who died during the whole expedition.

On October 3 the *Renomme* sailed for Quebec with four vessels laden with stores. A brigantine was sent to France with dispatches. The *Parfait*, a warship of fifty guns, was set afire, along with prizes from the West Indies and Carolinas and several New England fishing craft. According to some reports, several ships of war were also sunk on the eastern side of the Basin. The hulls were reportedly visible in calm weather for many years afterwards and there are stories of English settlers recovering wine from them in the 19th century.

The fleet sailed somewhere around mid-October 1746 with foty-two ships, heading for Annapolis Royal. There were five shiploads of sick and dying sailors and soldiers. Off Cape Sable, they struck more storms and the fleet was again dispersed. Two ships made their way to Annapolis, where they found the 50-gun *Chester* and the frigate *Shirley*. Dispirited, they chose not to attack but turned around and all headed back to France.

Duc d'Anville's remains were found in Louisbourg during excavations in 1932, buried under the Chapel in the King's Bastion. His remains had evidently been recovered from George's Island and removed to Louisbourg before the fortress fell to the British in 1758.

Local students of history have always had a fascination with this expedition, probably because of its tragic end. Naturally, over time, stories grew up about buried treasure. Ghost stories abound as well, including one that I had related to me first hand. Fact and fiction are inextricably interwoven into the story and, when a group of veteran divers gets together, still more fiction gets created as they tell their individual stories and pass on the latest rumours about some supposed find.

As long as there have been divers in the harbour, the lure of the *Parfait* and the other ships supposedly sunk in the Basin have held a certain magic. Reports of divers searching for the ships go back as far as 1835. In September 1955, local newspapers reported the attempts of a diver named John Sweeney to locate the wreck of another of d'Anville's ships, the *Caribou*. As far as I have been able to ascertain, nothing came of it and others have picked up the search in the years that have followed.

In 1995, the Geological Survey of Canada published the results of a survey of the harbour bottom. Using sidescan sonar, they had mapped the harbour bottom, finding a number of interesting anomalies in the process. One such anomaly was what appeared to be a wooden shipwreck. The computer-enhanced underwater map declared that the wreck could well be from the French fleet. It clearly shows the ribs of a wooden vessel, in eighteen to twenty-two metres of water in front of Mount St. Vincent University.

On November 12, 1998, I accompanied five other divers, including the director of the Maritime Museum of the Atlantic, in a search for the wreck. We were joined by members of the Nova Scotia Underwater Council and the Curator of Special Places aboard the National Harbours Board boat *Maintainer I*. We spent many hours in the water, but found nothing. Such are the vagaries of wreck hunting.

But that was not the end of the story. A few weeks later, using an underwater camera, the navy located the site again. We were engaged as divers to examine and survey the wreck and during the next few months, several of the group examined it thoroughly. Alas, it was not the wreck of a French warship, but that of a more modern wooden vessel, probably sunk in the

1940s after it had outlived its usefulness. The consensus among those who have seen old wrecks under the water is that the wood from the French ships is probably completely gone and all that would remain would be the ballast stones, perhaps some cannons (but they were valuable and would most likely have been recovered before the *Parfait* was discarded) and metal or ceramic objects. All of this has probably settled into the harbour bottom.

During a dive on the wreck in early January 2000, several of us had an experience we would be happy to forget. Dana, Jim Camano and I decided to take some underwater photos of the wreck, so on a Saturday morning we launched Jim's open boat and set out. Since the wreck site was well away from any traffic lanes and there was absolutely nothing moving in the harbour, we didn't bother to radio Halifax Traffic Control to advise them that we were diving in the harbour. Who would care?

It was blowing out of the northwest with snow squalls, so we put on our drysuits before heading out for the two kilometre ride to the wreck site. When we got there, we were thoroughly drenched and, since it was very windy and the temperature was below freezing, we were getting a little chilly. Jim had marked the site with a buoy, to which he tied the boat. When everything was secure, the three of us entered the water. If there had been four of us, we would have paired off, with one pair remaining in the boat while the first two dived, and then switching. Because there were three of us and because of the cold, we decided to leave the boat unattended.

We descended to twenty-one metres (70 feet) and found the wreck, the ribs towering over our heads, covered in anemones and very photogenic. Then Jim and I decided to swim off the stern to check for additional wreckage, as ships sometimes break in two while sinking and we suspected this might be the case with this one. After covering a large area, we had trouble finding our way back to the wreck, so we decided to surface and head back to the boat. After about fifteen seconds on the surface, with waves breaking over us, we both asked the same question: "Where's the boat?" It was nowhere to be seen.

After craning our necks to try to get some height to see over the waves, we located Dana off in the distance chasing the drifting boat to leeward. Jim decided to follow him and I headed for shore to try to find a telephone if that became necessary. It took me twenty minutes to snorkel my way to shore. There I was faced with twelve metres of water below me and, ahead of me, a wall of huge boulders, above which was a railway yard. Above my head, I could see the railway cars coming and going, being shunted back and forth by the diesel engines forming the trains that would take the containers coming ashore from a large container ship about a kilometre and a half away.

Our boat, in the meantime, was heading for this ship, with Dana and Jim in hot pursuit – so to speak. After a half-hour chase, Dana reached it first just before it struck the rocks behind the ship. Barely able to drag himself over the side, he managed to get his gear off and the engine going. He headed back upwind to pick up a very relieved Jim, relieved to be out of the water but doubly relieved that his boat was still in one piece. They then came and picked me up and we headed back to the boat launch.

When we were about halfway back we noticed a red inflatable heading our way, with two official looking occupants clad in survival suits. They came alongside and advised us that they were from the Coast Guard and that they had received a call that there was a boat in distress in the Basin. We told them our story and advised them that we were okay and thanks for the thought, but we could manage on our own. We continued on our way with the inflatable hanging back on our quarter. They followed us to shore and politely advised us that they would have to file a report, the end result of which would probably be a fine. To our great relief, nothing came of the incident.

The Founding of Halifax

On June 21, 1749, less than three years after the French fleet had left Chebucto, His Britannic Majesty's 20-gun sloop of war, *Sphinx*, entered the serene setting that had witnessed their suffering, followed shortly by thirteen other ships carrying 2,576 of the king's loyal subjects. They had departed Portsmouth, England, on May 14 and had come to establish a new settlement.

They did not come because they had been forced by persecution and conscience to leave the mother country as some had in the past, nor to take the gospel to "the savages," as some had, nor even to create an empire for His Majesty, for that matter was already well in hand. No such lofty ideals controlled their motives. Nor did they come for commercial reasons, to engage in that most Canadian of undertakings, the fur trade, whose tentacles were rapidly beginning to span the continent. The fact is, they were out of work and had been induced by advertisements encouraging "officers and private men lately discharged from the Army and Navy" to settle in Nova Scotia.

The government had recruited them and, in a manner that would become an honoured Maritime tradition, they were supported with government funding. (According to at least one historian, Halifax was the only North American city whose settlement the British government ever funded.) Their *raison d'etre* was to be the citizens of a garrison town, for the French were being troublesome in the land of Acadia. This land had been French land, having been settled by de Monts and Samuel de Champlain, Canada's first settlers, in 1604 near what is now Annapolis Royal. But by the Treaty of Utrecht of 1713, which had ended yet another of the interminable wars between England and France, it was now British. The problem was that it was still populated by French-speaking Acadians and, while they had no great love for France, they were not falling over themselves to embrace the English crown.

The only English presence in the colony was the so-called capital at Annapolis Royal on the Bay of Fundy and the fishing outpost at Canso near what the French had named Ile Royale. Today it's Cape Breton Island. On Cape Breton was the elaborate fortress of Louisbourg, which the French had built earlier in the century to protect the entrance to the St. Lawrence River, key to their dwindling North American empire. But the English considered the Louisbourg fortress to be a serious threat to their colonies and activities in the New World. Even though they had captured Louisbourg in 1745, and managed to hold on to it thanks to the ill fortune the French fleet had suffered in 1746, they were obliged by the Treaty of Aix-la-Chapelle to return it in 1748, to the great consternation of the people of Boston.

Boston was the closest English town of substance. Since it was so far away, Louisbourg needed, in the view of the governments of New England, to be counterbalanced with a closer English presence in Nova Scotia to act as a buffer to protect Boston. Chebucto was the perfect location, so the English government, responding to pressure and seeing the benefits, advertised for families to populate the new garrison town. Free passage, support for twelve months, arms and ammunition for defence, and tools and materials for clearing the land and engaging in the fishery were enough to attract 1,176 settlers and their families. On fourteen ships, they set sail from England on May 14 of 1749 and sailed into Chebucto on June 21.

During a period notorious for deplorable conditions aboard ships and long and dreary voyages often resulting in many deaths along the way, this voyage was remarkable in that only one death occurred on the passage, that of a child. The Board of Trade and Plantations, the sponsor of the undertaking, was credited with providing good ventilation below decks, a very modern addition to their ships. In the account of the expenditures for the settlement are the ventilators for six ships at a cost of just over £102.

This innocuous addition was significant because sailing ships were "battened down" in stormy weather. This was a process of sealing the holds in case water should flow in. Anybody in the holds would be cut off from any fresh air for weeks at a time. In the days of virtually no sanitation on ships, this could lead to a serious situation and many deaths occurred on sailing ships because of the lack of fresh air. The subject was getting attention. The authoritative *Boswell's Life of Johnson* states that in 1756 Samuel Johnson, the giant of eighteenth century English letters, critiqued a work on *Distilling Sea-Water, Ventilators in Ships and Curing an Ill Taste in Milk*.

"... And we shall soon have a very convenient and pleasant town built, which is to be called Halifax."

The President of the Board of Trade and Plantations, George Montague, the Earl of Halifax, had supported the plans for the settlement when they were submitted in 1748. In his honour, the new town was to bear his name. The man leading the expedition, Colonel the Honourable Edward Cornwallis, MP, has been credited with being a competent leader. One settler, writing home on July 25, 1749, in speaking of Cornwallis, wrote, "He seems to have nothing in view but the interest and happiness of all; his zeal and prudent conduct in the difficult task assigned him cannot be too much emphasised."

Like all such undertakings, the first winter was difficult and the climate and the necessity for hard work shocked some of the early settlers. Some died and some left, but more settlers followed. As the town thrived and because of its fairly well orchestrated beginnings under Edward Cornwallis, New Englanders saw a chance to make a dollar. They had supplied many of the materials initially used in building the town and knew an opportunity when they saw one, so many came and stayed. Late in the summer of 1750, the *Alderney* arrived from England with 353 new citizens and they received lots on the eastern side of the harbour, becoming Dartmouth's first citizens. Then, in September 1751, the ship *Ann* sailed into the harbour with three hundred German settlers, with additional Germans and other foreigners arriving in 1751 and 1752.

And so, for 250 years, with further immigration and normal population growth, people of European ancestry have called the area around Halifax Harbour their home. For much of that time, many areas within the harbour were considered remote regions, miles from the towns with no roads and accessible only by water. Their presence has changed the harbour and continues to have a lasting impact on its waters and shore.

What's it Like?

To a diving enthusiast, being underwater is pure magic and the joy of entering this peaceful world is unlike anything else that life has to offer. Topside, life is often hectic but the underwater world slows you down and takes away any desire or ability to hurry. It is a slow motion world without any limitation of movement. This world imposes strict rules that will not tolerate mistakes and when you become a part of it, it envelops your body and demands every ounce of attention you have. It is this very intensity – the challenge, the risk, the anticipation of what lies just beyond the range of visibility – that makes it so beguiling. Harbour diving presents its own unique set of joys for the small group who feel the call.

Not everybody warms up to the idea of diving year round in and about a busy northern harbour like Halifax. It is a far cry from the scenes we see on television, where colourful fish swim in warm, clear water past pink coral and white sand; where beautiful young women in designer diving outfits glide elegantly among the fish. These same ladies diving in Nova Scotia waters would be well-hidden under very complicated and unwieldy attire.

It starts with a neoprene dive suit, not likely to be in any designer's fall collection, even though manufacturers, in their advertising, try to attach sex appeal to their products. There are two kinds of dive suits. A wetsuit fits like a second skin. It is not watertight but provides an excellent insulator, is less expensive than a drysuit, and is adequate for most dives. A drysuit, on the other hand, is more expensive and complex. It is watertight and somewhat baggy, enabling the diver to wear light clothing. The upside is you're warmer. The downside is you're less streamlined and if you get a serious leak – which rarely happens – you're in deep trouble. Add a lead weight belt around the waist, ankle weights, tank, hood, mitts, boots, buoyancy vest, and this seemingly leisurely and laid-back sport quickly loses its simplicity. One of the greatest

Charlene Barker with 2 tanks strapped under her arm and 2 on her back, ready to dive on the Kaaparen, 240 feet below. Photo by Mark Gangl.

challenges in scuba diving in this country is being able to have fun while wearing all this gear.

For many, it's not worth it. The dropout rate among divers is around 75 percent of those who take the training and get certified. Most trainers feel it is because of the realization that it just isn't like in the movies. Much of the time, everything is brown, gray and drab, the fish are plentiful but camouflaged, or designed for filleting instead of photographing, the water is obscured by plankton and other growths and it is oh, so cold. That is why we human beings cannot dive below about nine metres without covering every inch of our bodies with rubber or neoprene, except perhaps our lips – and some even manage that.

Imagine yourself as a diver. The funny looking suit is your armour and that seven millimetres of neoprene enables you to safely enter this world where you were never meant to go. It is tight and tries to cut off your breathing, it is stiff and bulky, and makes your arms stick off from your sides as though you have starched your armpits. Its buoyancy causes you to float so high out of the water that you cannot swim. To overcome this tendency, you are obliged to wear up to eighteen kilograms of lead around your waist, causing a constant annoyance to the lower back, as you are prone for 95 percent of the time. The thick three-fingered mitts, made from the same material, reduce the functionality of your hands by 80 percent or more.

Throw a 16-kilogram tank on your back, stuff your mouth full of breathing apparatus and put on a mask which eliminates the ability to breathe through your nose, while seriously limiting your field of vision. In the process it cuts off visual contact with your equipment, which means you have to make any adjustments or handle emergencies by feel, with hands that have lost 80 percent of their dexterity.

No problem! Diving is for optimists.

Put on fins and now you know how a seal would feel downtown. You can't stand or walk, of course, because this extra weight has completely changed your balance and you can't see down. Now, if you can just make it across those slimy rocks . . .

Somehow, you get yourself into the water, and take a look around.

In the Water Column

The biggest single factor affecting the quality of a dive is the visibility, because it's hard to enjoy what you cannot see. Underwater visibility varies widely from week to week and even from day to day, depending primarily on the weather, especially wind and rain. The ocean's currents move great masses of water around and, with it, all the things that affect visibility. A typical harbour dive presents visibility in the three- to five-metre range. It can be much better – usually in winter – and it can be far worse.

With this limited range of vision, the area of water between the surface and the bottom – called the water column – is a bland, lifeless, disorienting, what some might consider scary, void. You don't know if you can see or not, because there is nothing to look at, even though it is not dark. You can be sinking or ascending and not know which way you're going, because there is absolutely no point of reference when you cannot see the bottom or the surface. Such times call for precise attention to detail and complete trust in your gauges, as improper control of your rate of ascent can lead to serious injury or even death.

You must control your rate of descent but even more important is the rate at which you come to the surface. When the dive is completed and it is time to surface, you must do so carefully and methodically. As the ascent begins, the bottom quickly disappears below you, much as the earth grows smaller and disappears below a rocket ship as it blasts off. The depth gauge is indispensable, for it is the only way that you can determine how fast you are coming up. Both descent and ascent are determined by your buoyancy, which varies depending on how deep you are. The deeper you go, the less buoyant you are.

What causes a diver's buoyancy to vary with depth? The pressure that the water exerts on your body increases as you go deeper. You quickly discover this when you dive into a swimming pool and feel the pressure against your ears. The pressure doubles at ten metres (33 feet) and adds another atmosphere every ten metres as you descend. In movies about submarines, we are constantly reminded that the sub can only go so deep before it is crushed like an egg by the enormous pressures hundreds of metres down.

The neoprene diving suit is full of tiny bubbles of air and is very buoyant, necessitating a weight belt to help you sink. As you start to go down, the pressure of the water compresses the suit, making it less buoyant, so you start to sink faster – which compresses the suit more, and so on. To compensate, you let air from your tank into your buoyancy vest. This counteracts the tendency to sink and with practice you learn how to become neutrally buoyant, so that you neither sink nor rise. When your buoyancy is neutral and you are at, say fifteen metres (50 feet) depth, you can lie perfectly still in the water, with no effort. Descend a little and you must continue to add air to the vest; come up a little and you must let some out.

As you go up, the pressure decreases so your suit expands again, making it more buoyant. The air in your buoyancy vest also expands for the same reason, increasing buoyancy even more. So you need to have your wits about you to expel this air before you start an unscheduled, and uncontrolled, trip to the surface. A diver must be vigilant to maintain as close to neutral buoyancy as possible and to stem any tendency to come up too fast.

Here's why. You are breathing compressed air while underwater. As you ascend, with the decrease in water pressure the air that is inside your lungs expands like the air in your buoyancy vest expands, and the tiny bubbles in your suit expand. There have been occasions when I needed to come up faster than recommended and have needed to get the compressed air out of my lungs as it expanded. The procedure is to keep breathing out. It is interesting, indeed, to breathe out steadily for twenty-five or thirty seconds without inhaling. Coming up too fast without getting this excess air out of your lungs can be disastrous. So, a proper rate of ascent is important.

An Unplanned Ascent

It happened to me one day. While on the bottom, I was negatively buoyant, so I pressed the little button on my inflator valve that allows air into my drysuit. A second or two is all it usually takes, because the air in the tank is under such high pressure. To my shock, the button jammed and my suit started inflating at an alarming rate, which meant I was about to head up in a hurry. Of course, I didn't want that so I grabbed the nearest heavy object I could find to weigh me down – a boulder, which gave me a few seconds to try and fix things. But, because my hands held me down, my feet became lighter so the air flowed up to my feet, leaving me suspended and "falling up," with more air pouring into my suit and making matters worse.

I managed to detach the hose from the valve, which stopped the air flow, but a lot of air had entered my suit, making me very buoyant, so I was quickly losing the battle to hold on to the rock. I had to get rid of the extra air but the valve through which the air vents from my suit is located in the shoulder. That is the logical place to put it, because the air is light and needs to vent from the highest place. But in my upside down position the valve was in the lowest place so I needed to get upright in order to get rid of this extra air. To do that, I would have to let go of the rock. When I let go of the rock, I knew I would not be able to flip over and vent the excess air in time to prevent an uncontrolled ascent.

All this happened in a matter of seconds. I found myself upside down, slowly losing my grip on the slippery rock that I was hugging, and breathing too fast because of the extra exertion. There was only one thing to do. I released my grip on the rock, and let myself go to the surface, flipping onto my back, spreading my arms and legs to slow my ascent, all the while exhaling at a steady rate as I had learned to do in my training, and purging air from my suit. It was winter so there were no boats to worry about. I hit the surface and, to my relief, was none the worse for the experience. I bobbed around for a few minutes, collected my faculties, and had a rest. Since I still had plenty of air left, I didn't want to give up the dive, but I also didn't want to take unnecessary risks, so I went into shallower water where the pressure was lower and I could continue the dive without needing to re-attach my inflator.

On the Bottom

Non-divers think that the dive is spent in some undefined place between bottom and the surface and rarely stop to realize that the majority of the dive takes place on the bottom where there is something to see – usually. I say usually because it is very easy to obscure the view while on the bottom; a careless wave of the arm or a poorly aimed kick of the fins will stir up the ever present silt, which slowly rises from the bottom in a swirl like a dust storm in a western movie. Two or three such kicks and you have a difficult situation on your hands, as visibility falls close to zero. Rise up a metre or so and you can often get above it, as an airplane gets above the white puffy clouds on takeoff. The puffy clouds, though, are brown and can ruin the dive, for you are now cut off from the same bottom that you came down to check out.

When several divers are poking around on the bottom a veritable blackout can occur, not a happy place for somebody who has trouble dealing with confined spaces. If the blacked-out area is large, you will need to keep your thoughts and fears under control for there may be no quick exit from the situation. In scuba diving, nothing is ever fast. If the silt has risen a long distance from the bottom, going up can be an unwise option if you're in the presence of boats or wharves because of the risk of hanging up in something. At such times, the only option may be to grope your way along the bottom to more clear surroundings. This usually takes only a few seconds.

The silt is virtually everywhere; it is simply a question of how deep it is. On all dives in the harbour, it is a factor that must be considered, so an experienced harbour diver will use any currents to his or her advantage, always heading into the current whenever possible. If the current is strong or you are obliged to go with it because that is the direction in which you want to travel, you can find yourself in the frustrating position of spending the whole dive in a cloud, like Pigpen, the *Peanuts* character, as you and the silt cloud travel along together.

Much of the harbour is bounded by steep banks and the bottom is covered with rocks, from marble sized to enormous boulders, some as big as a house. The kelp, which can attach itself to anything, easily reaches a height of three metres or more and in some places like the Northwest Arm it, too, is often covered with a thin layer of silt. When coming ashore from a long dive, you may find yourself separated from the bank by large boulders that sport a healthy growth of silt-covered kelp, a sure recipe for a blackout. The unwelcome alternative to going through it is to swim up over it, which will put you up in the void. The best option is often a trip to the bottom, among the stalks of the kelp and the base of the boulders, with a sharp eye on the compass to make sure you don't get lost and head out to sea.

Getting lost is a very real risk, because your line of sight is so short and you are not travelling on a track such as a road or sidewalk. It is essential to keep constant reference to the compass while swimming underwater, to avoid nasty surprises. The corollary is that you must have faith in your compass because at times you will instinctively want to take a different direction.

To get the most out of diving, you must enjoy your own company. Even when diving with others, it is a solitary sport because you are unable to carry out anything beyond the most basic communications. You are often physically alone and you are always alone with your thoughts. There are times in harbour diving when you need to keep a short rein on your thoughts and your imagination. This can be difficult when there is nobody to talk to and keep you focused.

It is also a parochial sport: you don't get to review the landscape. On life insurance forms, I have seen the question "Do you engage in dangerous sports such as skydiving or scuba diving?" It is ironic that they are linked together and even share similar names, because they are so different. The skydiver's world is measured in kilometres, while the scuba diver's world is measured in metres. The skydiver is literally on top of the world as he pursues his passion, with the world laid out below him. The scuba diver, on the other hand, is below almost everything, with a very limited field of vision. For example, when you are diving a shipwreck, the visibility is rarely good enough to enable you to see the whole wreck at once. This means that, as a diver swims around the wreck, he is constantly building a mental picture of what the whole thing must look like.

A great deal of mental energy is needed to interpret what you see or think you see. When the sun is shining and you're among big things — boulders, old boilers from the days of steam, submerged wharves, anchored boats — they cast dark and forbidding shadows that invite you to turn and go the other way. From outside the shadow it is impossible to see what lies within, such is the strange way the light acts underwater. There are but two choices: to swallow your pride and turn back or to keep going, with literally blind faith that what lies beyond is friendly. It usually is. And you never turn back. Harbour diving is for the incurably curious.

Just as challenging is the situation in limited visibility when everything is reduced to blurred shapes. Up ahead is a tall, dark (always dark) outline rising from the bottom. You blink several times to try and focus, and venture a little closer; the closer you get the more you have to crane your neck upward to take it in. It's covered in an enormous growth of kelp. There could be anything lurking in there. Closer, closer. The other fear is that it might be unstable and fall on you. (Might as well consider all the unpleasant possibilities.) It usually turns out to be part of an old abandoned wharf, or an old fishing boat, or yet another boulder.

Most high objects under the ocean are not unstable and are not waiting to fall down on you. This is not the case in fresh water. The ocean tides and storms make sure that weak things get beaten down. A wooden boat that has not collapsed to the bottom will fall on its own in due time. On the other hand, fresh water moves very little, so that a wooden wreck can be very unstable, and, if it has deteriorated sufficiently, the slightest movement of the water can send it tumbling.

There are other risks. There is the ever-present fear of entanglement in an old net, a coil of cable, or a mass of twisted metal dropped from some ancient dock or long forgotten construction project. And there is the fear of coming up under something and being cut off from the surface.

The harbour rarely freezes over, but in late winter there are patches of ice that can move around. Greg and I had the unpleasant surprise of entering the water only to come up forty-five minutes later in the same location and find ourselves cut off from shore, thanks to a patch of ice that had been blown in by changing winds. That meant we had a long swim around the patch, not life-threatening but definitely inconvenient. The thinnest ice is a problem, for even though you can surface through it, you can't swim through it, so it can block the route to your destination – the shore – and ruin your day. On a particularly cold day, we had a thin layer of ice form above us while we were in the water. The water was perfectly calm, so we couldn't see the ice until we came up through it. Being paper thin, it posed no risk but when we tried to snorkel through it on the surface, it cut into the tiny parts of our faces that were exposed.

Sounds

Those who don't dive think it is a quiet sport. It isn't. A dive in the harbour is full of weird and inexplicable noises. There is hardly a moment of silence in diving, even in the most secluded area because of the noise from your breathing. Each breath you take is a hollow, metallic rushing sound as your regulator, located near the back of your head, delivers compressed air through a hose to your mouth and on to your lungs. When you exhale it sends a rush of bubbles directly past both your ears: gurgle, rumble, rattle.

The harbour itself has a wealth of sounds, from the distant, slow groan of a faraway ship to speedboats, to a passing train, to the sound of trucks crossing the bridges, to those mysterious bang, bang, bangs of somebody working on something at the Dockyard or at a wharf somewhere. Sound carries long distances underwater and has no apparent direction associated with it. When it occurs it seems to come from everywhere. It is a most peculiar experience to hear an extremely loud whirring of a boat's engine until it becomes unbearable and you think it's about to run over you, so you slip into shallow water and head up to investigate, only to find that there is nothing there.

You mutter an inaudible "Huh?" put your face back into the water, something on the bottom catches your attention and the little incident is forgotten.

I have had many kinds of vessels pass over me, from canoes to container ships. In the early days of diving many years ago, we dove an area frequented by large ship traffic. Foolishly, we had no lookouts but simply kept deep enough for any ships that came along to pass over us. From that experience, I learned that you cannot hear a big ship approaching. The engines, which make the bulk of the noise, are in the stern of the vessel. Some ships are so big that when the bow goes over you, the stern and, therefore, the engine are still a long way away. You don't hear the sound until the ship is above you and when the noise is at its loudest, the ship has already gone past.

The loudest vessels are the supply boats used to service the offshore oil and gas drilling platforms. These vessels are generally sixty metres or so in length and serve a dual purpose: keeping the rigs supplied with everything they need and towing large loads – including the rigs themselves. They have very powerful engines and when they maneuver from the docks, they use thrusters that generate such a noise they seem to move the very stones on the bottom.

Even though the idea of having one of these ships pass over you when diving sounds disconcerting, if you are deep enough, there is not much more danger than with normal diving. The argument goes that if you have an emergency and need to come up and there is a ship above you, well, you aren't coming up. That is a legitimate argument. On the other hand, divers who penetrate wrecks or dive in caves are in the same predicament, and making an emergency ascent from twenty-five or thirty metres is fraught with a multitude of risks anyway. Be that as it may, I stopped diving under moving ships years ago and certainly don't recommend it to others.

The most dangerous craft, though, are pleasure boats. There are two types that are especially insidious to divers: sailboats and speedboats. The first problem is that when such boats are out, they are often out in large numbers on pleasant summer days. The second problem is that they can frequent shallow waters, which ships avoid, so there is always a chance of encountering one. On top of that, speedboats are fast and can come out of nowhere when you are on the surface. Sailboats, on the other hand, are slow, but because they are quiet, it is easy to surface with the false sense that there are no craft around, only to have one run over you.

Who Needs it?

With all the inconvenience, uncertainly and hazards, why would a sane "grown-up" wish to spend his or her precious leisure hours diving in Halifax Harbour? The short answer is because of the mystery, the discovery, and the voyage back in time. I have seen things nobody else ever gets to see and go places that are strictly out of bounds for 99.9 percent of the population. The divers with whom I associate are confirmed history addicts and most are maritime history addicts. In the harbour there is the evidence of our maritime history in the discarded china, the miscellaneous brass items, the occasional wreck, the ruins of old docks.

More than the maritime history is the connection with everyday life in an earlier time, centuries ago or just the other day. The bottles, clay tobacco pipes, crockery, dishes, glassware and the other castoffs of society are mundane objects; their owners probably never gave them a second thought. But to our little group they represent a peek into the way life was lived in the past.

Many people give up diving because it turns out not to be what they had expected. It is not what I expected either. It's better. It meets the criteria of any good hobby, with exercise *and* rest, mental *and* physical challenge, soothing relaxation *and* excitement, in heat *or* cold, as an all day event *or* a quick dive before breakfast. While many of my diving friends and I have participated in diving down south, and have certainly enjoyed the experience, we prefer the variety and the challenge offered on the Atlantic coast of Canada.

Bottle Diving

When word hit New England that a town was to be built at Chebucto, American craft shortly began to arrive with things for sale including liquid wares. Among the first settlers, William Steele, a brewer, was granted 101 hectares (250 acres) in Eastern Passage. The relationship between the settlers and the ancient pleasure of imbibing came early and has never gone away. Sailors, ferry passengers, navy men, fishermen, dock workers, ocean liner passengers, and ordinary town residents all discarded their bottles over the side and left a rich harvest of specimens for those with the interest to go looking for them.

One day on a routine dive looking at fish I came across my first 100-year-old bottle, which just looked like a curiosity. I took it home and decided I would like to find more. A few weeks later in twenty-five metres of water, I found myself staring at an area on the bottom with dozens of extremely thick glass pop bottles with cork tops and heavy embossed writing "Idris, London." I was hooked.

There are many enthusiastic bottle collectors all over the world and there is an abundance of interesting and unique specimens in Halifax for them to seek. In *The Bottle Collector*, Azor Vienneau has written that in 1865 there were 218 liquor dealers in Halifax, of which 28 were wholesalers. There were seven breweries, along with many pop bottlers. The level of alcohol consumption seems incredible. There was a time in early Halifax when a church or school had to service more than one thousand inhabitants, but there was a licensed liquor shop for every one hundred people, old or young.

Halifax is a port city so its contacts with the rest of the world have always been extensive and frequent. There was a steady influx of beverages on Royal Navy ships and other navies that sailed the world, along with the many shipping lines that called at Halifax. There were also countless schooners, brigs and other sailing vessels that came and went, so the potential for finding interesting bottles in Halifax Harbour is as good as anywhere in the world. In the harbour, there are bottles once used for liquor, soda pop, milk and medicine; bottles used for stove bluing, boot blacking and hair restoring. There are bottles for food, bitters, vinegar, beer, perfume, lubricants, and cod liver oil.

Finding Bottles in the Ocean

Any bottle diver with a large collection of high quality specimens has worked long and hard to acquire it, for bottle diving is an activity that requires tenacity, skill and physical fitness, and a willingness to go to unusual and uninviting places. Most bottles on the bottom of the ocean got there because they were cast from boats and ships or from wharves, as part of the household trash. To keep their passengers and crew well-fed and watered, ships had to carry plenty of food and beverages. For example, one ship – perhaps the most famous liner of all, the *Titanic* – carried 20,000 bottles of beer, 1,500 bottles of wine, 850 bottles of liquor, 3,000 tea cups, and 12,000 dinner plates.

There are two ways to look for bottles: using luck or being a little more scientific. Bottles that were dropped from moving boats can be found anywhere that a boat could go, so when hunting for them, a diver must rely primarily on luck. The chances of success are proportionate to the amount of area covered, as the pickings are not normally concentrated but are thinly spread far and wide. To cover a large area requires fairly shallow water because the deeper you go the faster you consume your air supply which, of course, limits your bottom time and consequently the amount of area you can cover. The second method is the "scientific" approach. It means you have to do some investigating beforehand, trying to determine where people lived dozens or hundreds of years ago. This method has an element of luck associated with it as well because when you locate a site where people once lived, the geography of the bottom still needs to be ideal.

The first requirement of the "ideal" situation is that the early occupants unwittingly cooperated with you and deposited their garbage into the water, for there is no guarantee that they did. Let's suppose they did. Now, the geographic and physical characteristics need to be in balance. Those characteristics are water depth, bottom conditions, shore geography and water movement. The best bottle dive site is a place with about six to twelve metres (20 to 40 feet) depth, going down a reasonably steep underwater slope from shore, not exposed to the open ocean, and located on a point of land.

You need these conditions to avoid the silt, which is the enemy of the bottle diver. Coves and harbours tend to collect silt naturally over time. Rain and melting snow running off the land deposit mud up to tens of metres deep in places. This material swallows up anything dropped into it, including those precious bottles. So when defining proper "bottling" conditions the silt problem is a big factor. The second enemy is wave action which will toss the bottles around in the water, breaking or scratching them or burying them in sand or gravel. The ideal dive site just described generally does not present these problems because at nine metres (30 feet), wave action is minimal or non-existent if the site is in a secluded area. A slope generally will have less silt than a flat bottom. By being on a point, the currents caused by the changing tides will keep the silt swept away, holding your treasures until pickup day.

In addition to patience, steady nerves and good presence of mind are also needed for much of this type of diving, as you find yourself in tight places that can be dark, or constricting in some other way. If the bottles were tossed overboard, they are probably in company with a lot of other paraphernalia forming an old dumpsite, so the general landscape can be pretty ugly. Dilapidated wharves, coal, slag from steam engines, tires, tires, tires, nondescript rusty iron objects, vast growths of seaweed, and huge boulders all have to be negotiated with minute care and some days it can be like looking for the proverbial needle in the haystack, especially when visibility is down to one or two metres.

Occasionally, I have found good bottling on a flat bottom if there is sufficient current to keep the silt swept away. This, too, will depend on the shape of the land. The waterway between two islands – what Newfoundlanders call a "tickle"– is an example. The constriction acts like the neck of a bottle and speeds up the movement of the incoming or outgoing tide. The problem is that if the current is keeping the bottom swept, it wants to sweep you away, too. The secret here is to dive during the "slack" tide, when the tide is high or low and is about to change. There is a lull of about a half-hour when you can scurry out to these challenging locations and reap a fruitful harvest.

Such sites call for good air conservation and precise underwater navigation. Good physical conditioning is also necessary, as you may be called upon to deal with the currents if your timing is not perfect, and it rarely is. Swimming against a strong current to get to shore is difficult because it means you consume more air than you normally would as a result of the increased exertion. The better shape you're in, the less air you will consume. And the one thing that is constantly in your thoughts when diving is "How much air do I have left?" There are many things to keep in mind when diving, but watching your air supply is at the top of the list.

On the Bottom

Most of the ocean's bottom consists of rock, sand or mud. Off Atlantic Canada the shore is typically rocky, eventually extending to sand at the bottom. A sandy beach is just an extension of the ocean's sandy bottom. Coves and harbours that are deep or protected from wave action contain a muddy bottom that comes from centuries of runoff from the land. If the cove receives water from a river or stream, it will often be muddier than usual.

In Halifax Harbour, this mud can be quite deep, existing in the form of silt in deeper waters that are not subjected to currents. While diving you can push your hand down to your elbow easily or to your shoulder with a little effort. The mud is often permeated with the same material that sits on a rocky bottom – tires, metal objects, rocks and bottles. In places on the waterfront or the Northwest Arm, it is easy to reach into the silt and find bottles strictly by feel. A fellow bottle diver speaks of reaching down with both hands and discovering a case of twenty-four pop bottles dating from the 1940s, still in the wooden case. It was impossible to pull the case up but the individual bottles could be coaxed up because of their tapered shape.

The biggest frustration in bottle diving is having to weed through the myriad of modern bottles to get to the gems. The short, stubby beer bottles and seven-ounce Coca-Cola bottles from that period litter the harbour bottom, especially at major picnic and boating sites like the Northwest Arm. You could almost end up believing that during the 1950s and '60s there was a municipal program to fill in the harbour with beer and pop bottles and every citizen was called upon to deposit as many "stubbies" and Coke bottles into the water as they could.

Through necessity, an experienced bottle diver learns to discern by sight what is modern and what has potential, simply by observing the size and shape. Many bottles are just a shape in the brown silt and you can develop an instinct for recognizing them, but in good bottling sites the bottle will be completely, or at least partially, exposed.

Modern bottles are of no interest to most bottle collectors. What is "modern"? Any bottle with a threaded top, with the possible exception of some preserving jars; screw top lids go back to the first preserving jars, as patented by John Mason in 1858. So, early preserving jars can have a screw top and still be old, but you cannot say the same for other bottle types. The presence of a screw or crown top is a quick and easy way to date many bottles.

The Evolution of the Bottle

The bottle is such an ordinary part of everyday life that we rarely if ever stop to consider its circuitous evolution. The movement and storage of liquids has presented peculiar problems throughout the centuries. Using heavy stone jugs, fragile crockery, wooden vessels, skins and bladders, and finally, glass and plastic, we have struggled through our history to get liquid goods from their point of manufacture to their place of consumption.

Before the glass container was perfected, there were three major issues to be addressed: the affordable and efficient manufacture of the container; the identification of the contents and other pertinent information; and the sealing of the bottle to keep the contents inside, especially challenging if the liquid were gaseous, as with beer and some wines. They needed to be isolated from the air, which could cause spoilage and shrinkage through evaporation. Until the invention of the automatic bottle-making machine at the beginning of the twentieth century, bottles had to be made by hand. For centuries, bottle makers blew a blob of molten glass on the end of a long blowpipe, shaping the bottle with a paddle or on a surface as they went. It required great skill and was slow and, therefore, expensive.

Molded Bottles

In the early part of the nineteenth century, a variety of molds came into use, allowing for more uniformity, but this improved method was still very labour intensive, because every item passed through several pairs of hands. Today, the process, like most manufacturing processes, is fully automated.

Identifying the contents of an early bottle was no trivial matter, when printing was very expensive and every label had to be applied by hand. Owners often wanted to identify their bottles, because bottles were not thrown away after only one use. They were intended to be re-used again and again. In seventeenth and eighteenth century England, it was quite common for individuals to order empty bottles from a manufacturer and have them filled by a beer or wine supplier, or do their own bottling. Specimens exist with the names of the bottles' owners scratched into the glass, such was their value. Another method of identification was to stamp an insignia into the hot, soft glass, much as was done in medieval times when the king would use his signet ring to stamp his identification into a blob of hot wax to seal a letter.

When the mold came into being, it became easy to produce bottles and to emboss product names and warnings against re-use on the side of the bottle. So we see imprecations such as "Property of Charles Gurd & Co Limited, Montreal. Anyone using, destroying or retaining will be prosecuted" emblazoned from top to bottom. Such warnings were placed on bottles because competitive bottlers, especially soda pop manufacturers, routinely placed their own products into any empties they found, and slapped their own label on the side. The Cook and Bernheimer Company, producers of Mount Vernon Pure Rye Whiskey, warned "Refilling of this bottle prohibited." I am unaware of what ghastly fate awaited those who ignored the warning. It is these embossed examples that make such interesting collection items because they represent a link to the past, complete with details.

Keeping Them Corked

The lowly bottle top has an equally interesting history. The problem of how to keep the liquid securely in the bottle was a serious challenge for bottlers for centuries. In the beginning, they used bundles of reeds and anything that could be inserted into the opening at the top. Cork was discovered at a very early date and found to be excellent, except for the problem that it dried out over time.

Like today's wine purchaser, users were expected to store their bottles of liquid with the bottles on their sides, to keep the cork moist. To ensure this rule was rigorously practiced, some bottle manufacturers ear-

A Schweppes torpedo bottle c.1870. From the author's collection.

ly in the nineteenth century did away with the flat bottoms now on virtually all bottles and made them with round or pointed bottoms. Today such bottles are welcome finds, especially the pointed specimens, the design of William Hamilton of Dublin in 1809. Most collectors call them torpedo bottles. These bottles contained soda pop, known in bygone days as "Aerated Waters." Torpedo bottles were placed in elaborate silver holders to grace the center of the dinner table.

As the production of soda pop increased during the nineteenth century, cork became too much of a nuisance, so the race was on for a better stopper. The British adopted an invention of Hiram Codd, who in 1875 came up with the idea of manufacturing bottles with a marble inside. The bottle had to be filled upside down, after which the marble settled into the neck and formed a seal against a rubber ring. The carbon dioxide in the drink soon went into the small amount of air space inside the bottle and the pressure kept the marble in place when the bottle was turned right side up. To consume the drink, the thirsty consumer had to push the marble back into the bottle. If she was in the mood for only half a bottle, she had to find a friend with whom to share, for the top could not be returned to its place without refilling the bottle with an aerated liquid.

Codd-stoppered bottles are serious "keepers," rare because children used to break them to get the marbles. This meant that the pop bottlers had a high loss rate and did not get as many returned as they needed. One Nova Scotia bottler used this type. Kempton Brothers of Milton, near Liverpool, bottled a variety of flavours under the name Milton Aerated Waters in the 1890s. They purchased the bottles from the English manufacturers for seven cents and sold the pop for five cents, a rather expensive proposition if the kids were scooping up the bottles to get the marbles, which, of course, they were.

American and most Nova Scotia soda pop manufacturers opted for the Hutchinson stopper, invented in 1879 by Charles Hutchinson of Chicago. It was based on the same principle of using the gas pressure to force a rubber stopper that was inside the bottle against the underside of the lip. A stiff wire extended from the center of the stopper out through the opening and above the lip and was used to push the stopper inside.

Up to the beginning of the twentieth century, there were several other types of closures of a similar nature in use, but they were clumsy and unsanitary because they got pushed into the bottles and interacted with the sticky contents. All fell prey to the simple, inexpensive and efficient crown top, which is still widely used today. Even it has been improved, eliminating the need for a bottle opener, which was a required household item for most of the twentieth century. The crown closure was invented by William Painter of

Baltimore in 1891 and eventually became the universal choice of bottlers everywhere.

Halifax Pop Bottlers

Making carbonated beverages was a fairly simple process. It consisted of adding a small number of ingredients in a tank to create the carbon dioxide gas that is characteristic of all such drinks. The gas was captured in another tank and bubbled through water to create carbonated water. The last step was to add flavouring and colour and put the finished product in a bottle. The first manufacturers got started in their homes and sold their products in the neighbourhood. Delivery to a store was difficult and slow in the days before the automobile.

It was common for the workers to wear heavy leather aprons and leather coverings on their arms. If they got the mixture wrong and put too much gas in the drink, the bottle was likely to explode. This explains why the first pop bottles were so thick.

The most interesting bottles have the name of the contents' manufacturer embossed in heavy glass lettering across the outside. The first pop bottler in Nova Scotia and one of the first in Canada was H.W. Glendinning, who started in business in Dartmouth in 1836. His descendants were also involved in the ice business. They were one of several firms that harvested ice from the Dartmouth lakes in winter, stored it in huge sheds and then sold it to householders and fishermen during the summer. Sometimes, they even shipped ice to the United States.

Glendinning produced mineral waters at 14 Commercial Street in Dartmouth and maintained offices and a warehouse at 206 Hollis St. in Halifax. His bottles are rare and valuable. Along the way there have been dozens of others, such as J.B. Baker, Duncan MacDougall, Wilson and Sullivan, and John Nash. Four are particularly common: Felix J. Quinn, Whelan and Ferguson, W.H. Donovan, and James Roue. The latter was the father of William Roue, who designed the famous racing schooner *Bluenose*, which graces the Canadian 10-cent piece. Most bottlers were located in the downtown area of Halifax. James Roue was in the Collins Building, which

James Roue crocks, four of them dated 1898, 1900, 1902, 1903. From the author's collection.

still stands as part of the Historic Properties complex on Upper Water Street. William Roue was employed at this plant while he worked on the *Bluenose* design and the company eventually adopted the name "Bluenose Beverages."

Some of these early bottlers used earthenware crocks to purvey their wares. Sometimes called stoneware, these crocks were used to bottle ginger beer, a drink particularly popular with the British army personnel stationed at Halifax. Many crocks have attractive designs and are real prizes to collectors. Nova Scotia is second only to Ontario in the number of different crock designs used in Canada. Several have the dates of use printed on them; for example James Roue issued different dated designs in 1898, 1900, 1902, and 1903.

Milk and Drug Bottles

Although not as old, milk bottles are an interesting item to collect. The oldest Nova Scotia example of which I am aware is from the Scotia Pure Milk Co. Limited with the inscription "Pat Sept. 17th 1889" embossed on the bottom. Halifax and Dartmouth had a surprisingly large number of dairies during the early part of the twentieth century, including Farmer's Pure Milk, Army and Navy Dairy, Maple Leaf Dairy, Woodlawn Dairy, Ideal Dairy, Oxford Dairy, and others.

Almost all milk bottles used clear glass, but the Scotia Pure Milk Co. used two designs of an amber coloured bottle for a brief period. The idea of using coloured bottles for milk did not go down well with careful housewives. These were the days before refrigeration and they wanted to examine what was inside the bottle to make sure they were getting a fresh product.

Hence, the appearance of the word "Pure" on many milk bottles to reassure buyers that they were getting milk — and not buttermilk.

Before the days of pharmacy chains and the big drug companies, druggists prepared many of their own concoctions for their customers. They needed bottles in which to deliver their products, which they could buy in bulk from companies such as Whittal Tatum of New York or Richards Glass Co. of Toronto. For a little extra, these companies would provide the same bottles embossed with the name of the drug store, names such as "E.S. Blackie, 17½ Spring Garden Road, Halifax"; "Taylor's Drug and Prescription Store, Halifax"; and "Avery F. Buckley, Medical Hall, Halifax." I once found a baby's nursing bottle from the 1920s; put out by the Richard's Glass Co, it was called the "Rigo Nurser." Since Greg's wife, Anne, was about to deliver their first child, I gave it to him, a little gift from one collector to another.

Patent Medicines

In addition to drug stores, some enterprising individuals – doctors or otherwise – were in business up to the early years of the twentieth century producing patent medicines with colourful-sounding names. If the medicine didn't exactly cure your malady, it at least let you forget about it for a while, thanks to the extremely high alcohol content. Some were also known to contain morphine, heroin or cocaine. Pendleton's Panacea, Graham's Pain Eradicator, Dr. Kilmer's Swamp Root Kidney Cure, Fellows Syrup of Hypophosphites, and Dr. S.N. Thomas Eclectric Oil hold prominent positions in my collection.

Many of these bottles can be quite attractive and amusing. Warners Safe Cure is a large amber bottle with an elaborate safe embossed on the front. The company was started and built by a retired safe salesman in New York. Being told that "75 in Every Hundred Refused Life Insurance on Account of Kidney Trouble," readers of their ads were enjoined to purchase Warner's Safe Cure, which claimed to cure a multitude of kidney related diseases, along with diabetes.

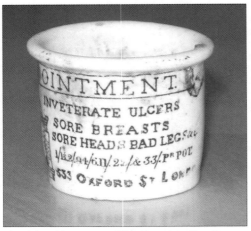

An ointment to cure everything. From John Hagell's collection.

If you think that modern drug ads make fantastic claims, they are merely a shadow of their predecessors. Perry Davis' Vegetable Pain Killer, which author Mark Twain mentions in his autobiography as one of his more unpleasant memories of childhood, professed to cure everything from baldness in people to diarrhea in chickens. In a 1905 newspaper ad the makers of Dr. Chase's Nerve Food stated that "the blood is thin and watery in the spring," while the Burdock Blood Bitters people recommended their product because at the same time of year "the blood becomes thick and sluggish." Radway's Ready Relief cured coughs, colds and pneumonia and one satisfied customer supposedly wrote to the company that it had cured "frosted feet." Yet another in the long line of wonder cures took care of "sore breasts, sore head and bad legs."

At the beginning of the twentieth century, these products were exposed for what they really were and legislation passed to try to control their manufacture and sale. On July 2, 1906, a law came into effect in Nova Scotia requiring strict labelling of patent and proprietary medicines.

Coloured and Clear Glass

One of the challenges for the first bottle manufacturers was to get rid of the ever present green colour on many of their so-called clear bottles. The green and aqua cast of early bottles was caused by iron oxide in the sand from which the glass was made and was very common. Because many customers wanted perfectly clear bottles to show off the purity of their products, bottle manufacturers rose to the challenge.

It was known that if certain materials were added during the manufacturing process, the resulting glass would be coloured. The best known example is the addition of cobalt to make the glass deep blue. Gold was used to produce red glass, making it very collectable. Around the end of the nineteenth century, manufacturers tried several methods to remove all colour from the glass, one of which was the addition of manganese. It worked fine, but little did they know that, over time, the sun's ultraviolet rays would turn the glass a very engaging amethyst colour. Now known as "suncast" bottles, such types are favourites with collectors. Seventy-five or a hundred years of lying on the bottom of the ocean did not retard the process. An amethyst suncast bottle is easy to date because manganese was not available after 1915 as a result of a war shortage.

Free Blown Bottles

Modern bottles are made by inserting a blob of molten glass into a mold. Like all modern processes, it is fully automated and has become increasingly so since the invention of the automatic bottle-making machine by William Owens in 1903. The process leading up to this involved a glassmaker blowing the blob into a mold that was held by an apprentice. Throughout the nineteenth century, molds evolved from a very crude affair to being fairly uniform and efficient, but they still required a good deal of human intervention.

Before molds came along, the whole process had been manual. A glassblower took a blob of molten glass at the end of a two-metre long blowpipe and, with great skill, fashioned a bottle through a combination of blowing and shaping until he was satisfied with the result. Collectors call such a bottle freeblown and they are at the top of the desirability scale for many. No two such bottles are alike, so they present a lot of personality as they sit on display tilted to one side, sometimes distorted with varying thicknesses and generally showing solid character and independence.

Because of the difficulty in maintaining a consistent size when manufacturing these bottles, getting a predictable amount of product with each purchase of wine or beer was next to impossible. The English system of measure was very confusing, with the Queen Anne gallon, the ale/beer gallon, the Irish gallon and a bewildering assortment of Scotch pints, Scotch ale pints, pints, pottles, Winchester half pints, and so on. The most confusing of all were the many sizes of "quart" in use in different parts of England and in different industries. In *Cylindrical English Wine and Beer Bottles* Olive Jones states that ". . . because the bottle makers do not appear to have tried to make quarts of official sizes, it is difficult to know which systems of measure are represented by the quart capacities." The introduction of the imperial gallon in 1824 was meant to bring some order to things. The imperial gallon contained ten pounds (4.5 kilograms) of distilled water, so it was consistent because it was based on weight.

Somewhere along the way, English wine merchants came up with a system that, in a crude and amusing way, compensated for the varying bottle capacities. Ms. Jones continues: "This system was based on a dozen quart bottles that, ideally, should have held three gallons of wine. As the bottles generally did not hold a full quart the three gallons were taken as a substitute and the number of bottles per dozen was adjusted accordingly so that the dozen could be anywhere from 12 to 18 bottles."

She quotes one ad in a London newspaper that advertised fine Old Red Port at 1 shilling 6 pence per quart, 6 shillings per gallon, 18 shillings per *dozen consisting of 13 bottles* (my emphasis).

Bottles were not the only containers with hard to measure capacities. Ships bringing staple goods to Halifax supplied butter by the firkin, rice by the tierce and molasses by the puncheon; sugar arrived in hogsheads, tobacco was packed in kegs, gin was sold by the pipe, figs came in drums and olive oil came in casks.

Crocks and Crabs

In addition to the major categories including pop, liquor and medicine bottles, and ginger beer crocks, there is a wide variety of other bottle types in Halifax Harbour. They include many kinds of crocks that held just about any liquid – molasses, varnish, boot blacking, ink, glue, wine, rum and so on. They range in capacity from a couple of ounces to more than ten gallons

(45.5 litres). There are also preserving jars with upbeat names like Gem, Perfect Seal, Ball Ideal, Improved Crown, and Canadian Jewel, all embossed in very attractive lettering.

When bottles are first recovered from the bottom, they can be a sight to behold. Because they invariably sport every imaginable growth from coraline to barnacles to seaweed, cleaning them is a daunting task. Combine that with a host of occupants that have taken up residence on the insides and only the most committed will bother trying to clean them up. Mussels are the most common of these squatters; they begin life inside the bottle and grow so that they become prisoners. The occasional milk bottle will arise containing a crab or two in the same predicament – protected from predators but also isolated from the food supply.

Newly recovered bottles and crocks. The bottle on the left is at least 200 years old. From the author's collection.

The most effective way to get these bottles into a presentable state is to soak them in an acid solution, which will destroy the coral and other growths. When cleaned they may or may not be presentable for the glass might have deteriorated over time. Early glassmakers were not too careful about mixing their base ingredients in precise proportions, with the result that 150 years later the glass is beginning to break down. Bottles will often have a condition that collectors refer to as "sick glass," whereby the glass falls off the bottle in paper-thin layers, like the skin of an onion. Even though a long period in salt water can be hard on glass, it does not seem to hurt crockery.

Bottle History

Bottle collectors tend to have a well-developed interest in history. Holding a 200-year-old bottle gives you a very personal connection with the past, not necessarily because the item is old but because it belonged to somebody. For example, when you contemplate a bottle with "Lung Tonic" embossed on it, it is easy to picture a person during a time when many were ravaged by tuberculosis, perceiving this humble product as a little bit of hope. We do no less with medicines today.

There is a humorous side as well. During a period when temperance was all the rage, men who would not let liquor pass their lips could, with a clear conscience, take a nip of one of the many kinds of patent medicines containing 90 percent alcohol. In an early account of the Newfoundland seal hunt, I once read of sealers on pack-ice hundreds of kilometres from land, spiking their very humble noontime meal with a few sips of patent medicine, for their health, of course.

Nova Scotia Bottle Manufacturers

Along with identifying a bottle's use and user, bottle collectors also try to identify the bottle's manufacturer. Two Nova Scotia factories manufactured bottles in the late 1800s. Both were located in Trenton, near New Glasgow. Humphrey's Glass Co., owned by five brothers, operated from 1890 to 1917 before moving to New Brunswick under new ownership. Lamont Glass Co. started in the same year and lasted until 1899. Between them, they produced many of the bottles found in local collections, especially the pop bottles used by Nova Scotia bottlers. Humphrey's is generally believed to have produced a wider variety of bottle types, such as fruit jars and medicine bottles, probably because they were around longer.

There was a third glass producer in Trenton. The Nova Scotia Glass Company was the first and it became the largest, operating from 1881 to 1892 and producing pressed glass. The name refers to the mold type. Unlike bottles, which are molded only on the outside (which accounts for the varying thickness of bottles), pressed glass products are molded on all sides. Their products were tableware such as bowls and plates. As far as is known, they did not manufacture bottles.

On very rare occasions, the bottle manufacturers added their "maker's mark" identifying the producer of the product. After years of searching, I finally found a medicine bottle that can be positively identified with the Lamont Glass Company. A small addition to the bottom of the bottle reads "LG Co N G", standing for Lamont Glass Company, New Glasgow. The bottle contained a medicine called Prussian Oil, produced by A.J. Cox and Sons, of Halifax.

Old Nova Scotia bottles can come from several sources: digging at the manufacturing sites in Trenton; digging in old dumps around the province; or from the water, whether it be from the ocean or from lakes and streams. Diving for them is excellent exercise because of the need to cover such a wide area. On many occasions, I have spent an hour and a half in shallow water swimming continuously. The activity reminds me of diving for scallops, which is normally done in six to nine metres (20 to 30 feet) of water, carrying a net bag and swimming, swimming, swimming, while picking up the occasional scallop until the bag becomes too heavy to carry. The difference, of course, especially to those who have no interest in bottle diving, is that the scallop diver is doing something that's useful.

Diving Where the Tugs Dock

The large ships that frequent Halifax are difficult to maneuver within the confines of the harbour and need the services of tugboats to move them about. These busy, powerful vessels nudge ships dozens or even hundreds of times their own size into position at dockside and pull them out again when it's time to go.

A tugboat is little more than a floating engine with propellors, fuel tanks and steering wheel. Extremely nimble, its sole purpose is to push, pull, tow, prod and generally coax other ships to go where they cannot go under their own power. The Navy maintains a tug fleet at Halifax, but commercial shippers rely on the services of Eastern Canada Towing Limited, known as ECTUG, to maneuver their vessels. The two ECTUG docks are on the southern part of downtown, next door to the Maritime Museum of the Atlantic. From here they maintain a fleet of boats in Halifax with others elsewhere on the East Coast of Canada.

ECTUG docks and tugs in winter. Photo by Greg Cochkanoff.

With enormous engines driving two 2-metre, 4-bladed propellors that can turn in any direction, these boats easily keep the bottom in a state of turmoil. A dive below the tugs' berthing area is a chilling experience and each time I have gone there, I did so with a sense of unease that, of course, added to the excitement of the adventure.

The author between a tug's propellors. Photo by Greg Cochkanoff.

Each boat has scoured a deep pit in the bottom from the thrashing of the water when they come and go at dockside. Being caught on the bottom when one of these brutes fires up would be like diving in an eggbeater. That's why Greg visited the president of the company and asked his permission for us to check out the bottom around his docks. He graciously agreed, and we were treated to some of the most interesting dives I have done anywhere.

Preparing for the Dive

Pretend for a moment that you accompany us on one of these dives. Each visit requires a separate clearance. After discussion with the manager beforehand and having received his general agreement, our next step is to check in with the dispatcher at dive time. It is difficult to plan a dive too far in advance because in a busy harbour like Halifax, these boats can get dispatched like floating taxicabs, with only a moment's notice. There is always a crew on standby to respond to a call, but most trips are booked in advance.

The dispatcher sits on the second floor of a small building situated at the seaward end of the company's longest dock. Over time, we have become acquainted with most of them. The person on duty today is a Dalhousie University student in his last year of astrophysics, who seems to be perpetually locked in mortal combat with the mother of all math assignments. After the obligatory small talk regarding the weather, which neither of us cares about, we state our business and get a clear idea of when the tugs will be moving. Obviously, as recreational divers, we have to work around their schedule. With a three-hour window before the next job, there's plenty of time, so now we will check in with Halifax Traffic Control to let them know that a dive is about to take place. They need to know when and where, so they can post a notice to mariners over Marine Radio.

Suiting Up

The parking lot south of the ECTUG premises is an appropriate location to don our diving suits and equipment, a process fondly referred to as "suiting up." It's minus 18° Celsius in January with a northeast wind off the water, so we orient the van to afford at least some shelter while getting ready. Dealing with equipment at these temperatures requires a well-practiced routine because bare flesh can freeze in a few minutes.

Each of us attaches the breathing apparatus—called the regulator—to our tank. Normally, we would take one or two breaths from the regulator to make sure it is functioning and air is flowing freely, but it is so cold today that the moisture in our breath would cause it to freeze open and we would lose precious air. That first breath will have to wait until we are under the water, which is a break from normal diving practice but, as the saying goes, extraordinary circumstances call for extraordinary measures. Next, we check the pressure gauge, which reads 3,000 pounds, indicating that the tank is full with enough air for about an hour underwater at our planned depth.

In winter, we normally wear drysuits made of neoprene or rubber, with tight seals at the wrists and neck to keep the water out. As the name suggests, this suit keeps a diver dry (usually) and enables the wearing of clothing underneath – a jogging suit, sweater, and three pairs of woolen socks. It's a one-piece suit, including boots, and we step into our individual suits through the zipped portion across the shoulders. After being zipped up, on goes the hood, which covers everything from the neck up except the bare essentials — mouth, nose and eyes. Even our chins and foreheads are covered.

A drysuit is more buoyant than a wetsuit, so in addition to the normal weight belt, we will need to attach weights around our ankles. After that, a knife gets strapped to the inside of the right or left calf. It goes on the inside, where it won't be an impediment, in case we need to get rid of our weight belts in an emergency. Using the quick release buckle a diver can easily undo the belt with a single motion of one hand. Its weight naturally causes it to slide over the hips and down the body on its way to the bottom.

I have never ditched my weights, although I have found and recovered two weight belts while diving, so divers feel they need to do it at times. I never intentionally ditched my weights, but I accidentally released my belt one day in shallow water as the buckle struck the bottom while I was coming ashore. Some wreck divers wear two buckles for just such an eventuality. The last thing you want to do is lose your weights while inside a wreck, as you would rise up to the ceiling and be stuck there, utterly helpless, with lots of time to think about your impending death.

Next come the all important scuba tanks. They must now be strapped to our backs, after which we must attach the inflator hose to the valve on the chest portion of our suits. Its job is to facilitate the movement of air from the tank and into the suit in order to control buoyancy. Next, we snap the 16-kilogram belt of lead weights around the waist, walk to the shore and step into the water up to our knees. On go masks, mitts, and fins. Set compasses on a westerly bearing for coming back to shore.

The Dive

We fall into the water, do a quick gear check and begin the descent, while placing our regulators into our mouths to breathe. Opening your mouth under the water in January is a bit like chewing ice cream – cold on the teeth.

On a normal shore dive, the water gets deeper and deeper as you go from shore, but because the parking lot has been constructed hundreds of metres out into the water, we descend almost vertically to nine metres (30 feet) below the surface. On the bottom, we press the inflator button to adjust buoyancy for comfort so that we are neither sinking nor ascending, make sure everything is working, give the OK sign and begin the dive by turning left and swimming fifty metres or so north to the first wharf.

The main ECTUG dock is on the other side of this one, so from below the surface, we save time by swimming through this wharf. We carefully wind our way among the forest of posts as we note the wide selection of metal objects that have accumulated underneath, including cables, engine parts and other castoffs from an industrial waterfront that has played a central role in two modern wars and hundreds of years of shipping. The bottom has eroded away in one place and one of the posts that once supported the wharf is itself being supported, its pointed end at least half a metre up from the bottom, just dangling there. We won't touch this post as it may be unstable.

To swim through a dock as we are doing, we must first travel uphill to the crest of a mound that has grown under the pier, and then go down the other side. Currents and ship movements over the years have caused gravel and mussel shells from the bottom to accumulate among the posts that hold up the wharf. This accumulation has piled up perhaps two or three metres.

We have chosen to go through the wharf under the water and not on the surface for several reasons. On the surface there is wave action, which makes the trip much more difficult. Waves would cause us to move laterally, bouncing us against posts that often have nails and broken pieces of wood sticking from them. Waves also cause vertical movements which can slap a diver against one of the supporting braces that run at a 30- or 45-degree angle from post to post on large docks. Besides that, the sides of many docks are often covered with planking for aesthetic reasons or to keep ice out, presenting a wall to a diver on the surface. Such planking ends just beneath the surface.

Compared with these complications it is a relatively simple and safe procedure to pass through on the bottom. It is important to stay near the bottom in the limited visibility and close quarters, for the bottom makes a good point of reference. If anything protrudes up, we will see it more quickly and be able to take evasive action to avoid a collision. When we start to swim through, it is fairly dark and eerie but our eyes adjust and as we work our way among the supporting posts and hit the top of the mound, we soon see light on the other side. Down we go, staying close to the bottom, emerging on the other side under the forbidding shadow of the first tug.

Under the Tugs

There are three tugs in this very confined space, one of which is tied to the dock from which we just emerged. Alongside and almost touching this one are two more, which are secured to the next dock. Their dark outlines are visible from the bottom; they are about three to four metres (10 to 15 feet) above where we are. The bottom undulates so much that the clearance varies a great deal as we move around.

Here, the bottom is completely free of the silt that normally covers everything in the harbour. It is kept clean by the powerful sweeping motions of the tugs' propellors. The bottom is very uneven, composed of large rounded stones the size of basketballs, among which are dinner plates, cups, bottles, brass objects, cabling, unrecognizable rusty iron objects, waterlogged wood, pieces of crockery, broken clay pipes. And, below the stern of the tug is the gaping pit that its props have chewed out of the bottom. The hole is at least three metres wide and one to three metres deep, running most of the 33-metre length of the tug.

Only through first-hand observation of the inside of the pit do you get an appreciation for how much has been dumped into this area, for there are layers of litter along the sides of these hollows. Extending out from under the dock and hanging out over the top of the hole is what looks like a metal mat about a metre thick, composed of cable, iron, glass, brass, bottles and tires all seemingly woven together and cemented with a mortar of rust and corrosion. Piece by piece, year in and year out, debris went over the side of ships or off the dock without a second thought. In the pit is everything imaginable that could survive, from door locks to telegraph keys, broken portholes, ceramic doorknobs, broken instruments, rings, washers, cogs, bolts, door keys, hinges, coconut shells, rubber boots, firehose nozzles, knives and spoons.

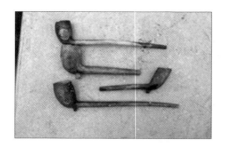

Clay pipes from the 1700s and 1800s. From the collections of Dana Sheppard and Dave Lemly.

It is this apparent debris that excites history buffs like those of us who dive the harbour, for it speaks first hand of events and times that we have only read about. It is a private museum of admittedly worthless objects, but for us it is a step back in time, for much of it is a connection with everyday life from the past. Every pop bottle belonged to a person, every broken cup contained somebody's cup of tea, each clay pipe was clenched between somebody's remaining teeth, perhaps on a summer's evening on the deck of an early steamship, perhaps by a humble crewmember of a fishing schooner, perhaps by the mate of a great square-rigged ship for which Nova Scotia was famous, going to England with lumber, or to Chile for copper or to Australia for wool or to China for tea. And here it has sat, untouched for 150 years or more.

After a short stay in this area, it's time to swim through the next wharf. This is a more significant undertaking for this dock is larger – more than 107 metres (350 feet) long – and covered in concrete, and big enough to support the two-story building where the dispatcher is slogging it out with his math assignment, far above us. It easily bears the dozen or so vehicles parked on it. After following the same routine as before, we emerge on the other side to a similar scene. The water is not so deep here, but there are more tugs. There are three on this side, tied one behind the other. It's a fair distance to the next wharf, so we will not have a reference point to help us navigate. It will be necessary to check our compasses to avoid having to come to the surface to confirm our location.

A right turn puts us on an easterly heading, away from shore, and parallel to the dock. It also puts us into another deep hole below the outside tug. At the same time, the bank goes down steeply and we descend into deeper water, down to fifteen metres (50 feet). A short swim and we're now off the end of the longest dock, with the slope continuing down. The long legs of the dock go up from the bottom and out of sight. If the dispatcher could see what his building is perched upon, he might have other things on his mind besides integrals. Turning north, we parallel the shore and enter an area with an almost unbelievable amount of rubble. It looks like a garbage dump, except there is no colour because any biodegradable items have long since disappeared. Everything here is made of metal, glass, ceramic, concrete or plastic.

There are huge slabs of concrete from the surface of an earlier dock that was allowed to fall into the water after its useful life had ended. Long poles that once supported this dock appear at odd angles out of the gloom, partly buried in the mud and silt, which has reappeared at this depth because it is out of reach of the churning waters from the tugs' props. The farther we go from the surface, the darker it gets. There is almost no colour, for colour is filtered out at this depth and everything is covered in grey silt anyway, which also absorbs the diminishing light. Looking down the bank is pointless. There is nothing to see; it is almost like looking at a black wall.

Although such a situation may sound intimidating, to an experienced diver this is quite normal, for he or she has often experienced poor visibility and minimal light, as we all do during the night. One's overactive imagination might conjure up all sorts of scenes and even creatures lurking past the visible zone, but it's just a few metres farther down until the bank levels off to the bland desert-like sea of mud that characterizes the bottom in this area of Halifax Harbour.

It's left again and up the bank as we move closer to shore. The light increases and the bottom is again clear of silt. Here begins the remains of another earlier dock, its posts sawn off by commercial divers sometime in the past. Its clear outline is easy to follow with the short posts poking their heads up, a third of a metre in diameter and a few centimetres from the bottom. This was probably the wharf of F.W. Bissett, that is identified on a 1957 harbour chart and was removed sometime after that date. Several of the post stumps have been ripped out of their holes by the violent churning of the tugs' props.

Not far off to our right is the third modern pier, referred to as Farquhar's Wharf. The pilot boats tie up here, when not engaged in ferrying the harbour pilots who escort the container ships, oil tankers, bulk carriers, and cruise ships into and out of the harbour and to and from their docking locations. Here the depth is a shade over six metres (20 feet) and the evidence of the tugs is everywhere on the bottom. Anything breakable has long since been smashed after being hurled among the rocks; there is no seaweed and the rocks are brown with the dispersal of rust from the ever-present iron. Broken china abounds from steamship companies such as the Red Cross Line, which had a regular passenger and freight service between St. John's, Halifax and New York at the beginning of the twentieth century.

Yet, like something very much out of place, we occasionally come upon a milk bottle or soda pop bottle that is in pristine condition, probably recently arrived from spending the last fifty or one hundred years in the mud that we just left. It has probably been dislodged by a departing tug at low tide. It will not last long unless it gets wedged among the large rocks or finds its way into a diver's goodie bag.

Left again and we are on the last leg of a square, heading back towards the tugs and the large dock. We come to the familiar deep pit and feel the light diminishing as we pass under the tug, carefully moving to avoid sharp objects that could entangle or worse, tear a hole in our suits, a very serious accident in waters measuring minus 2° Celsius (28°F) with nowhere to get out in an emergency.

Now the long legs of the dock reappear. Up the bank we scurry through the semi-darkness, over the crest, down the other side and into another hole beneath the first tug we visited at the beginning of the dive. A quick check of the gauges shows we have been in the water for 42 minutes, depth is 30 feet (9 metres) and 800 pounds of air remain. That's enough for a few minutes of poking around this area, although our hands have become numb from the cold and the rest of our bodies are starting to cool down, as well.

Returning

Five minutes later, with 500 pounds of air left, it's time to travel back through the first dock, back down to twelve metres (40 feet) and swim the remaining fifty metres to our point of departure. At the base of the large stones supporting the parking lot, we will do a quick assessment before starting the ascent. We have been to a maximum of fifteen metres (50 feet) and have been in the water for forty-eight minutes, well within the limits of safe diving. With no need to worry about decompression stops, we remove much of the air from our suits so that, when we start the ascent and the remaining air expands from the reduced water pressure, we will be able to control the rate to a safe speed. We are now slightly heavy so that it becomes necessary to swim up to start ascending at the rate of no more than a foot per second, all the while carefully bleeding air from our suits at a comfortable pace.

We arrive at the surface about six metres from shore and immediately feel the cold air. We put our faces down and swim to shore. Waves are breaking on the rocks, so we come ashore carefully, staying prone and letting the waves carry us in to shallow water. This is a tricky part because of the change in equilibrium. After being so light and maneuverable on the bottom, we become like the proverbial fish out of water — heavy and ungainly. Timing is important; as soon as a wave goes by, we stand up as quickly as possible, turn sideways for stability and to present a smaller target, and brace for the next wave.

After it passes, off come the fins and we carefully negotiate our way among the rocks up to the parking lot. Before long, ice has formed on the outside of our masks and is beginning to cover our suits, even though we are relatively comfortable, but the cold air and wind will soon change that. We make for the van as quickly as possible, remove weight belts and tanks, open the van and retrieve an important item — a large insulated jug of warm water, which will keep our hands working as we remove the rest of our gear.

With the water jug strategically placed in position, off come the mitts and we thrust our increasingly cold hands into the water for marvelous relief. With warmed hands, it's now time to get out of our suits. By now, there is a thin layer of ice on everything and we are each working with bare, wet hands in a temperature well below freezing. With some effort, we undo each other's frozen zipper and out through the opening comes a small cloud of steam from the warm body inside.

At this point, there is a great deal of animated conversation as we discuss what we saw. The very basic communication possible while diving creates a pent-up desire to talk, so there's a lot of catching up to be done after the dive. To a bemused onlooker, the enthusiasm is evident, with plenty of sentences commencing with an excited "Did you see the . . . ?"

Through intermittent warming of our hands in the water and with the practice of having done this hundreds of times, we coax our very tight-fitting hoods off, to be immediately replaced by a woolen cap. Neck seal and wrist seals are opened and each diver steps out of his suit and into a winter parka. We don winter boots and mitts and head for the dispatcher's building to let him know we are out of the water and to satisfy his curiosity by dealing with the usual question that everybody asks, "What do you see down there, anyway?"

The Diver's Motivation

With a quick call to Halifax Traffic to let them know we're up, it's off to the nearest coffee shop and another half an hour of excited discussion. The highlight of today's dive was the "fid," a large version of a marlinspike, a pointed tool, about ten centimetres long, used by sailors to help separate the strands of a rope for splicing. This fid is almost a metre long, so it was used with very large ropes. Made of lignum vitae, the hardest and densest of all woods, it was lying on the bottom, too heavy to float. It looks rather uninviting right now, but it is still sound and will make a very nice decoration when cleaned and polished.

Somebody else found a chamber pot, adorned with a large crest of a shipping line. Well known to our grandparents, these china pots were a necessary part of life before the days of flush toilets. One would have been placed under each bed on a steamship, ready for service.

There is animated talk about how everything has changed since the last dive here. Several new holes have been scoured, exposing more of the bottom. And, there is the usual discussion that follows all dives — everybody's opinion on the "viz," or visibility. Today it was good, as it often is in winter, when the water is colder and harbour traffic is reduced. In addition, there has been no rain for several weeks and the winds have been light.

It is the joy of discovery that makes this dive so captivating, and the challenge of dealing with the unique set of difficulties presented here. Those interested in things maritime and things associated with the past, interested in machines, the ocean, ships and shipping find such a visit fascinating, and the challenges associated simply go to make the whole package a unique experience. In January, some people fly to tropical paradises and dive in the warm water among colourful plants and fish, followed by a session on the beach. Some of us derive no less joy from diving among the wharves in Halifax Harbour, followed by a hot coffee and warm fellowship.

Underwater Pioneers
of Halifax Harbour

Before Canadian Pacific entered the North Atlantic market, the major Canadian steamship company was the Allan Line of Montreal. Many new Canadians departed Europe in Allan Line ships. Its large passenger liners crossed the Atlantic on a regular schedule from the mid-1800s to the second decade of the twentieth century, with service to major Canadian ports, including Halifax.

On March 26, 1905, the SS *Parisian,* launched in Scotland in 1881 as the flagship of the fleet, stopped at the harbour entrance to take on a pilot, who would guide the ship into Halifax. As the pilot was about to come aboard, many of the *Parisian's* nine hundred passengers and crew watched in disbelief as the Hamburg-Amerika Line steamer *Albano* came into view and rammed into their ship. The *Parisian's* perplexed captain had seen the *Albano* coming and, realizing that a collision was imminent, ordered full ahead to try to get his ship out of the way. The *Albano's* captain, also appreciating what was about to happen, ordered full astern. But they were both too late.

The *Albano* struck the *Parisian's* right hand side abaft, near the stern. The stricken vessel began to take on water through the hole and the ship was in danger of sinking by the stern. Captain Johnston decided the only hope for his ship and passengers was to make for the dock, gambling that the bulkheads, which separated different parts of the ship's hull, would hold and keep the ship from flooding completely. Coaxing as much speed as he dared from his injured ship, he headed into the harbour. He made it. An hour after the collision the *Parisian* was tied up at Pier 2 and the passengers disembarked without any loss of life. Powerful pumps were put to work to remove the water but the ship continued to settle by the stern while the bow rose out of the water, like the end of a lever.

Shortly afterward, the bulkhead that was keeping the ship from flooding gave way and water rushed into the hull, flooding the engine room. The news became the talk of the town and great crowds came to see the stricken 134-metre-long ship with her stern on the bottom ten to twelve metres below and the bow towering above the dock. She was in grave danger, teetering as her rounded stern rested on a hard bottom, with a serious risk of rolling over against the dock or breaking in two from the stress of having the bow out of the water.

Three divers, employed by Beazeley Brothers, went to work patching the gaping hole in her side. The plan was to temporarily repair the hole and then to pump the ship out and refloat her. Within two days, they had the hole patched and were ready to make an attempt at raising the *Parisian*. They started the pumps and the water began to recede. But two days later, the ship filled up again and they were back where they had started. The divers were obliged to go back down to find what had given way and make further repairs.

In the meantime, there was an inquiry to ascertain blame for the accident that could so easily have turned into a major disaster. The captain of the *Albano* admitted to the inquiry that he could have been quicker in giving the order to go astern. He testified that he had seen the *Parisian* when she was about six kilometres away and expected that they could pass without incident. As he came closer and realized the *Parisian* was stopped, he ordered full astern but too late. The *Albano* struck the *Parisian* at right angles. He felt that the *Parisian*'s Captain should not have ordered full ahead; if he had not, the *Albano* would have passed the *Parisian*'s bows.

The divers continued to work, this time with better success. The salvagers rounded up all the pumps they could find. With four companies participating and with six high capacity pumps averaging 11,000 litres per minute of throughput, they started to gain on the water. On April 4, the temporary repairs done by the divers held, as the 3440 tonne ship finally rose out of the water, the first step in the vessel's resurrection.

Early Divers

The divers who worked on the *Parisian* were involved in a mysterious and risky pursuit, about which there was still much to learn. Diving in 1905 was not a sport, as it is today. It was a deadly serious business – more deadly than the participants realized. They worked to meet the challenge of maintaining a constant air supply, but they were unaware of the consequences of subjecting their bodies to the long periods of pressure that are associated with working underwater. The long-term risks were understood only in the most rudimentary way. This was before the days of scuba tanks, decompression tables and dive computers.

The first scuba divers called themselves "menfish," because they could move around in the water like a fish. Unlike their earlier colleagues, they were completely mobile. Jacques Cousteau and Emile Gagnan are generally recognized as the inventors of the apparatus that made such mobility possible hundreds of years after commercial diving began, but they were just contributors in a long line of men who solved the problems one at a time. Because they were so enthusiastic, Cousteau and Gagnon attained a much higher profile than most of their predecessors.

Pressure, visibility, buoyancy, physiology, and equipment all presented challenges that had to be met one at a time and some gave up their secrets slowly and painfully. The effects of pressure on the body were particularly brutal and many divers died from the bends before a way to decompress had been developed and the effects of time and depth were fully understood.

Cousteau and Gagnan perfected a device to overcome the biggest problem in diving. Getting air wasn't the problem. There were already several proven ways to do that. The challenge was in getting the *right amount of air* when and where needed. Because pressure increases with depth, a diver needs air at the right pressure to overcome the pressure that the water exerts on the body. The deeper the dive, the more air he needs to consume with each breath. The demand regulator, a simple device attached to a cylinder of compressed air, made the Self-Contained Underwater Breathing Apparatus – scuba – a reality. As the pressure increased or decreased with depth, the combination of regulator and tank – which Cousteau called the "aqualung" – delivered just the right amount of air. The diver carried it strapped to his back, so there was no longer a need to be supplied from the surface.

The First Dive Gear

Prior to the invention of the regulator, divers wore a cumbersome and heavy assortment of equipment, and needed a support group to get them ready and assist them from the surface throughout the dive. Wearing a suit of canvas and rubber, lead boots, and a copper and brass helmet, their air supply was pumped down from the surface, initially via a hand-operated pump and later by a motor-driven compressor. To the public of the time, they were "deep sea divers"; today we call them "hard hat divers". Their world was limited by their ability to walk with 9- to 13-kilogram boots, their ability to see through the tiny windows in the brass helmets they wore and the headache of working with the hoses and other umbilicals from the surface. They were in constant danger of falling over and not being able to get up, and they relied for life itself on their crew above.

Dive gear from the early 20th century in the Musé de la Mer, Pointe-au-Pere, Quebec.

Diving under the ocean was not something that a visionary dreamed up and then perfected. It evolved over hundreds of years and is still evolving. As long as men and women have been able to swim, there have been those who found the means and the stamina to get under the water and stay there for longer periods of time than others could. Some believe the *ama* of Japan may have plied their trade for up to two thousand years. These women do up to a hundred dives a day for shellfish and edible seaweed without using any external air source. Pearl divers and Mediterranean sponge divers have worked the same way for centuries.

Diving Bells

The first air sources used by divers were inverted containers that held a trapped bubble of air. Aristotle described such an invention in the fourth century B.C. and Alexander the Great is supposed to have descended beneath the ocean under such a "diving bell." If you invert a cup and place it on the surface of a pan of water, it will trap air. Keep the cup level and push it into the water and it will keep the air trapped. Make the cup as big as several men, weight it properly and you have a diving bell. It is incredible what men have been able to achieve with these primitive contraptions throughout the centuries. For example, in 1663, salvagers working from a diving bell recovered cannons from the recently sunken ship *Vasa,* in Stockholm harbour.

In the first bells, the "diver" breathed the trapped air until it became more and more stale, and he was forced to surface. Some pushed their luck and died from lack of oxygen. Next came the idea of pumping air into the bell from the surface, but pumps didn't have enough power until the late 1700s. Late in the seventeenth century, Edmund Halley, known as the discoverer of the comet that bears his name, built a diving bell that resembled a giant inverted wooden bucket, lining it with lead to get it down and breathing the air trapped inside. It was an improvement over the first diving bells because more inverted chambers could be sent down to replenish the air, while a valve at the top exhausted stale air. Amazingly, on one job, divers stayed and worked at a depth of fifteen metres (50 feet) for two hours. One diver could venture from the bell by breathing through a hose that his partner held inside the bell – the first successful attempt to achieve mobility.

There were variations on this basic design, but they all lacked one critical characteristic — the ability to move around, easily or otherwise. The workers were stuck under the bell and could only get about with great difficulty and risk. It would have been an easy problem to solve if not for the water pressure exerted on the diver. Simply forget the bell and give the diver a sufficiently long snorkel, a long hose from the surface. But, it is much more complex, as a snorkel any longer than perhaps half a metre is useless because the pressure exerted at the surface is not sufficient to force the air down the tube. The answer was to pump air down to overcome the pressure, to a person in a waterproof suit. Augustus Siebe designed such a suit in 1819. Now a diver could, albeit with great difficulty, walk around on the bottom. This became the accepted method of working underwater and remained so until Cousteau came on the scene over a century later and scuba diving took off.

In a little lagoon on the French Riviera, Cousteau tested their invention in June, 1943. With elation, he described the experience: "I took normal breaths in a slow rhythm, bowed my head and swam smoothly down to thirty feet [9 metres]. I felt no increasing water pressure, which, at that depth, is twice that of the surface. The aqualung automatically fed me increased compressed air to meet the new pressure layer. Through the fragile human lung linings this counter-pressure was being transmitted to the blood stream and instantly spread through the incompressible body. My brain received no subjective news of the pressure. I was at ease. . . . "

It is difficult to imagine how the divers who worked on the *Parisian* managed to get anything done. They would have worn the canvas suit, helmet and heavy boots, with air supplied from the surface. The bottom would have been in turmoil from their boots as they moved about, causing clouds of silt to rise, so it would have been dark. Their heavy boots would sink in the soft bottom, so it would have been difficult to handle the tools and heavy items they needed to use. They often worked with bare hands, which is also hard to imagine, considering how cold the water gets in this part of the world. And they would have needed to work part way up the side of the sunken ship to get at the hole. This means they would have dangled off the end of an umbilical cord or been stationed on a platform like a window washer, moving laterally with a great deal of effort, all the while trying to riv-et or bolt iron plates to cover the hole in the ship's side. They did this with the knowledge that, at any minute, the ship could roll onto them and snuff them out.

Early Diving in Halifax

Commercial divers were descending under the waters of the harbour much earlier than most of us realize. Dartmouth historian John Patrick Martin writes: "In the autumn of 1835, a diver named Hawkesworthe, equipped with a new diving apparatus invented by Mr. Fraser of Halifax, made some researches into the waters of Bedford Basin for the purpose of recovering the supposed treasure of Admiral d'Anville's expedition. At that time, and for years afterwards, the old hulls were visible off Rockingham and in the wa-ters near Steven's Island."

Probably the same Mr. Fraser appears in a reference by John Camp-bell, Superintendent of St. Paul Island, who made the following interesting entry in his journal on July 24, 1843: "Charles Muggan, with Mr. Thos. R. Frazer the diver on board arrived today from Sydney to work again at the wreck." Unfortunately, he does not give the name or any other details re-garding the shipwreck to which he is referring. St. Paul Island is off the northern tip of Cape Breton Island and snagged many ships on their way up or down the St. Lawrence River.

James Farquhar

A wreck off St. Paul Island got Halifax resident James Farquhar into the diving business in 1867. His first job was with the Halifax salvage firm of Larder Brothers, recovering pig iron from a barque which had wrecked off the island a year earlier. His account of getting into the business is remark-ably quaint and indicative of the early days of diving. Having witnessed William Larder's exploits, he simply convinced them to let him try and he went to work.

Farquhar writes: "On deck it was all I could do to stump around in my heavy rubber suit, with the big brass sphere of the helmet bearing down on the collar on my shoulders and my heavily ballasted soles dragging at my feet. But once over the side and under the surface, and I became as light as thistledown. It was no trick to jump as high as my head, in my two hundred-pound outfit, so long as I was under water. It was the air in it, which made the difference.

"This very lightness and ease of movement, I found was one of the pitfalls besetting the diver. It begot overconfidence and carelessness — and a little negligence, such as allowing the air to get into the lower part of my dress, would trip me up as though I were falling downstairs. Only I would fall not down but up. Twice, when in deep water, I have been turned topsy-turvy and shot to the surface, feet foremost. Bad enough, for the sudden change in pressure is enough to paralyze or kill you with cramps, but what would have happened had I not been near an open hatch . . . ? I might have struck the deck above me and burst my dress or become entangled and died before I could be rescued."

He would, as he said, "fall up" because the air trapped in his feet would have no way to escape, as happened to me the day my inflator valve stuck. Under normal diving, as he exhaled, the breath would leave his helmet as bubbles. If there were too much air in his helmet, he could turn a valve to let some of it bleed off. But if he were inverted, the air would build up in his feet and would force him to rise. Because he was often working inside newly sunken ships, this would be disastrous if it happened when he was inside the ship and unable to complete the trip to the surface.

A hard hat diver like Farquhar died while salvaging the wreck of Canada's worst sinking, that of the *Empress of Ireland*, which sank after colliding with another ship near Rimouski in the St. Lawrence River, with the loss of more than a thousand people. In June, 1914, while working forty metres (130 feet) below the surface, his air hose snapped, probably as the result of a fall.

There are many other instances of divers working in Halifax Harbour over the years. In the spring of 1873, divers worked on the wreck of the White Star liner SS *Atlantic* just outside the harbour, recovering valuables and the bodies of victims; in a tragic yacht race on September 2, 1876, the Royal Nova Scotia Yacht Squadron yacht *Cygnet* sank while racing in the Narrows. She took two of the crew down with her. Divers searched the bottom for several days but the bodies were never found.

In 1884, James Farquhar was retained to work on the wreck of the *Daniel Steinman*. It was carrying passengers and freight from Antwerp to Halifax when it struck on the Sambro Ledges, about a half-mile from the Sambro light. This wreck is a popular dive site for experienced wreck divers, many of whom have recovered bottles of wine from the cargo that Farquhar salvaged. He didn't get it all.

What became of the *Parisian* and those involved in the collision? She was repaired and continued to sail until being taken out of service and scrapped in 1914. On one voyage she even picked up a few survivors from the wreck of the *Titanic*.

Even a collision at sea can be turned to somebody's advantage. The day before the *Parisian* was towed to dry dock on April 8, 1905, for repairs to her side, the A. O'Connor Co. advertised in the Halifax papers that "This morning at 9 o'clock, we will sell 2652 pairs of assorted Ribbed, Plain, Cashmere, and Lisle Thread Hosiery at 18¢ a pair. These goods are nearly all damp and wet as they came out of the after hold of the *Parisian* on Wednesday, but as they were purchased by us to sell from 25¢ to 60¢, you cannot fail to procure a bargain."

Just three months after working on the *Parisian*, the Beazeley brothers were called again to check the damage to another ship. The 2740 tonne SS *Salerno*, en route from Cadiz, Spain, to Halifax with a load of salt, ran aground on the Litchfield shoal while coming into the harbour. Tugs and support vessels from the Dockyard could not get her off, so the divers were engaged to make an assessment of the damage. The news was not good; two holds were filling with water. *Salerno* slid off the shoal and was lost. It now lies at a depth of twenty-five to twenty-eight metres off the little fishing village of Herring Cove, in the outer part of the harbour.

The *Salerno* was one of the first wrecks I visited when I started diving. One of the group of five with whom I dove that day informed me that this was a terrific dive, being one of the prettiest wrecks he had ever seen. I was disappointed. There was nothing pretty about the scene. Instead, I found a lot of rusty iron, covered in seaweed, which I have since come to expect of all wrecks. Many years and many wrecks later, I still have not learned what constitutes a "pretty wreck."

Another early harbour diving incident is an amazing story of survival. Two navy divers survived the worst non-nuclear explosion in history — the great Halifax Explosion of December 6, 1917, which is discussed later in this book. When it occurred, the two divers from HMCS *Niobe* were in the water at the Naval Dockyard. Six men were tending these divers, manning the air pumps, maintaining communications and generally being available to assist. The explosion killed four of them, but it did not kill the divers. They got a severe shaking up and their hoses became entangled, but with admirable attention to duty, the surviving tenders managed to keep air going down to them and to get them untangled and out of the water before going to make sure their own families were safe.

Do You See Any Sharks?

On a selected Monday evening in winter I sometimes go to a Sunday School classroom, put on all my dive gear and make my grand entrance into the church hall. It's my annual presentation to the Boys' Club and is a time when I get to tell my wide-eyed little friends all about my favourite hobby. They find all the paraphernalia pretty interesting, the little ones being especially fascinated by the hollow, metallic sounds of breathing, which, no doubt, reminds them of *Star Wars* villain Darth Vader. Boys being boys, they all want to get their hands on my diving knife, a privilege I must deny them.

After I have told them all about the gear, it's time for questions. The first one is as predictable as the tides, "Do you ever see any sharks?"

"Actually, I carry my knife to deal with sharks."

"Yeah?"

"Uh-huh. Here's how it works. When a shark comes along, I whip out my knife . . . and stab my buddy. Then, while the shark is busy eating my buddy, I get away!"

Silence. They're very impressed and a little shocked. Sometimes, there is a "Wow!"

Finally, one of the bigger boys will declare with confidence, "He's kiddin'!" and there is relieved laughter all around.

Everybody is fascinated by sharks and those who don't dive want to know not only about sharks, but also about all the challenges and dangers that confront the diver. At the top of the list are questions about sharks and the bends.

Scuba diving is often described as a dangerous sport, which never fails to bother those of us who love it. Rather than calling it dangerous, implying that there is an inordinate number of injuries or even deaths – which is not the case – it would be better to describe scuba diving as an unforgiving sport. Because the environment is hostile, the consequences of mistakes and carelessness are severe. Flying in an airplane is no different. To counteract this, the equipment standards are very high (who would want to buy cheap diving equipment?) and the training is thorough.

I have had my share of close calls but most have actually happened on land. One of the challenges of harbour diving from the shore is finding a suitable place to get into and out of the water. The shores of the harbour have been built up so much that it's easy enough to get in, but, of course, it is unwise to get in until you know where you're going to get out. Getting out at a site where you can't stand up in the water is a headache. The normal way to end a dive from shore is to swim in to waist-deep water, remove your fins and walk up on the beach. To get back into a small boat, you would remove your weight belt and tank and hand them to the person in the boat. You are then very buoyant so it's a simple case of kicking your feet and flipping in over the rail of the boat. But on some occasions, such as climbing a ladder, you have to remove your fins.

With no fins on, you can't build up the momentum to help get out. As strange as it sounds, you lose your balance in the water. On one occasion, where the shore had been filled in with smooth stones about the size of grapefruits, I was obliged to leave my fins on and crawl up the 45-degree bank on my hands and knees. The smooth stones would roll down the bank, but I managed to claw my way out. Just as I stood up, the rock I was standing on rolled and I fell – literally – on my face, like a cartoon character. Splat! I still had my mask on and the regulator in my mouth. The mask is indestructible, so instead of breaking, it got pushed into my face. The regulator went in pieces. The inflator valve on my drysuit stuck into my chest. My tank valve clunked me in the back of the head as my tank fell forward. But other than suffering from severe annoyance, I was okay.

I was not so lucky on another day five years later. It was a similar scenario in which I had just come out of the water. Again, I was in full gear, this time among big boulders. The rock I stepped on rolled and down I went. I instinctively reached out to break my fall. But with the tank and weight belt, I was carrying too much weight. I put my hands out to catch myself but I couldn't hold the weight. My right hand buckled in between my chest and a large rock as I landed, and my clenched fist went into my chest, breaking a rib. And breaking my heart, too, because the doctor gave me very clear instructions to stay out of the water for six weeks.

Winter provides special challenges when diving. Once, on a winter dive, I had to cut across a snowbank in full gear. I sank to my hips in the deep snow and became utterly helpless, thanks to the extra weight I was carrying; my dive buddies had to dig me out. Greg has provided some lively entertainment in winter. On cold days, when the tide recedes, the wet rocks freeze and get covered in a paper-thin layer of very slippery ice that is difficult to see. At the beginning of a dive, he stepped onto the beach and literally went flying through the air, landing with a thud among the rocks and kelp. I had to help him into the water. On another occasion while crossing a railway track, he slipped and, thanks to his rubber (i.e. slippery) drysuit, slid down a long bank of snow through the woods, plowing down all before him and landing in the water.

When wearing dive equipment, it is definitely safer in the water. But more than sharks or the bends, my greatest respect is for currents. Currents are everywhere in the ocean, they are unpredictable and they are deadly because they can carry a diver away to heaven knows where. I was diving with a group of six divers at Seal Island at the entrance to the Bay of Fundy near a rock called Devil's Limb, which had claimed many ships in the past. The home to the world's highest tides, the waters roar into and out of the Bay of Fundy like a river, so we carefully planned our dive to occur at the slack tide.

Everything went fine on the dive but, as we came up, the tide turned and we were dispersed on the surface ten kilometres from land. While the boat went to pick up the person who had drifted farthest away, the rest of us watched helplessly as she steamed away and we rapidly drifted apart. Luckily, the boat had a sharp-eyed spotter aboard for such an eventuality and we all got rounded up.

In a similar experience outside the harbour entrance, we were diving the SS *City of Vienna*. The currents were strong, so I went down the anchor line and made sure that I was always ahead of it, so it would be there when I needed to surface after the dive. I would let the current take me downstream and back to the line. When you are diving a shipwreck and currents are strong, you can hold on to the wreck and move yourself around with your hands. But when it's time to go to the surface, if you don't have a line to hold, you're going to rapidly drift away. That happened to a couple of the group and off they went, away from the stern of the boat. It took all their strength swimming to retard the rate at which they were being carried downstream. Fortunately, the well-equipped boat carried lots of rope, so, with a buoy attached to a rescue line, the captain flung it to the divers. By the time it got to them, there was perhaps a half-kilometre of line out but we got them aboard.

These incidents stayed in my mind on another occasion in the spring of 1999. Ten years after the dive at Seal Island, we were visiting the wreck of the *Good Hope*. It lies in twenty-seven metres of water, directly in the narrow shipping lanes off McNab's Island. It was a beautiful Sunday afternoon, the first good day of the season for sailing and there were sailboats out in abundance. Divers are very wary of sailboats because such vessels are completely silent. A power boat can easily be heard from below, inviting caution. But a diver who breaks the surface in the path of a sailboat is in for a nasty surprise.

We were using a 10-metre Cape Island dive boat and there were eleven divers. With the dive flag fluttering, the skipper radioed Halifax Traffic Control for clearance. We received clearance but were cautioned that a 40,000-ton ship would be leaving the harbour in half an hour and would pass near us. However, we were well marked, the ship's pilot was advised of our location as Halifax Traffic put out a notice to all vessels in the harbour, and the weather was fine. Over the side we went. As we went down the yellow anchor line, I was impressed by how quickly the darkness descended upon us; visibility was much poorer than we had anticipated. We finally got to the bottom and started to look for the wreck, which we would have been able to easily spot if the visibility had been normal.

As we searched, I heard an unusual sound, so unusual that I just had to find out what it was. I swam briefly in the direction from which it seemed to come and to my shock an anchor clunked and clattered its way past along the bottom. It was moving fairly quickly so I had to swim fast to catch it. Realizing it was from our boat, I hoped it would soon hook into something. But the bottom was flat and covered in small stones, and there was nothing to stop its advance.

The boat was drifting away from us. "Surely they realize this on the surface!" I thought. I was tempted to grab the line and head up, but felt obliged to advise the others, so I headed back in the direction of the wreck. The other divers were nowhere to be found. My heart sank and I had this terribly lonely feeling descend upon me as I thought of what was above me. I was in the middle of the shipping channel with dozens of sail boats, a 40,000-ton container ship was coming our way, the shore was out of reach, and the dive boat was drifting away. I envisioned everybody being safely on the boat while I was left to fend for myself.

I didn't want to risk surfacing, so the only option was to chase the anchor, which by now was out of sight. Using my compass to guide me, I took off in the direction in which the anchor should have been heading, all the while hoping it had snagged something, but fearing that the skipper of the boat had pulled it up. In the meantime, his dilemma was that if he hauled the anchor up, the boat would drift even faster and he would have to start steaming back to the dive location, all the while risking striking a diver coming to the surface.

It's hard to swim fast when you're twenty-seven metres (90 feet) underwater, but I kept hoping against hope that the anchor had snagged, and I really didn't have any other options. But you just can't gulp air from a regulator — it comes at a prescribed rate — so, despite my good physical condition, I was quickly getting out of breath. Just as I was about to give up and head to the surface to face whatever awaited me, I was pleasantly surprised to spot the anchor still scraping its way along the bottom. But I had mixed emotions as I realized that the skipper still wasn't taking any action to correct things. I went up the line as fast as I could safely ascend to discover that only one other diver was up. I got aboard and we retrieved the anchor. In the meantime, the container ship appeared in the inner harbour just as a diver appeared a half-kilometre upwind. Fortunately, the sailboats were giving us a wide berth, seeing our dive flag and many having been monitoring the radio as we spoke to Halifax Traffic Control. Up popped another diver and then another and for twenty minutes we steamed around picking up tired and shaken divers, but all got up safely.

On another occasion, off the south coast of Newfoundland, we were diving on a large wreck a few kilometres offshore. As is common in this area, the fog rolled in just as we were entering the water. The divers of Canada's east coast are used to fog, so that didn't stop us. The wreck lay in eighteen metres (60 feet) on a flat, sandy bottom, with the dive boat's anchor line attached to the stern of the hulk. We went down the line and investigated the wreck. It was very large and flattened out from the constant pounding of the sea. I decided to swim along the right side with the plan to take a 90-degree left turn, swim across the wreck, and then swim back to the stern on the opposite side.

I took the left turn and started swimming across a mass of debris, but after going what I had estimated to be the appropriate distance, I did not come to the left side of the wreck; I found myself in an endless field of twisted iron plates and girders. I looked all around. Maybe I should go more to the left – or did I already turn a bit to the left? The truth was dawning on me that I was lost and I really didn't know which way to go.

"No problem," I thought, "I can't be far from the boat, so I'll head to the surface, swim to the boat and come back down the line." Then I remembered the fog. What if I got to the surface and couldn't see the boat? I would be obliged to go back down to the wreck and be more disoriented than ever. Or, worse, with the current, I could be moved off the wreck during the ascent and subsequent descent. Then I would find myself on a flat bed of sand with absolutely no idea which direction to take. Just great! My most vivid recollection of this incident is the sound of my own heart pounding in my ears.

I checked my air supply. Fortunately I had plenty. I calmed myself down and collected my thoughts. I decided that if I swam in the completely wrong direction, the worst that could happen to me would be to end up at the bow of the ship. At least then I would know where I was. I would then know how to return to my starting point at the stern. I made an educated guess at what I thought was the proper direction and started swimming. After a few minutes, to my immense relief, I found myself back at my starting point looking at my two buddies, whom I should never have left. The incident served to reinforce in my mind the importance of keeping calm. Not only is your air supply limited, but getting upset will only speed up its consumption.

So, to my little friends at Sunday School, I have to say that I have never known a diver who was bothered by a shark or any other creature in the ocean — notwithstanding the overly dramatic television diving documentaries that love to exaggerate the dangers. The dangers in scuba diving lie elsewhere, and are more mundane. It is not the sharks and the bends that sneak up on you, but the currents, the freak happenings and the most dangerous thing of all — overconfidence.

The Northwest Arm

The native Mi'kmaq called it Waegwoltic; the first settlers called it the Sandwich River; military planners called it the Hawke River, but it has held its present name of the Northwest Arm since 1752. It is easy to understand why the first visitors mistook it for a river because it is narrow and about three kilometres long. It is a very deep inlet of the sea, which almost cuts Halifax off from the mainland and makes the city an island. It thus situates the city on a large peninsula and severely complicates traffic movement. Because the original part of the city is on a peninsula and newer neighborhoods overflow around the western side of the Arm and the Basin, the people of Halifax commonly refer to two major parts of the city – "on the peninsula" and "on the mainland."

The Arm is strikingly beautiful in summer, full of pleasure boats, and bustling with yacht and rowing clubs, but a hundred years ago it was fairly isolated. The shores of the Arm were in the country and were settled by those who wished to emulate the life of the English country gentleman. Estates like Belmont, Jubilee and Oaklands boasted fine Victorian mansions, some of which still exist. At his estate, called Armdale, lived the Right Honourable Sir Charles Tupper, Companion of the Bath, Knight Commander of St. Michael and St. George, holder of the Grand Cross of St. Michael and St. George, member of the King's Imperial Privy Council, Father of Confederation, and Prime Minister of Canada. Today the house is a set of apartments but it still stands.

On land now occupied by the Atlantic School of Theology, Joseph Howe was born. He ran a newspaper in Halifax and is credited with winning freedom of the press for Canadians. Sir Sanford Fleming, a driving force in the building of the Canadian Pacific Railway, which linked Canada from coast to coast, also lived on the Arm. His estate was called Blenheim Lodge and his house survives essentially as it was when he moved into it in 1872. Fleming was an interesting man, who became frustrated with the lack of any coordinated system of time from country to country and even from city to city. He proposed and saw adopted the international system of time zones that we use today.

Across the Arm from his house, he donated a large piece of land to be used as a park. Not surprisingly, it bears the name Sir Sanford Fleming Park but it usually gets referred to by the name "Dingle Park." That is because of its distinguishing feature – a stone tower, called the Dingle tower, built in 1908 to commemorate the 150th anniversary of responsible government in Nova Scotia.

The Dingle sits on the narrowest part of the Arm at a point where the water achieves its greatest depth of eighteen metres (60 feet). You could walk off the sandy beach and drop almost vertically to the bottom eight stories below. This is deeper than many of the bays of Nova Scotia. Generally, the waters of the rest of the Arm are nine to twelve metres (30 to 40 feet) deep. Most of the bottom is flat and covered with silt, although, like the rest of the harbour, there are some sites that contain very large boulders. There are a couple of other places where great piles of basketball-sized rocks rise up from the bottom, as though some giant had scooped them up and placed them there. Called eskers, they are the result of early glacial activity and pose a serious danger to boaters.

At the entrance to the Arm near Point Pleasant, Charles Brister had a tug and salvage business at the beginning of the twentieth century. Older residents of the area tell of playing as children during the 1920s around a World War I vintage submarine. I once dove there with a team under the auspices of the Underwater Archaeology Society of Nova Scotia, but we found no trace of the sub. We did, however, find the skeletons of numerous ships that Brister's had decommissioned, scrapped and sunk in the area, leaving a large field of debris, including several hulls.

Across the Arm from Brister's lies a large navy tug that was bought at auction and tied at the Quarry dock, but came free and sank. Like thousands of other wooden vessels that have gone to the bottom in Nova Scotia waters, it is quietly disappearing. It lies off an area that was known as the Queen's Quarries, where the British military authorities quarried stone for the early fortifications of Halifax, including the Halifax Citadel. The area later provided material for public buildings in the city, such as St. Mary's Basilica on Spring Garden Road.

Crossing the Arm

The Arm may be beautiful, but to a traveler it is very inconvenient. To travel by land around the Arm from Point Pleasant to Purcell's Cove is more than ten kilometres but by water the distance is hardly worth considering. That is why, throughout the years, the Arm has had many ferries.

The first ferry communication with the outer part of the Arm was through Royal Navy vessels stationed at the Dockyard and other military establishments along the waterfront. A regular service between Purcell's Cove and Point Pleasant started in 1853 and was run by Joseph Purcell. A person wishing to cross raised a flag at Point Pleasant to signal Mr. Purcell that he had a customer. His descendants continued to run the service until the middle of the twentieth century and, in the process, they were credited with saving many lives as pleasure boats swamped or were overturned in the rough waters at the Arm's entrance. When the tides are running and the wind is from the southeast, this normally benign area takes on a whole new personality.

Samuel Jollimore supposedly started operating a ferry at the centre of the Arm near the Dingle Park in 1880. As already mentioned, this is the deepest part of the Arm. Because of the intense recreational activity in this area for a hundred years, the bottom has accumulated an immeasurable number of bottles, most from the mid-twentieth century. Such bottles originated with ferry riders but they also came from the great crowds of bathers, canoeists, and rowers. This was a favourite play area for Haligonians and continues to be, despite the significant reduction in bathers brought about by the high power boat traffic and harbour pollution.

The constriction in the Arm at the Dingle point causes strong currents in this area, which keep the bottom constantly in motion. Except on the best days, this is a very gloomy dive. It is, in essence, a hole, which means the light enters from a small area. The currents keep the silt swishing back and forth as the tides change, which also reduces the visibility.

Farther in the Arm, there was a ferry from Deadman's Point to Jubilee Road and evidence remains of a large wharf off Deadman's Point. It was probably used by the ferry and I could speculate that before that it was the wharf where dead French and American sailors from the nearby Melville Island military prison landed for the last time. I have seen references to Longley's Ferry from Jubilee Road to Melville Park, so it is probably the one that serviced this area. Halfway between Jubilee Road and the Dingle, at Coburg Road, Adam Marr ran a boat slip early in the twentieth century, from which you could get a boat to any part of the Arm. And there were others, including Boutilier's Ferry, which operated from South Street.

In October, 2001, New Dawn Charters operated a ferry across the Arm for a couple of weeks. Using a 9-metre tour boat, they conducted a test to see if there was sufficient demand to justify a regular service. It turned out that there were enough people who were tired of sitting in their cars, inching their way towards a local traffic bottleneck called the Armdale Rotary. Between seventy and ninety people used the service each morning, taking about thirty minutes off their commute, and encouraging the promoters to approach Halifax Regional Municipal Council to put a ferry in the Arm on a full time basis.

Playing in the Arm

At the beginning of the 1900s, when the harbour was getting too crowded with steamships and other vessels, the Northwest Arm became the dominant ocean playground for the citizens of Halifax. Rowing was the rage and the calmer waters of the Arm lent themselves nicely to this civilized sport.

On the other side of the harbour, the Dartmouth lakes bustled with the Mic-mac Amateur Athletic Club and the Banook Canoe Club. Large clubs were forming in the Arm as well. The Northwest Arm Rowing Club, the Jubliee Boat Club, St. Mary's Amateur Athletic Club, the Waegwoltic Club and others had large boathouses and floating docks to handle the hundreds of little shells and canoes that their members used. Rowing is still very popular in the Halifax-Dartmouth area, which has produced many world-class competitors.

Huge regattas took place in the first half of the century, and the Arm would be clogged with every kind of floating conveyance, such as rowboats, steam launches, sailboats, even the harbour ferries. The Halifax ladies in long white dresses, huge feathered hats and parasols were escorted by mustachioed gentlemen in black suits and bow ties, all there to take in the events. There seems to have been plenty of guzzling, for the patrons of these and other activities have covered the bottom of the Arm with beer and pop bottles.

The Waegwoltic, a private club founded in 1908, is still very much alive, and with a healthy waiting list. It has succeeded in maintaining its Victorian charm, while subtly making those necessary additions that keep it up to date and running smoothly. The St. Mary's Aquatic Club, after languishing for several years, has been renovated and the traditional lines of this building nicely complement the Waegwoltic. Both continue to grace the Arm, as more modern buildings encroach upon the shoreline.

In addition to that most ubiquitous of debris items, the pop bottle, the bottom of the Arm also shows the evidence of a century of pleasure boating. There are many abandoned or lost moorings up and down the Arm. They usually take the form of a large concrete block or a rusting engine. There are also several generations of submerged docks.

Today, the Arm is alive with boaters almost year round. The rowers come out in the early morning, in their flimsy but graceful racing shells or kayaks, skimming the flat waters, accompanied by the occasional pair of loons, a flock of ducks or a hunting osprey. With the arrival of the winds in late morning, the sailors start heading out towards the open sea for an afternoon of sailing, accompanied by cabin cruisers and other powerboats. And on the warmest and sunniest Sunday afternoons, there are always a few long and rakish cigar boats, with a deep, throaty idle, driven by a tanned, muscular young male with a beautiful young lady seated next to him. I have often wondered where these boats and their occupants come from and where they go. They seem to materialize just in time to round out the scene and disappear with the fog and the rain.

The Halifax Islands

At almost a quarter of a million kilometres in length, Canada has the world's longest coastline and certainly one of the most convoluted. The Northwest Arm is evidence of that. As further evidence, Canada's coastline includes more than 52,000 islands. An island is a hill or mountain that rises above the water's surface. Most significant bodies of water have them. Halifax Harbour has been blessed with several that contribute to the interesting geography of the area. Each has its own engaging history.

McNab's Island

My favourite place to visit in the whole harbour is McNab's Island. Almost five kilometres long and more than a kilometre at its widest, McNab's Island is the sentinel that guards the harbour's inhabitants from intruders and from the wild Atlantic storms that plague the east coast of Canada, especially during winter. The largest island in the harbour, it makes a significant contribution to the well being of all who reside within the harbour boundaries. A whole book could be written about this interesting place, whose history goes back to the earliest visitors to Chebucto. Before any Europeans gave a thought to settling in the area, the large sandy beach which faces west and looks out into the shipping channel hosted fishing fleets that used the beach to dry their catches.

In the early days of Halifax, it was not uncommon to see a body or two dangling from a gibbet on the point at the end of the beach, a grizzly reminder to Royal Navy personnel of how England treated those who did not toe the line. In the fall of 1809, six men were publicly executed for mutiny aboard HMS *Columbine* and hung in chains on the beach, a sight that would have made an impression on every sailor entering or leaving the harbour.

In addition, McNab's Island has been key to the defence of the harbour and city and some of the first of the harbour's fortifications were established on it. An intruder coming in the harbour would have to get around the island, so guns were placed on its shores and high places to repel an attacker. There are numerous ruins of gun emplacements and fortifications, and other military odds and ends everywhere on the island. During the Second World War, a long steel net stretched across the harbour entrance to keep enemy submarines out, running from the west side of the island to the mainland of the outer harbour. The guns of Fort McNab looked menacingly down on each ship as it was checked by the Naval Boarding Service before the gate-ship opened the net to permit entrance into the safety of the inner harbour.

Most of Halifax's islands have had several names during the centuries and this one is no exception. During the early days of Halifax, it carried the name of Halifax's founder, Edward Cornwallis. Not long after the city's founding, Cornwallis granted the island to three of his nephews — as a reward, no doubt, for being born into the right family. They never lived there and offered it for sale in 1773. There was still room, though, for ordinary citizens to find a place to live. Joshua Maugher had been granted the beach mentioned above and to this day it bears his name, though it is pronounced "Major's Beach." He had left Halifax by 1760. The Ives brothers occupied a small portion of land on the inside part of McNab's and have left us the island names Ives Cove and Ives Point, as well as Ives Knoll, which refers to a nasty little shoal just north of the island and barely out of the shipping lanes.

But the name most associated with this area is that of Peter McNab and his descendents. McNab purchased the island from the Cornwallis family on Christmas day in 1782. His descendents continued to farm and live there for a century and a half, playing a role in the business and social life of the area. Peter McNab is mentioned in historical records as being a member of a Grand Jury looking into the matter of press gangs in 1782. His son, Peter McNab II, was listed as Surveyor of Highways for Eastern Passage in 1806. The last sale of property by one of Peter's descendents was transacted by Ellen McNab in 1931. There is a McNab family cemetery on the south part of the island, which bears evidence of the extensive McNab presence on the island spanning three centuries.

Besides the McNabs, others have occupied the island during most of the centuries following the founding of Halifax. There were several farms and estates. In 1885 Frederick Perrin, of Lea and Perrin's Worcestershire Sauce fame, purchased a large parcel of land and an estate and moved to the island. By the late 1950s there were around a hundred residents. Today, only the Parks Canada caretaker remains. When I spoke with him in 1997, he told me of taking his children to school in Dartmouth by boat each morning. On three occasions during the previous winter there was too much ice and his daughter had had the privilege of being taken to school by helicopter, much to the envy of her classmates.

McNab's Island has always held a certain attraction for the locals. Beginning in the late 1700s the island became a favourite picnicking area for the people of Halifax and Dartmouth. In 1790 there was a house of entertainment kept by Mary Roubalet for tea parties in the summer and called the Mansion House. With the coming of the automobile came the Sunday afternoon drive, and, ever since, we like to drive somewhere in order to feel that we have had a proper outing. In the days before the automobile, the locals often went somewhere by boat and a visit to McNab's Island always had an air of excitement about it. After the steam-driven harbour ferries began operating in the 1830s, it was relatively easy to get large groups to the island.

And they came. In the summer of 1839, shipping pioneer Samuel Cunard returned from England after winning a contract to carry the mail from London to Halifax and Boston by steamer. Local merchants, appreciating the significance of this revolutionary undertaking, gave him a banquet at McNab's Island in honour of his achievement. In July, 1845, close to 4,000 people gathered at McNab's for a bazaar held to raise funds for the building of a Mechanic's Institute in Dartmouth. The Steam Boat Company, which operated the ferry service between Halifax and Dartmouth, provided two of its ferries for transportation. The next year the Mechanic's Institute drew nearly 6,000 people to the event.

With this kind of potential, it was only a question of time before a major facility was established on the island. On July 8, 1873, Woolnough's Pleasure Grounds opened with two large pavilions for dancing and dining, grounds for quoits and football, and walks on a piece of beautifully wooded highland nearly a kilometre from the shores of Ives Cove. Even the Governor General of Canada, Lord Dufferin, made his way to the island, being honoured at an elaborate civic picnic just a month later. Woolnough's became so popular that a competitor, Findlay's Pleasure Grounds, opened for business in the 1890s with the usual accoutrements and the added attraction of a merry-go-round run by steam.

To slake the many thirsts that sprang up among the picnickers, A.J. Davis operated a bottling plant for a few years up to 1912, turning out aerated waters and other beverages. His bottles have become very collectable. With a couple of exceptions, bottle divers have been frustrated in their attempts to recover Davis bottles from the ocean. I was fortunate enough to find one on a very lengthy swim along the island's shores one hot summer's day. As if to rub our noses in it, in 1978, a local bottle-collecting club did a dig at the site of the plant and found about three hundred A.J. Davis bottles and crocks. Oh, well.

Diving around McNab's means covering a lot of area in shallow water. Ives Cove, in the north part of the island, seems to have seen the most activity as the bottom of the cove is dotted with wharves, tires, bottles, anchors, and derelicts of coal boats and construction barges. This was the location of Woolnough's Pleasure Grounds and where most of the residents lived, as it faces in toward the harbour and is nicely tucked away from the open ocean. There is a substantial barge beached in the cove and another in nine metres (30 feet) of water on the outer part of the cove. There is a tugboat wreck not far from the barge and on the beach are the remains of a boat used to deliver water to ships anchored in the harbour during World War II.

On the other side of the island (the Eastern Passage side which faces toward Dartmouth) there are more derelicts that were left to rot away in Back Cove. Most of them were coal barges used by the local power utility. With the decline of coal as a fuel, they were no longer needed so, in keeping with an ancient tradition, they were, once again, bequeathed to the ocean. I've checked them out but with shallow water and a muddy bottom this latter area makes for rather boring diving.

Garrison Pier, a long dock built in 1895 on Maugher's Beach near Findlay's Pleasure Grounds, shows evidence of a past devoted to recreation. It juts out from the long sandy beach into the shallow cove. A quick underwater examination reveals that reconstruction took place, because the first dock was built on top of the original. Plenty of old bottles from the turn of the century reside in the sand of the cove.

Like many parts of the harbour, this island has seen its share of human suffering. Before the days of communications and radio, ships carrying any of the dreaded diseases of the day would enter port flying a quarantine flag. Depending on the port, there might be quarantine facilities available where the sick could receive treatment. But, too often, they were forced to suffer and die aboard ship, taking other passengers and crew with them. Even the first steamship to cross the Atlantic, Samuel Cunard's *Royal William,* had been quarantined in Halifax Harbour in 1832.

In 1866, the SS *England,* whose 1,300 passengers had been reduced by 300, arrived in Halifax with cholera on board. The ship was quarantined on McNab's Island, where 200 more people died and were buried, including the Port Health Officer, 37-year-old Dr. John Slayter. He, along with three other physicians, a priest, and three Sisters of Charity, had worked on the island to help treat the sick. The victims are buried on Hugonin Point across from Garrison Pier.

McNab's Island is one of the most interesting places in all of the harbour because few people have lived there but many people have been there and left an impression. History is everywhere, both on the land and in the water, not in the well-manicured form for the casual visitor but in its raw, unsanitized form. The forts and gun batteries have not been restored, the farms lie idle and slowly growing over. It is an unusual area to explore and is excellent for walking, biking, boating or diving.

Lawlor Island

Sharing responsibility for guarding the entrance to the harbour, Lawlor Island is located east of McNab's and is about one-fifth the size. Its presence means that there are three channels or passages out of the harbour. From shore, it is difficult to distinguish this island from McNab's. Because it is very close to McNab's Island, it appears to be part of the latter, but boaters can easily tell the difference.

Its history is connected with suffering and death, for here the incurably ill spent their last days. Five years before the SS *England* incident, four ships arrived from the West Indies with yellow fever aboard, which resulted in fifty-two deaths in Halifax. Because there was nowhere to quarantine the victims, the hospital ship *Pyramus* (a retired Royal Navy sailing ship berthed in Halifax from 1832 to 1879) was used as a quarantine station.

The Nova Scotia government eventually recognized the need for a quarantine station and decided on Lawlor Island. Before it could be opened, HMS *Eclipse*, contaminated with yellow fever, had to be sent to Bedford Basin. In 1871, another cholera scare came aboard the SS *Franklyn* resulting in several more deaths in the town and county, which pushed the government to complete the temporary quarantine station on the island. And not a moment too soon, for in April, 1872, the SS *Peruvian* sent two smallpox patients to the island, one of whom never left.

The permanent quarantine facility was completed in 1878, described as two hospitals, a steward's residence and some other buildings. In the winter of 1899, the SS *Lake Superior* arrived with 2,000 refugees from Russia, one of whom, an 8-year-old child, had died of smallpox on the journey. All 2,000 were sent to Lawlor Island, to somehow manage in barebones facilities meant for a maximum of 1,400. None of the "guests" succumbed to smallpox and the hardworking immigrants managed to contribute by constructing several buildings during their stay.

In 1901, nine more cases of smallpox ended up on Lawlor Island, with two proving to be fatal. After that, the facility remained unused and eventually fell into disrepair and closed in 1938. A newspaper article mentions what was probably the last case handled there. It happened in 1938, when a crewman from a freighter collapsed while the vessel was being fumigated. His malady was diagnosed at the Camp Hill Hospital as smallpox and he was transferred to Lawlor Island where he died two days later. Unfortunately, the poor man infected two orderlies who had ministered to him, so they were sent to what remained of the quarantine station. They were taken there on March 18 and were greeted by frozen pipes and a complete lack of equipment as the station was in the process of being transferred to the mainland. They ended up in the doctor's cottage along with the male and female nurses sent to take care of them. They were sealed off from the rest of the world, without even a telephone. A boat came to the island daily with supplies and three doctors to see how they were progressing. After much suffering they recovered and left the island on May 10, after close to two months of isolation. The two nurses received commendations from Ottawa for their faithful service.

Today, Lawlor Island is quiet, showing little evidence of the pain that its unwilling visitors had to endure. It is home to numerous eagles and ospreys, which make for spectacular watching on clear days. At low tide, you can almost walk across Eastern Passage from the outer Dartmouth side of the harbour and visit the island.

Greg and I dove at two sites on the island and we quickly lost interest. On a dull February day in the early 1990s, we visited the trawler *Fort Louisbourg,* which sank in 1972 near the north end of the island, and did a second dive at another location, which turned out to have nothing of interest. There were no boats available in midwinter to take us to the island, so we decided to use my canoe. We are both over six feet tall and with our weight belts, tanks and other equipment, we were overloaded, to say the least. But, it was calm and, after all, we were scuba diving.

As a precaution, we wore our dive suits in the canoe. We got across and did the dives without incident, but the wind came up in the meantime and we were unable to canoe back by the same route. We ended up walking half way around the island towing the canoe in waist-deep water in high winds and freezing rain. Along the way I slipped on the rocks and took a nasty spill, striking my head against the gunwale of the canoe. I was spared serious injury by my dive hood, which cushioned the blow. Somehow we finally managed to coax the canoe across Eastern Passage and got to the car, very tired, very cold and disgusted with the whole undertaking.

Across the same route during the American Civil War, on August 20, 1864, the 61-metre Confederate blockade-runner *Tallahassee* made a daring midnight escape from Union gunboats that were waiting for her outside Halifax. The British colonies were officially neutral in the war so the *Tallahassee* came in for repairs and coal. But the neutrality laws required that she be on her way again within twenty-four hours. Her captain knew that as soon as she left the harbour, capture or sinking was inevitable, so he decided on a desperate gamble – to sneak inside the islands in the dark of night and escape to the east.

The gamble was a success thanks to the local pilot's skilful maneuvering of the big ship through the narrow and shallow passage. This incident has been hailed as one of the greatest feats of daring and seamanship associated with the harbour's seafaring history. While I was sitting at dinner with some friends in the spring of 1999, the story of the *Tallahassee* came up for discussion; I was interested to learn that one of the guests, whom I had known for years, was the pilot's great-granddaughter. Like many Nova Scotians, she, too, is descended from skilled and daring men who lived a life of adventure while making a living the only way they knew how – from the sea.

Devil's Island

The local pilot was Jock Flemming and he was dropped off the *Tallahassee* with his little rowboat near another of the harbour's outer islands – Devil's Island. Today, it is a flat, bleak-looking rock facing the open Atlantic, with nothing but a lighthouse to decorate it. But it has a history, too.

The island was densely wooded when the first settlers arrived in Halifax and was occupied in the 1700s. The first permanent settlers came in the

1830s and by the 1920s there were twenty-eight families, most, if not all, engaged in the fishery. There was a lifeboat station on the island from 1882 to 1937 to render assistance to ships that became entangled in the surrounding reefs and shoals while entering the harbour.

Melville Island

At the innermost end of the Northwest Arm is a little island situated so close to land that many Halifax residents think it to be part of the mainland instead of an island. A short causeway runs to Melville Island, which houses a modern yacht club. It is well suited to this purpose, for the island is small, almost round, and surrounded by relatively deep water.

It, too, has an interesting history. It was originally called Cowie's Island, after Robert Cowie, who in 1752 received a land grant of sixty-four hectares, which included the island. On it, he built a 21- by 6-metre storehouse and a defensive building called a blockhouse, and set about trying to rent it out. On November 18, 1752, he advertised in Canada's first newspaper, the *Halifax Gazette*, for prospective tenants who might like to undertake the manufacture of "shingles, clapboards, laths, hoops, etc."

Ownership passed to James Kavanagh in 1784 for the price of £65, and it became known as Kavanagh's Island. He sold it to the Admiralty, the government department that ran the British Navy, and they promptly renamed it after Viscount Melville, First Lord of the Admiralty from 1804-6. Under Melville, it was turned into a prison, which it remained for nearly 150 years.

In 1793, the Governor of Nova Scotia, John Wentworth (best known as the man who championed the building of Government House on Barrington Street in Halifax, now the official residence of the Lieutenant Governor) had recommended the island as a suitable place to detain French prisoners of war. By 1797, the British had begun to keep them there. But at that time the Admiralty didn't own the island so they acquired it from Mr. Kavanagh in 1804 – for £1,000. With the Napoleonic Wars still dragging on four years later, they decided to build a permanent prison of stone, which was completed in 1809. The foundation stone is still there, bearing the date September 1, 1808.

The new prison filled quickly. At one point, in the second decade of the 1800s, England was at war with both the Americans and the French. After the building of the prison, the town of Halifax and its vicinity abounded with French prisoners of war. Men taken from captured American ships increased the population and the prison was often overcrowded. To keep the prisoners in line, the guards circulated a story that they kept a shark cruising the waters near the island and fed it regularly, to keep it hanging around. Sharks have traditionally been held in such fear that this little scheme was probably all that was needed to keep the prisoners in their place.

Many of the French prisoners were ingenious workers in wood and bone and made articles that they sold to the numerous visitors who were freely permitted access to Melville Island. Going to the Melville prison to purchase the prisoners' handicrafts became a popular winter outing for some Halifax residents. The visitors would travel from Halifax by horse-drawn sleigh (today, Melville Island is within city limits) and would cross on the ice by walking or skating from what is now Jubilee Road.

Despite the shark stories, the attitude towards military prisoners of the time was fairly benign as the following announcement attests: "The inhabitants of Halifax and its vicinity having either American or French prisoners of war in their employment are hereby required and requested to send them to the prison at Melville on Monday next, 21st inst. for the purpose of attending muster."

The interesting thing to observe is that the notice, dated February 13, 1814, told the citizens to *send* the prisoners to Melville Island, implying that they could find their own way there and could be trusted to arrive. Even though living in prison was no picnic, it was probably preferable to serving in the military and fighting a war and it was definitely preferable to escaping into the Nova Scotia forests.

After the wars with the French and Americans, the prison was used from time to time as a hospital. The British Army took it over and used it from 1856 to the early 1940s as a military prison for soldiers sentenced to hard labour for desertion, unauthorized absence from duty, drunkenness and other such iniquities. It again housed prisoners of war during World War I. The stone building which remains from the prison today is probably part of the large cellblock that was built during 1880-82. Today it is used for storage by the Armdale Yacht Club, which has occupied the island since 1948.

On one point of land near Melville Island are the graves of prisoners who died during incarceration. The spot is appropriately called Deadman's Point. There is no indication from looking at the land that it was once a cemetery, but a local association studying death records to support their opposition to the residential development of the area estimates that nearly two hundred Americans died over a one-year period during the War of 1812. Nearly 8,100 were imprisoned on the island at some point. More than a hundred people of French, Spanish and Irish descent were also buried at other times. There are also estimated to be about one hundred black slaves buried in the area. In June 2000, during a training visit to Nova Scotia, a group from the Tennessee Air National Guard came to remember their fallen comrades. It is assumed that most died of smallpox and typhoid in the crowded prison.

This is an interesting island to dive. Being at the end of the long Northwest Arm it is the terminus for the tides that slosh in and out of the Arm twice a day. They swirl around the island with a good deal of force, which means that the bottom is surprisingly firm. Where you might expect to find a wasteland of mud and silt, there is a field of bottles and the usual assortment of bric-a-brac. They do not appear to have originated with the prison but with an amusement park, which was here at the beginning of the twentieth century, and the yacht club.

The geography of the bottom is unusual as well. There are several large eskers, the piles of underwater stones that rise up from the bottom as though a submerged bulldozer had piled them there. Most likely caused by glaciers, they are a constant headache for yachters and have snagged many an unwary boater in the area.

George's Island

George's Island, with downtown Halifax on the left. Note the gun emplacements.

Pound for pound, the most significant island in the harbour has been George's Island. Located within swimming distance of what is now downtown Halifax, it was the heart of the harbour defenses and its importance from a military standpoint has far outweighed its size. Acting as host to Fort Charlotte, with its big guns facing out to sea, it was meant to be the last holdout against an invader. Having somehow run the gauntlet among the guns of York Redoubt, Point Pleasant, McNab's Island, and Fort Clarence, the intruder would finally face an impregnable fortress if he hoped to gain access to the town. During World War I, a submarine net stretched across the harbour, using the island as an anchor at its centre. In World War II, it was equipped with anti-aircraft guns. As time went on, the defenses moved farther out the harbour, until today the island has no military value and is owned by Parks Canada.

In the 1870s, the British located the Submarine Mining Establishment on George's Island. In several buildings on its northern tip, they manufactured electrically detonated mines, which they intended to use to mine the harbour in the event of an attack. However, the harbour was never mined because it was and is a major commercial harbour with a great deal of ship traffic that would have been placed in danger.

Historians generally accept that Duc d'Anville was buried on this island, which the French called Ile Racquet, or Snow Shoe Island, because of its shape. His remains were later removed to Louisbourg, where they were rediscovered during the excavation and reconstruction of the fortress more than two centuries after its destruction. Apparently, the Duke had had a pig's tooth inserted to replace a tooth he had lost and its presence in the skull served as a positive identification.

The island also served another purpose during the first days of settlement. The area around downtown Halifax was heavily wooded and, considering that England and France were at war, an excellent place to ambush a landing party. First reports of the arrival of Cornwallis and his settlers state that they landed on George's Island, probably fearing an unwelcome reception from the natives, who were allied with the French. Six years later, the original Europeans that settled Nova Scotia, French Acadians, were incarcerated on the island en route to being deported to the French territory of Louisiana. Today their American descendents are no longer called Acadians, but Cajuns.

Diving George's is unlike any other dive I have done. This almost round island is the top of a knoll that rises up twenty-five metres (80 feet) from the bottom. It is simply a large drumlin, a bigger version of the piles of rocks that rise here and there throughout the harbour. The bank is quite steep, which is not unusual, but what makes it a little unnerving is that the island is in the stream, which is another way of saying that it is directly in the traffic lanes. Ships go along both sides of the island, as do the sweeping tides. The bank is steep and it is also smooth, with few hand holds or little hiding places, so it is easy to imagine yourself being disconnected from the island and being swept into the great beyond. That's unlikely, of course, but the feeling of vulnerability is a characteristic of diving around this island.

Other Islands

There are other islands in the harbour. Spectacle Island, at the mouth of the Northwest Arm in Purcell's Cove, used to shelter the schooners that transported an earlier generation of harbour pilots.

On the eastern side of Bedford Basin is a cluster of small islands, the largest of which is Sheppard's Island. These islands contain the remnants of a group of cottages from the early 1900s. All that remains are foundations of buildings and, underwater, some small wharves that were probably used for pleasure craft. This would have been a lovely area for a cottage earlier in the

115

twentieth century, before the area got developed for industry. Apparently, a little footbridge once led from the mainland to the islands. Today an industrial park and bulk loading facility dominate this area, and large ore carriers load gypsum.

Near Sheppard's Island is Navy Island, where many divers over the years have searched for the remains of Duc d'Anville's ships. Reports seem to indicate that several may have been sunk in this area. After one dive, Greg and I walked around and dug spent bullets from the high bank on the west side of the island. It looks as though a passing ship used the island for target practice and strafed it with machine-gun fire. We found two different calibre of bullets in the soil of the bank above the beach.

With the exception of McNab's Island and its neighbours at the harbour mouth, almost all the harbour islands rise sharply out of the water and are surrounded by fairly steep banks. The islands add to the diving opportunities open to a harbour diver, because they increase the amount of shoreline that is available to be explored. Islands always were and continue to be curiosities for visitors and anybody with a boat is naturally drawn to check them out. Even though they lie quiet today, they have a good deal of interesting castoffs lying on their banks that testify to their military and social history.

On the Waterfront

Historic Properties

The Halifax waterfront is dotted with historic places, topped by what is appropriately called Historic Properties. This is a stretch of the original waterfront and contains a group of old buildings that came perilously close to feeling the touch of the wrecker's ball in the 1970s. During the '60s there was a continent-wide push to "modernize" and it became the rage throughout North America to build expressways, office towers and parking garages. The Halifax city fathers, falling over themselves to establish Halifax as a real city and to shed what some saw as its dreary past, envisioned a modern downtown, bereft of those stone buildings that were so old. Fortunately, some saw value in what was old and felt that the city's future was connected to its past, and they fought to keep it from being destroyed. Today, the old waterfront is pulsing with new life as the area attracts visitors from around the world.

The oldest part of the Halifax waterfront lies directly off downtown. The original shoreline has been filled in and has seen many generations of docks come, deteriorate and be replaced. The locations of the Queen's Wharf and the ferry terminal have stood throughout the centuries but the other areas have evolved. The first wharves bore the names of local merchants, and hosted barques and brigs going on and returning from trading voyages. Interspersed among them were the premises of harvesters of the sea – fishing, sealing and whaling companies. Many of these wharves eventually went away, to be replaced by the docks of larger shipping companies, tugboat and salvage companies, almost all of which are now gone themselves. The downtown waterfront is still commercially alive, not with fishing boats or steamers, but with cruise ships, pleasure boats and tour operators. The Maritime Museum of the Atlantic and the Pier 21 Museum bustle with visitors, eager to learn about the part the historic harbour played in the history of the nation and North America.

It is abuzz in summer and fall, but all lies quiet in winter, which entices the harbour divers to visit those normally inaccessible places. During the winter and early spring, it is possible to dive the giant Ocean Terminals docks, along with the Cable Wharf and the site of the Pickford and Black's wharves. The latter was a locally owned shipping line, founded in 1876, whose ships sailed in and out of Halifax for a century. They traded between Eastern Canadian ports and the Caribbean, carrying passengers and freight.

Pickford and Black's ships landed at what today is the liveliest part of the Halifax waterfront, popularized by bars, restaurants and outdoor cafés. Their offices were in one of the Historic Properties buildings, near where James Roue bottled soda pop. The Casino Nova Scotia Hotel is next door. Underwater, the bottom has a very extensive area of wharf remains, with multiple ballast piles that reach far out into the harbour. The area is heavily silted because of the lack of large vessel traffic, whose propellors would keep the bottom swept clean. Should it be dredged, it would yield a rich harvest of artifacts from the city's past. This area was also the place where privateers landed their goods two centuries ago, so there is no doubt that the thick layer of mud and silt covers an interesting assortment of relics.

Privateers Warehouse is the name that has been given to one of the oldest Historic Properties buildings. Before Pickford and Black occupied the spot, a different kind of trader frequented the area. The 10-year period after the founding of Halifax was a time of seemingly endless European wars, which led to a marked increase in the risky but immensely profitable enterprise known as privateering. The first privateers would have set out from the harbour in the days of the American Revolution, the Napoleonic Wars, and the War of 1812. Privateers were, in essence, legal pirates who roamed the seas during times of war, searching for ships belonging to the enemy.

Upon finding a ship, the privateer attacked and if they prevailed – which they usually did – they took the ship and crew to the nearest friendly port, where the prize and cargo were sold at auction. Often that port was Halifax, and the common place at which cargoes were stored and auctioned was what is today called Historic Properties. As a result, many fortunes were made in Halifax. The captured crew might be imprisoned or released or sent home on a prisoner exchange.

Privateers used privately owned warships, usually small and fast, operated under the authority of a Letter of Marque, which was issued by the government of the host country. They were not considered pirate ships – at least not by the host country – but simply free enterprise warships out to make a profit. Their legal capture of enemy ships and cargoes and the subsequent sales were a significant factor in the commerce of the North Atlantic, whether the ships were British, French or American.

Privateering was usually profitable for both sides. The Commonwealth of Massachusetts commissioned more than five hundred privateers during the American Revolution. The Continental Congress started issuing Federal Letters of Marque in April of 1776 and recorded a total of 1,700 during the war. In 1777 alone, American privateers captured a total of 733 British merchant vessels and warships. At one point during that year, the English port of Liverpool was forced to close because more than 250 of their vessels, with cargoes worth in excess of $10 million, had been captured by privateers operating off the coasts of England and Ireland. Over the course of the entire war, New England privateers alone recorded a total of 1,450 ships captured or sunk. On the other hand, between 1777 and 1814, nearly 800 prizes were escorted into Halifax Harbour by privateers and ships of the Royal Navy.

In the three years 1778-81, 900 sea-going craft of all descriptions entered the port of Halifax from colonial ports, New York, the West Indies or the British Isles. This same period saw the modest beginnings of the Nova Scotian trade with the West Indies, a trade that grew in volume and importance in the early nineteenth century and in time brought Nova Scotia into the domain of international affairs. It also brought Pickford and Black's Steam Ship Lines into existence.

The important docks have all moved away from downtown to other parts of the harbour, where large trucks, cranes and trains can gain access. In the past, gangs of men did the work; today machines do it all. The large docks today are at Halterm (general cargo containers), Ocean Terminals (cruise liners), HMC Dockyard (warships), Richmond Terminals (general cargo), Fairview Cove (general cargo containers), the Navy Magazine (warships), the National Gypsum pier (bulk ore carriers), the Bedford Institute of Oceanography (oceanographic research vessels), Nova Scotia Power's generating station (oil tankers), the Dockyard Annex (warships), the Coast Guard Base (icebreakers and buoy tenders), Industrial Estates (offshore oil and gas supply), Irving Oil docks (oil tankers), Imperial Oil docks (oil tankers), Shearwater (warships), and Autoport (automobile carriers). Something on the order of 100,000 automobiles pass through Autoport each year. The ungainly ships that carry them from Europe and Japan have to be among the most unsightly ships afloat.

Symonds' Foundry and Iron Works

Across the harbour from downtown Halifax and just north of the harbour-side parking lot which occupies much of downtown Dartmouth was the Dartmouth Iron Foundry, owned by W.S. Symonds, the first mayor of Dartmouth. Opened in 1849 as IDA Foundry, it manufactured iron and brass castings, hydraulic presses, steam engines, boilers, safes, and stoves. Symonds became its third owner in 1863 and built a large wharf to handle castings for ships' propellors and deck machinery. Much of the premises, including the wharf, were destroyed by a hurricane on October 12, 1871.

Symonds rebuilt and became more prosperous than ever, adding furnaces, fire hydrants and water pipes to his product line. The latter would have come in handy in 1887, for the foundry was struck by a devastating fire that destroyed the business. It was sold at auction the following year, two years before W.S. Symonds died. It was finally torn down in 1915.

The water in this area is surprisingly shallow, being part of a plateau that runs out from the Dartmouth shore to the deep stream that runs up the harbour and is the route of the largest ships. Wharves had to be long in order to attain sufficient depth to enable larger vessels to come alongside. An 1845 advertisement for a neighbouring property includes two 61-metre (200-foot) wharves. This area is four and a half to six metres (15 to 20 feet) deep with a soft and flat bottom. The Symonds workers left a clear signature of their presence by dumping considerable amounts of coal ash from their furnaces over the wharf. There is also a substantial quantity of coal, no doubt accidentally lost in bits and pieces over the years as coal ships and schooners would have unloaded this very necessary fuel at the dock.

Interspersed in this field of ash is the occasional bottle from the late 1800s in the form of triangular ink bottles (probably from the office), liquor bottles and pop bottles. They are a long way from shore, which would indicate that the dock extended well out. The few photographs of the premises show that this was the case. The stone ballast from the dock is still there but the wood has, of course, completely disappeared. There is wood on the shore but there is no way to tell if this is from Symond's wharf because the practice was to tear down a decaying wharf and build a new one in its place. Sometimes from the bottom you can look inside an existing wharf and see a couple of generations of earlier ones. It is very reasonable to expect that another dock was built on top of the original.

The ash is light enough to sit on top of the naturally occurring silt which covers most of the harbour bottom. It creates a base for other items to accumulate. Because this area now has a small marina and anchorage for pleasure craft, the glass, metal and ceramic artifacts are mixed in with plastic items. This shore is one of the few places in the harbour that were settled early but have not been completely buried by development. At low tide you can walk on the original shoreline.

Pier 21 – The Gateway to Canada

In 1996, local divers discovered what is always referred to as Pier 21. This is just one of the large Ocean Terminals docks that were built in the first quarter of the twentieth century. The name has gained additional profile in recent years because of the interest in genealogy that characterizes the baby-boomer generation. During the mid-twentieth century Pier 21 housed the immigration gateway to Canada. Over a 40-year period, one and a quarter million immigrants walked down a ship's gangway, passed through its doors, and entered Canada as their new home. Pier 21 is part of a 610-metre (2,000-foot) dock that was completed in 1928, receiving its first group of immigrants on March of that year. The first group landed from the ship *Nieuw Amsterdam* of the Holland-Amerika Line. Their new home must have appeared dreary indeed to the little company of fifty-one people as they landed at 8 a.m. on March 8.

Immigrants arriving might have been tired and bewildered but most were optimistic at the prospects that lay ahead of them. This was not the case for some others who landed here. In 1940 the crew of the German warship *Graf Spee* came ashore here on their way to a prisoner of war camp in the Canadian hinterland. At the same pier, 3,000 British children came in 1940 and 1941 to escape the ravages of war. And from this pier others went to fight and some to die, as multitudes of Canadian servicemen went overseas aboard the world's great liners to fight in World War II. As an example, in late 1942, the Cunard steamship *Queen Elizabeth* departed for Europe with 14,000 Canadian troops aboard. They were just a few of the estimated 300,000 military personnel who departed from Pier 21.

The most common sight in the 15-metre (50-foot) deep water off this dock is china from the shipping lines that tied up there. Hailing from the glory days of the great ocean liners are the plates, cups and saucers – and assorted fragments – of companies such as the Italian Line, Furness Line, Cunard, White Star, and Compagnie Generale Transatlantique. The bottom here is very rough, having been churned for years by the propellors of some of the world's biggest ships.

Dinnerware from the Royal Mail Steam Packet Co., Red Cross Line, and Mississippi and Dominion Steamship Co. From the author's

John Hagell made quite a splash on a winter dive at Pier 21. The dock is made of granite blocks and from the water's surface, it looms up to the height of a two-story house. At long intervals, there are iron rungs inserted between the blocks of stone to act as a vertical ladder. They make a challenging climb at the best of times, but in full dive gear, it's more than I ever wanted to attempt. I have looked up at them in the past and, though tempted to try and save myself a 300-metre swim to the place where we normally get out, I have always opted for the swim.

John made the ascent, only to arrive at the top and find there was no convenient place to hold on while doing the precarious climb over the last rung and onto the surface. His hand slipped on the snow and back he went, down, down, with his tank on his back, weight belt around his waist, mask still on. He landed on his back and, by a stroke of luck, did not strike his tank valve against the back of his head. He was shaken up, but only his dignity was severely injured. Five minutes later, Dwayne McLaughlin was swimming along the bottom and found a fin, then another. Puzzled, he gathered them up, unaware that poor John was wallowing his way along the front of the dock trying to manage the 300-metre swim without fins.

Sandy Cove

Back across the harbour in Dartmouth is an area of sandy beach, just south of the Coast Guard base. There are many sandy beaches in Nova Scotia, but given the geography of the area, a sandy beach is very unlikely in Halifax Harbour. This is not a natural beach, but one that was constructed. In the 1880s the Hessleins, proprietors of the Halifax Hotel, erected a row of bathing houses on the shore. They installed a lengthy arc of tall wooden posts, running well out from the beach, driven in and sheathed to keep the enclosed water calm and sheltered from northwest winds and waves. Into this pool and far up on the beach, hundreds of tons of sand were spread. On both sides of the breakwater, diving stands and landing stages were set up.

The facility opened in July 1880, and attracted hundreds of people each day that the weather permitted. The *Morning Chronicle* advertised that the steam launch *Arrow* would take people from the Market Wharf in Halifax to the "Sandy Cove Bathing Establishment," with trips between 6 and 10 a.m. and from 3 to 7 p.m. for ladies and children only. How could people stay away from a place with such an enticing name? The cost was fifteen cents, including "bath," or ten cents if you arrived in your own conveyance. People came in pleasure boats from Halifax and Dartmouth, taking advantage of the novel attraction. Rowboats and yachts packed with the whole family and laden with picnic baskets sailed to Sandy Cove in those pre-automobile days when people sought their summer recreation on the waters of the harbour.

This area has the best anchorage in the whole harbour. The water is not as deep as it is on the Halifax side, but is deep enough for the largest sailing ships. This meant not having to put out as much anchor line, an important consideration in the days when the heavy anchors had to be set and hauled using manual labour. It is also nicely sheltered from southeast gales in an area sufficiently open to accommodate a large number of ships. Even before its settlement, early fishermen and traders accustomed to the port would anchor in this area either to seek shelter from a southeast gale, or to avoid riding the deeper waters in mid-stream.

Historians believe that many ships of the substantial British fleet that assembled in Halifax Harbour to prepare for the second siege of Louisbourg in 1758 must have anchored near the eastern side. This is inferred from a record of that year which reveals that General James Wolfe frequently drilled his troops, making landings on the Dartmouth shore. The most logical place for these exercises would have been the broad hill southward from the Coast Guard site, because of the steep incline of the forested slope, and the large boulders that would have provided training for the landing parties on the beach.

I have done many dives in this area. The bottom inclines quickly down to six to nine metres (22 to 30 feet) deep and then levels to a very gradual slope, which runs hundreds of metres out from shore before descending again to fifteen to eighteen metres (50 to 60 feet). It is a very broad area of bottles and debris covering the whole range of times since the founding of Halifax and Dartmouth. It contains the remains of several wooden vessels, probably beached there in days past when they were no longer serviceable and allowed to decay. The ballast stones from a large dock are still there, which might have serviced the estates of the area or been used to dock the steam launch to enable bathers to disembark. Judging by the bottles on the bottom, this area remained a popular picnic site long after the Hesslein establishment had closed. I have always found the area interesting because of the range of debris. Being well inside the harbour but never having been used for commercial shipping, the bottom was left alone and quietly collected its castoffs for two and a half centuries. Unfortunately, in the mid 1980s, the Coast Guard filled in about half the area to build a storage yard and covered up a lot of artifacts in the process.

The Harbour's Innocent Victims

Halifax was born because of war and conflict. It has been a place from which to attack the French, a last holdout against the American rebels, a colonial stronghold from which to support the "mother country." Much of its history has been dedicated to keeping an enemy at bay or preparing for a war or sending troops to a war. The gun batteries built to protect the harbour are silent today, overgrown with grass and bushes, but they have witnessed the departure of thousands of ships and millions of men heading to war and destruction. And today ships still leave Halifax going to this war zone or that trouble spot.

June 1998 saw the biggest concentration of warships in Halifax since the Second World War. These ships of the North Atlantic Treaty Organization fleet, Canada's naval allies, were engaged in exercises off Newfoundland, but their presence in the harbour served as a reminder that Halifax still deals in instruments of death. Halifax has forts, batteries, and redoubts and its history is inextricably linked with the soldiers and sailors who have, for a short time, called the place home. It has been home to different fleets for close to three centuries. But even though the city has lived with the news of war and the threat of war, the big guns at the thirty or so forts and batteries surrounding Halifax Harbour have never been called upon to repel an attacker.

Like most Canadians, the people of the communities surrounding Halifax Harbour think of their military as a means of defending themselves

126

and their loved ones. Yet, in numerous twists of irony, instead of protecting them, the military presence has brought trouble and misfortune to the citizens who have lived near the harbour. The bad luck began prior to the English settlement of the harbour. When the French armada visited Halifax in 1746 with its thousands of dead and dying, the only inhabitants at the time were the native Mi'kmaq who visited during the summers. They were the allies of the French, so they came in contact with the diseased men, who were dying, according to different accounts, of scurvy, dysentery and typhus. Several historians report that some acquired the clothes of the dead soldiers and sailors and took disease back to their villages, wiping out large numbers of the indigenous population. The presence of their military allies had brought death and suffering to them.

The Halifax Explosion

On December 6, 1917, the harbour and its people suffered the worst of all its disasters, in a well-documented event called the Halifax Explosion. A French munitions ship caught fire and blew up in the Narrows after colliding with another ship. All the explosives, ammunition and fuel that the *Mont Blanc* carried were supposed to be used against the German enemy but it was turned upon the people of Halifax instead. In the worst non-nuclear explosion in recorded history, 2,000 died and 6,000 were injured. A large number were blinded because so many people – many of them mothers carrying toddlers – went to their windows to watch the burning ship; the ensuing explosion blew the window glass into their faces.

It took years for the city to recover and rebuild. The victims who survived carried both the physical and emotional scars for the rest of their lives. The living continued to suffer in other ways, for many lost their homes, their possessions and their livelihood, at least for the short term, because there is always work during wartime. The railway station, the Richmond docks and railway yards, the sugar refinery, the textile mill, and other parts of the industrial base were all obliterated.

Describing one teenage girl who lost her whole family, consisting of five brothers and sisters and her parents, Janet Kitz writes "Of her old life, there was practically nothing left. Her home, furniture, clothes, photographs, and the people who meant most to her were all gone."

It wasn't an enemy's bomb that brought the disaster. It was the day-in, day-out proximity of the instruments of death and war that finally caught up with the city, killing more people of the area than four years of war in Europe had.

I often get asked if I have ever seen anything from the explosion when I dive. If I ever did, it would be difficult to positively identify without bringing it up and then going through a lot of effort. There is plenty of old metal on the bottom and one piece looks like another. The place where the explosion took place is quite unappealing because today it is covered by a huge floating dry-dock. I was in the vicinity of the explosion site, not far from the dry-dock, in the summer of 2001 when I located what I suspect is a relic of the explosion. It is a piece of iron plating about two metres long by a metre wide, bent and twisted, especially on the edges. It is in twenty-three metres (75 feet) of water. As I swam past it, I thought it was a flat rock and paid it no heed, but I found myself thinking "That was no rock!" and I turned back for another look. The edges are ragged and bent inwards, indicating a great deal of stress. It is sitting on a flat, bland bottom with nothing else like it in the vicinity. The absence of any other pieces of metal in the area makes me believe it might have been a part of the exploding *Mont Blanc*.

The Schlesien

The "war to end all wars" did not live up to its billing – but there was a period of peace. On March 14, 1937, with one war over and the next one a mere two years away, there was another harbour accident involving, of all things, a German warship. About 135 men, women and children boarded the *Thor II* and were taken to visit the 14,000 ton pre-World War I German battleship *Schlesien*, anchored in the harbour. She was the first German naval vessel to visit the harbour since 1913 and, for many, she was an unwelcome sight. She certainly brought bad luck to some, for while *Thor II* waited, the latter's engine blew up, catching people's clothes afire and hurling others into the icy water. Several people suffered severe burns but, fortunately, none died. The *Schlesien* went on to serve in the German Navy during World War II and almost survived that conflict, until she struck a mine in the Baltic Sea in April, 1945, and sank.

The Trongate Incident

Halfway through the Second World War, in the early morning hours of April 10, 1942, the captain of the SS *Trongate*, a British cargo ship, watched in disbelief as the Canadian warship HMCS *Chedabucto* fired upon his ship within the supposedly safe confines of Halifax Harbour. The *Trongate* went to the bottom.

The skipper of the *Chedabucto* had not lost his mind. He was acting under orders from his superiors. With the vivid memory of December 6, 1917, still fresh, they had decided to take no chances with the *Trongate*. The ship had a fire in the hold and its cargo of 10,000 cases of ammunition and nearly 2000 drums of toluene, a prime ingredient in TNT, held the potential to flatten downtown Halifax and Dartmouth. The *Trongate*'s captain had considered scuttling and sinking the ship in shallow water, but never got the chance. The ship's crew was ordered off and the *Chedabucto* commenced firing.

Here was another ammunition ship, burning in the centre of the busy harbour, in the midst of two hundred other vessels, docks, houses and people. It was happening again! So, while the Allies were losing dozens of ships to the enemy and were going through so much to protect them, here in the best fortified harbour on the coast, they were sinking one of their own ships to the sound of rockets and shells exploding in her cargo holds.

The *Chedabucto* carefully fired about twenty-five 4-inch non-explosive practice rounds at the *Trongate*'s waterline. Regular ammunition is explosive and would have had the very result they were trying to avoid. All the projectiles found their mark except one, which is said to have landed next to a desk in a building on the waterfront, having ricocheted off the water's surface. Now, there's a souvenir worth having. I wonder where it is today.

The *Trongate* went down in twenty-three metres (75 feet) of water and came to rest with the tops of her masts sticking above the surface. There she sat for thirteen years until a British salvage firm brought the wreckage to the surface in 1956 and transported it to the Dartmouth Marine Slips nearby, where it was cut up and shipped to Sydney for melting down as scrap. Even after the years under water she still posed a hazard as the occasional hidden piece of .303 ammunition fired when the cutters' torches heated it up, sending workers scurrying for cover.

Surveys show a depression in the bottom where the *Trongate* sat, just east of mid-channel and due north of George's Island. It is one of the anchorages for large vessels that need to anchor for extended periods of time. Several of us decided to dive the area and see what was left. Using a depth sounder, we located the site, radioed the harbour traffic control office for clearance to dive and got flatly refused. They pointed out that diving in the area was prohibited because of the large amount of explosives scattered around the bottom. We took the refusal with a chuckle, because we knew that there is ammunition all over the harbour.

Three More World War II Mishaps

There had already been other accidents and deaths in the harbour associated with World War II, especially collisions between large merchant freighters and smaller vessels, which resulted in violent deaths to men and sorrow to Halifax households. On March 26, 1941, HMCS *Otter*, a converted yacht used to patrol the mouth of the harbour, caught fire and burned, resulting in nineteen men out of a crew of forty-one losing their lives.

On June 30, 1942, scores of downtown office workers were horrified to witness a terrible sinking as they worked at their desks. The Canadian National Railways tug *Lavaltrie* was towing two barges not far from where the Maritime Museum is currently located. The barges were lashed one on each side of the vessel. A passing freighter sliced into one of them, plowing wreckage onto the tug. The wheelhouse of the tug got swept away, taking the captain to his death, and the tug then rolled over and went to the bottom in less than a minute. Five more men died and four survived.

The fireman on the steam tug, William Basker, lived to tell a miraculous story. He was at work in the stokehold below deck, when he felt the lurch of the collision. But as the freighter had struck the barge, and not the tug, the impact had been cushioned and Basker thought they had just been swirled about by the wake of a passing ship. It didn't take long for him to realize how wrong he was, as the tug rapidly started to roll over. He headed to a doorway and was met by an inrush of water. Somehow he got out and had to start crawling toward the bottom of the tug as it turned turtle. The tug began to sink but he was buoyant and started to rise, only to find himself beneath one of the barges. He struck his head against the bottom of the barge and started to sink again. As he struggled to surface the suction from the sinking tug kept drawing him down. After a superhuman effort he fought his way to the surface, to find that he had gone completely under the freighter and emerged on the other side.

He had the comfort of finding himself in the company of a fellow survivor of the crash, but quickly realized that he was not out of danger. They were in the path of the ship's great, spiraling propellor and its huge blades chopped the water as it wound its way towards them. Then, just as it was about to consume them, it stopped turning, as those aboard the freighter were taking action as a result of the collision. The four survivors were pulled from the water by small boats, which had begun to assist.

This was not the first close call for William Basker. He had already survived one wreck off the Newfoundland coast before serving for two years on a British tanker, a distinctly dangerous profession during wartime. He decided not to sign on for another voyage of the tanker and not a moment too soon, for on her next trip, she was sunk by enemy action, with the loss of the entire crew.

In another wartime incident, an allied freighter cut down the shipyard tug *Erg* in Bedford Basin. She had been heading towards another ship that needed work before going to sea, when the Norwegian freighter *Norelg* struck the 17-metre tug and sent her to the bottom, taking nineteen of the twenty-four men aboard to their deaths.

The *Norelg* had just entered the Basin on a rainy and foggy morning, and was heading to her assigned anchorage. The anchors were already dangling from the hawseholes in the ship's bow as she maneuvered into position at a speed of about five knots. According to witnesses, the *Erg* was travelling ahead of the ship and to one side on the same course, but slightly slower. Because of the high bow of the *Norelg*, the tug soon disappeared from the pilot's view. The next time anybody on the ship saw the tug, she was bottom up and beginning to sink.

At the inquiry into the sinking, all aboard the *Norelg* maintained that the tug must have changed course drastically and suddenly, for the ship struck and ran over her without anybody realizing it was happening. The big ship struck the little tug on the port quarter just aft of amidships – on the left side just rear of centre. The tug's stern was pushed down and the bow rose as she skidded across the water. In a second she flipped over, trapping her victims inside, and headed for the bottom, seventy metres (230 feet) down.

This incident happened on the morning of Tuesday, July 6, 1943. The *Erg* was no stranger to disaster. Built at Halifax in 1915 and called the *Sambro*, she sank during the Halifax Explosion of 1917. She was later re-floated, fitted with diesel engines and renovated for service. She began her new life as the *Erg* in 1930. Two weeks after the *Norelg* struck her, she was raised for the second time and beached on the Dartmouth shore. Ten bodies of the nineteen men lost were recovered from the derelict. It was felt that the missing nine probably got out but were dragged down in the vortex created as she sank to the bottom. This time, the tug had been damaged beyond repair. She was transported out into the Basin and allowed to sink for the third and final time.

But that was not the end of the story. Her location had been long forgotten, when surveyors from the Bedford Institute of Oceanography rediscovered the site while doing a survey of the harbour floor fifty years later. Armed with the survey results, Jim Camano was towing an underwater camera from his boat in the early fall of 2000. As he watched the monitor, he saw what seemed to be riveted iron plates at very close range, in fifteen metres (50 feet) of water. He took note of the location for later reference.

A couple of months later, several divers from the Nova Scotia Undersea Exploration Society returned to the spot to check out what Jim had seen. There sat the tug, upright and bearing the marks of her encounter with the large freighter. To those of us who saw her, she was a mystery, for the B.I.O.

survey had simply identified a possible wreck site. Her wheelhouse was buckled down, there was no glass in the windows, and the doors were missing. She seemed like a vessel that had been condemned, but she had not been scrapped for her valuable brass; the portholes and brass propellor were still intact. Everything pointed to it being the *Erg*, but we could not find a name on the vessel and, besides, this was in the wrong part of the Basin.

After Jim consulted old newspaper articles and the Nova Scotia Archives, it became clear what had happened. He uncovered a photo of the boat just after she had been raised in the summer of 1943, and we were able to positively identify the *Erg*. Fifty-seven years after her sinking she looked exactly as she had on the day she was raised. Jim contacted Halifax Shipyards, the owners of the tug, and they constructed a memorial plaque, to be placed on the wreck in memory of the men who were lost.

Dana's future father-in-law, a wartime shipyard worker, was supposed to have been aboard that day, but he missed the incident and got to live to an old age. He died almost fifty years later, fully aware of the tug's tragic loss but never realizing that she had been raised, for such things were not reported during wartime.

The VE Day Riots

The Second World War ended on May 7, 1945, but not for Halifax. Its population of 65,000 had swollen to 120,000 during the war. There were close to 30,000 members of the Armed Services in the city, either in barracks or aboard ships in the harbour. The city was full of people who had lived with the fear of death and violence for years. It was finally over and they were ready to party, but the authorities, fearing excesses, decided there would be no celebrating.

The frustration and wrath of the thousands of sailors was vented on downtown Halifax that day as they rioted, breaking into stores and looting their contents, smashing hundreds of windows and destroying millions of dollars worth of property. Close to 600 businesses were pillaged, as the mob guzzled 65,000 quarts of stolen liquor and 8,000 cases of beer. Three people died as a result of the orgy of drinking and looting that lasted two nights and a day, before authorities finally succeeded in restoring order.

The Magazine Explosion

The city was just recovering from that one when another disaster struck. This time it was in the familiar form of explosions and fire. At war's end, Canada had the world's third largest navy and its ships converged on Halifax to be decommissioned. Enormous amounts of ammunition were removed from the fighting ships – depth charges for destroying submarines, torpedoes, anti-aircraft ammunition, artillery shells, rockets, and bombs. There was more than enough to completely destroy the cities of Halifax and Dartmouth.

The magazine where all this ammunition was stored is still located on the Dartmouth side of Bedford Basin. It was constructed of separate buildings so that an explosion in one building would not ignite the contents of another. But there were so many explosives being unloaded from the warships that it was everywhere. In the early evening of July 18 there was a blast that caught the attention of the people in the cities and surrounding area. It ignited fires and in the midst of a steady rumble of minor detonations of ammunition, there were three more huge explosions that night. The fires continued and there seemed to be no way to deal with the impending danger. Ships in the Basin and inner harbour struggled to get to the outer harbour, out of range, as the north end of Halifax and much of Dartmouth were evacuated.

At dusk, Naval Headquarters had broadcast a message suggesting the area be evacuated. That was all the war-weary citizens of Halifax, Dartmouth and Bedford needed. Within an hour there was a line of traffic sixteen kilometres long snaking south, away from the Basin and the magazine, in a scene reminiscent of the many peoples of Europe who had fled from the German invaders. But there were no invaders – only our own ammunition firing in all directions, like some gun-toting lunatic gone wild. The people crowded onto Citadel Hill and into the parks on what was, fortunately, a hot, dry evening. They also spent the night in yards, gravel pits, by the roadside, anywhere they could find a place to lie down, terrified of what might come at any moment if the whole magazine went up.

The worst explosions came at 4 a.m. on the 19th, breaking windows and knocking down those few people who remained close enough to be affected. The fires continued all that day and by 6 p.m. the Navy announced that the worst had passed and people could return to their homes. The cleanup operation was extensive, as live ammunition had been hurled all over the surrounding woods and the Bedford Basin. But they didn't get it all. While diving, I have seen intact artillery projectiles under the MacKay Bridge and other types of ammunition in many parts of the Bedford Basin.

More Tragedy

The war's end didn't end the dying. On July 16, 1947, the Canadian destroyer, HMCS *Micmac* was outside the harbour, undergoing speed trials following a refit. While heading back to port, she encountered a fog bank. Within seconds of entering the fog, she collided with an outgoing freighter, killing ten sailors and a civilian Dockyard worker who was aboard.

Harbour fog caused another accident a few years later. On November 8, 1954, the navy's duty boat, a type of floating taxicab that transported naval personnel to the navy's sites around the harbour, collided in dense fog with the harbour ferry, *Scotian*. Two civilians and one sailor died as a result.

Ten years after the incident with the *Micmac*, HMCS *Magnificent*, a Canadian aircraft carrier with forty-eight airplanes aboard, was being maneuvered by three tugs in the harbour. The port bow tug, the *Glendyne*, swung across the bow of the moving carrier and was hauled over. The *Magnificent* immediately went full speed ahead on both engines to take the strain off the line, but the tug did not right herself. Two men were trapped inside and went to their deaths as the *Glendyne* was dragged under and sank. She was later re-floated and was ultimately sunk and raised many times as a training vessel. The *Glendyne*'s wheelhouse now sits outside the Maritime Museum of the Atlantic and is used as a ticket booth.

There are other stories of death and disaster because of the military presence in Halifax. They serve to remind us that this harbour has always been used as a place to keep ships of war and of all the large, powerful devices and dangerous activities they bring with them. Through much of her history, Halifax has prospered during times of war and languished during peacetime. The citizens of Halifax always meet cutbacks in military spending with dismay because the military – especially the navy – means jobs and prosperity. But while there has been prosperity for some, for others the military presence has meant just the opposite – suffering and sadness.

Crossing the Harbour

The Ferries

The cities of Halifax and Dartmouth face one another across the harbour, their downtowns separated by about two kilometres of water. From the very beginning, people and goods have needed to cross the distance between the two cities. In 1752 one of Dartmouth's first settlers, John Connor, who had arrived on the ship *Alderney* in 1750, received a three-year charter to provide a regulated ferry service across the harbour. It ran daily from sunrise to sunset and once on Sundays to take the people of Dartmouth to church in Halifax and back home again.

The population of Dartmouth was so small that Connor had trouble making a living, so he gave up his franchise two months later to undertake a trading expedition. But the town grew and there were others waiting in the wings to take over the service. Soon there were two competing ferry services, operated by James Creighton and John Skerry. They boarded passengers in Dartmouth Cove and landed them at essentially the same downtown Halifax location that is used today.

In 1815 the leading Halifax businessmen of the day formed the Halifax Steam Boat Company to provide a more substantial ferry service. This group, which included Samuel Cunard, the founder of the famous steamship company, wanted to build a ferry powered by the new and exciting medium of steam. They ended up, instead, with one powered by eight horses, cleverly dubbed the "Team Boat." Bearing the name *Sherbrooke*, this 18-metre paddle wheeler, which was launched at Dartmouth in 1816, made its first crossing on November 3 of that year. It could cross the harbour in a very respectable twenty minutes, thanks to the efforts of the eight horses walking continuously on a treadmill.

Cunard and his associates eventually got their steamboat which replaced the *Sherbrooke* in 1830. It is generally accepted to have been the first steamboat built in Nova Scotia. Called the *Sir Charles Ogle*, after the commander of the Royal Navy then stationed in Halifax (promoted to Admiral of the Fleet in 1857), it was also a paddle wheeler and was thirty metres long. It was built by Alexander Lyle in Dartmouth and served its clientele – the people, horses, cattle, sheep, goats and oxen of Halifax and Dartmouth – for an incredible sixty-four years.

Photographs show the name "Sir C. Ogle" emblazoned across the side of the vessel. In her memoirs published in 1900, a Mrs. Gould writes that as a child she and her friends called it the "Sircy Ogle." During her long life, this ship experienced more than her share of adventures, including rescuing the brig *Cordelia* from Thrumcap Shoal in January 1834, and towing her to Dartmouth for repairs. The hull of the *Sir Charles Ogle* found its final resting place as part of the cribwork of the Dartmouth Marine Slips. It was not unusual to use an old vessel for such purposes by filling it with rocks until it sank and then modifying it as required to form part of a wharf. There is still one such example easily viewed from the water. Directly below the Mac-Donald Bridge is the outline of an iron craft forming part of the shore. I examined it one day and found what appears to be the remains of a steam-driven tug.

A sister ship of the *Ogle*, the *Micmac*, transported the delegates of the Charlottetown Conference for a day's outing and picnic in the Bedford Basin in August 1864. They were in Halifax following their historic conference to consider the Confederation of the provinces of British North America into a single country to be called Canada. Additional ferries have come from builders in Dartmouth, Yarmouth, New York, Glasgow, Lauzon, Pictou, and Lunenburg.

Other services besides the main ferry service came and went through the years. The Upper and Lower ferries operated from Dartmouth for a few years after the Steam Boat Company got its act together. In 1845 a competitive ferry started providing service across the Narrows. It could carry a hundred people and was powered by four men turning a crank that drove the propellor. If you were a passenger in a hurry you could lend a hand and speed things up. In 1856 the Steam Boat Company inaugurated what it called a north end service, crossing south of where the MacDonald Bridge spans the harbour today.

Two hundred and fifty years after John Connor and nearly twenty boats later, the ferry continues to ply the harbour waters. The service became such an integral part of life for Halifax and Dartmouth residents that one of the local papers carried a gossip column called "Ferry Tales." The author of the piece supposedly participated in mythical conversations that took place on the ferries, and passed on what he heard. The service has survived hurricanes, collisions, drownings, groundings, the 1917 Explosion and the loss of a ship of the fleet in 1944.

The lost vessel, the *Governor Cornwallis*, was designed by William Roue many years after he designed the *Bluenose*. She caught fire while crossing from Halifax on December 22, 1944. After the 300 to 400 passengers and twenty vehicles were off, tugs towed the ferry to George's Island where it burned to the waterline. It had been launched in Dartmouth just three years earlier, one of the largest wooden vessels ever built in the harbour. She quietly slid from the bank of the island and today the burnt out hulk lies on a slope off the southeast tip of George's Island, having disappeared into twenty-five metres of water. The end of any ship is a sad occasion but somehow it seems more noble to go to the bottom in the waters where she served than to end up at the wrecker's yard, as her sisters did.

Ferries have departed from several Dartmouth locations over the years but have landed almost exclusively at one Halifax site – virtually where they land today. The present terminal and floating dock started operating in the early 1980s next door to the traditional location closer to the Cable Wharf. On the bottom are the remains of the docks that served for many years when the ferry was much larger and carried automobiles. The wood is near-

139

ly deteriorated but the stone will never go unless it is removed. The cozy arrangement which permitted the ferry to snuggle between two docks is clearly visible in the shapes of the stone ballast piles and large, squared timbers. The top of the ballast piles is about six metres (20 feet) below the surface in water that is about nine metres (30 feet) deep.

Thousands of people have used the ferries daily and if you look at the bottom where the terminal was, you get the impression that every passenger threw a pop bottle overboard. A diver can follow the route of the ferry by the trail of pop bottles on the bottom. They are several generations deep from the years of being tossed over the side and off the docks.

The harbour's propensity to obstruct traffic continues to be a major factor in people's lives, and so does its ability to provide a means of transportation. Through the years, the ferries have come in all sizes and shapes, propelled by oars, sails, horses, steam, hand cranks, and diesels. The latest high tech propulsion system to be talked about is a hovercraft, running from Bedford to downtown. No doubt it, like its predecessors, will stay for a while, to be replaced by something better or cheaper.

Dreaming of a Bridge

The ferries achieved what they could, but the people of Dartmouth dreamed of a bridge to take them to Halifax and to accelerate the growth of their community. As early as 1796, a petition had been presented to the House of Assembly praying for an act to authorize the building of a bridge across the Narrows. That year, Jonathan Tremain incorporated a company to build a bridge of boats strung across the Narrows from Dartmouth to the Dockyard. Nothing came of it. On another occasion in 1835, a newspaper writer suggested a drawbridge across the Narrows.

Ten years later, there was another move afoot with a scheme to build a floating bridge. Arthur Godfrey of Dartmouth and John Starr of Richmond incorporated the Richmond Bridge Company. Their plan was to anchor a series of large boats across the Narrows, connected by stringers, which would be planked over. Rails would be constructed for protection. Such bridges were common in Europe, the promoters alleged, particularly on the

Rhine River, but the scheme went nowhere on Halifax Harbour. It is hard to imagine it working in a harbour so big and with so much traffic. Even though it is not far across the Narrows, large waves regularly get whipped up in the area, so the bridge surely would have bobbed and lurched about, providing the walk across with more excitement than most people were interested in experiencing.

The Railway Bridges

The dream of connecting the two towns finally became a reality in 1884 with the building of a railway bridge across the Narrows just south of where the A. Murray MacKay bridge crosses today. The Narrows Bridge was started in May 1884, coincident with the building of the Acadia Sugar Refinery in Woodside, south of Dartmouth. The bridge was constructed with hemlock pilings and pine, both of which are soft, brittle woods. It curved north from the Richmond terminal of the Intercolonial Railway and had a straight section, which included a swing bridge near the Dartmouth shore to allow harbour traffic to pass. This 61-metre steel swing could be operated by one man and was designed and built by Starr Manufacturing of Dartmouth, a company best known as a major manufacturer of ice skates.

The bridge then curved south and ran across Tuft's Cove via a trestle, crossing the area occupied today by a large electric power station. It was four hundred metres long and eight to thirteen metres wide with supports reaching down eighteen to twenty-three metres. The bridge foundation had been built of piers, which held twenty tons of ballast and came up about two and a half metres from the bottom. Long, spindly legs attached to these piers and then traveled to the surface where they were covered with the superstructure of the bridge. It had a single track. The first train crossed in March 1885 and passenger service was inaugurated on January 6, 1886.

The passenger service was less than ideal. Phyllis Blakeley in *Glimpses of Halifax – 1867 to 1900* writes that the passenger service was so slow that one man who missed the train in Dartmouth drove the considerable distance to the ferry, crossed to Halifax, took another horse-drawn cab, and still caught the train at the Richmond station in Halifax. A good swimmer could have done it in less time.

The bridge was curved to withstand the ice that moves out of the Basin in the spring. But the traffic passing over caused very high stresses on the turn as the inertia of the heavy trains tended to throw the bridge northward toward the Basin. Because there were no lateral braces angled out from the bridge and going into the bottom, these stresses weakened the whole structure. The strong currents that pass through this area twice a day in each direction would have weakened it still more. So the poorly designed and poorly built bridge never got a rest.

A day of reckoning was approaching. On Monday evening, September 7, 1891, it came in the form of a hurricane that swept up the harbour. Along the way, the hurricane washed away part of the ferry wharf at Dartmouth, blew down the chute of the grain elevator at Cornwallis St., and destroyed the Fish Market and Slip. By midnight, most of the bridge was gone.

It was hastily rebuilt early in 1892 and was less than two years old when it just floated away in the early morning hours of July 23, 1893. The passage of the trains had loosened the piles, some of which were twenty-six metres long and containing two joins. Reports state that they had been simply driven into the bottom without the benefit of ballast to hold them down. As I observe what remains of this bridge on the bottom, it's difficult to imagine how it ever remained stationary. Where the bottom is not soft mud, it's a slope of boulders and cliffs. It seems that the weakened structure just floated off the bottom at high tide and went on its way, leaving thirty-five railway cars stranded in Dartmouth.

Both bridges, or what survived of them, are still on the bottom, in twelve to twenty-five metres of water. Corroded railway iron, stone cribwork and occasional scraps of wood are all that remain. It is impossible to tell which of the two bridges provided the railway iron that remains, because both of them collapsed. The iron rails are spread over a large area which, at first, seems puzzling, but can be explained by the fact that the tracks would have been attached to the wooden bed that floated around during and after the hurricane. According to reports, there were collisions and near collisions with large sections of the bridge up and down the harbour, as it caused a serious hazard to marine navigation. The schooner *Ellie*, belonging to Halifax merchant Daniel Cronan, was blocked from docking at Cronan's premises near present day Purdy's Wharf because of a large mass of floating wreckage.

For those of us who dive for pleasure, there is a special aspect to this dive. Diver Edward Whebby of Dartmouth, employed by contractor Duncan Waddell, died while participating in the construction of the first bridge. It was reported that after working underwater, he complained of not feeling well and died within a few hours. At that time little was known about the dangers of decompression sickness associated with staying in deep water for extended periods.

The Narrows area is one of the more challenging dives in the harbour. By harbour standards it is relatively deep, going down to more than twenty-seven metres (90 feet) at high tide. Because of the size of the Bedford Basin, a substantial amount of water passes through this constriction when the tides change, so the currents can get quite strong. Getting pushed along by these currents has rather unpleasant consequences because it means you can end up in the Basin with a long swim to shore or you can get swept out the harbour with nowhere to get out of the water. So it requires careful planning, observing the direction and speed of the currents, taking precise compass bearings, and adhering to a pre-planned itinerary.

But it is also one of the most interesting dives anywhere. The currents have a positive effect as well. They keep the silt away, which makes the scenery very attractive. Filter feeders need strong currents to bring nutrients to them so they abound in this area, along with scallops, lobster and long-legged snow crabs. On a sunny day it is a veritable garden. Massive boulders, cliffs and rocky seascapes surround you. And a virtual museum lies on the flat areas of the bottom, provided you are observant enough to spot the artifacts, for to the unaccustomed eye everything looks the same.

A Close Call

On one of my first dives in this area many years ago, I learned a valuable lesson about sticking to the dive plan. Dana and I were diving for bottles in the early hours of a winter morning. Snow was falling from a grey sky as we walked to the point below the MacKay Bridge that marks the shortest distance across the harbour. We swam down the bank, which descends at a very steep angle. We eventually got separated, but I continued the dive, thoroughly enjoying all that I was seeing and finding. Keeping a steady eye on my air supply, I was about to head back when I got into a particularly interesting area that was strewn with 150-year old bottles. I succumbed to the temptation to pick up more bottles than I could easily manage and hung around until I realized I had just enough air to get back to shore. I had been careless in a very unforgiving environment.

Normally, I like to go all the way in along the bottom because I feel vulnerable on the surface, especially in an area with currents. If you get caught in strong currents, you can always claw your way along the rocks on the bottom or anchor your hands into the mud. I checked my compass and followed my return bearing, concerned that my air was getting low. I was at twenty-one metres (70 feet) facing a dilemma.

Should I go slowly and, by minimizing my exertion, consume my air slowly, or should I speed up to get in before running out of air? It's the same predicament you face on the highway when your car's fuel gauge approaches empty. I swam and swam and swam. The bag of bottles was heavy and slowed me down. It was becoming harder to get a breath as my tank approached empty and I knew I would have to surface soon. With great relief I came to the bottom of the bank and headed up to 18, 15, 12, 9 metres. Then, to my shock, I reached the end of the bank and the bottom dipped back down. It was a shoal and I was lost.

Still worse, I was out of air. I had no choice but to head up – fast! I hit the surface gasping, and was greeted by a blinding snowstorm. Waves were breaking over my head and I couldn't tell which direction to take. Because I had followed normal procedures for surfacing and purged all the air from my suit, I was heavy on the surface and prone to sinking. The emergency fix

144

for such a dilemma would have been to drop the bottles or ditch my weight belt, but I was too stubborn to part with $75 worth of lead that I would have to replace before I could dive again. And I certainly wasn't throwing away the bottles!

With great difficulty and the help of my compass, I managed to make out the shore and started the long swim home. As the shore came into clearer view, I could see Dana's black form in the blowing snow, cleaning his bottles and obviously basking in the memory of a good dive. The going was difficult and I struggled to stay on the surface. Occasionally, when I was just too tired, I relaxed and would start to sink. The short rest was pleasant, but I would then have to fight my way to the surface for my next gasp of air. I was getting spent. On one particularly long rest which felt just too good, a voice in my head shouted, "You idiot! You're about to die for a bag of old bottles!"

I dropped them and as I looked down to watch them go out of sight, I was surprised to see them land about three metres (10 feet) below me. I was in shallow water and nearly ashore. I had been so preoccupied with staying alive that I hadn't realized I had made it. I finished the swim, stood in waist deep water to get a badly needed rest and went back for the bottles. But I had learned my lesson. I had let the interests of the dive so preoccupy me that I forgot the consequences of complacency, that my first priority was to do the things that ensured my safety. Ever since that day, I now head back with ample air to cover emergencies and if I expect the dive to be long or deep, I wear double tanks with independent regulators.

Still Dreaming of a Bridge

The railway bridge across the Narrows was the last bridge to cross the harbour for more than half a century. But the dream did not die. In 1911, the Dartmouth Board of Trade renewed their request to Ottawa for a permanent bridge across the Narrows and, by 1913, federal government engineers were making estimates of the cost. The Halifax-Dartmouth Bridge Association incorporated in 1928 and got down to business, drawing up plans and choosing a site. Then along came the depression of the 1930s and with it another frustrating setback, as the whole project went on hold while the depression ground its way through the Nova Scotia economy, only to be followed by the Second World War.

In the bright morning following the long night of war, the 1945 edition of the municipal planning book for the city of Halifax showed that bridge fever was very much alive and in the air. It expressed hopes for a bridge across the harbour at the Dockyard or the Narrows, and at least one other bridge across the Northwest Arm. If a new bridge were to be built across the harbour, it would come with prophetic baggage, for somewhere out of the foggy mists that envelop the harbour comes this little ditty, said to be of Native origin:

> *Three times a bridge o'er these waters shall rise*
> *Built by the white man so strong and wise*
> *Three times shall fall like a dying breath*
> *In storm – in silence – and last in death.*

The first had gone in a storm and the second went silently according to the prophecy, both without loss of life. This is almost a miracle when we consider that there were two passenger trains a day that crossed the bridge, along with the freight trains, and that both bridges had been in such poor condition when they succumbed. It remains to be seen if and how the third will go and if it will take human lives with it. However, when the time came to open the new bridge, officials took no chances, and opted to wait an extra day while April Fool's Day passed.

Driving Across the Harbour

A motor vehicle finally drove across the harbour on October 25, 1954. It was the first vehicle to cross the bridge even though the bridge was still under construction. The brand new suspension bridge opened for business on April 2, 1955, and was named after Angus L. MacDonald, who had served Canada as Minister of Naval Affairs during the Second World War and had served the province as Premier. Unfortunately, he died just before the bridge was completed.

A year almost to the day after the bridge opened, the operators of the north end ferry shut down after running a service with four boats for thirty-five years. That same year, the Halifax-Dartmouth Ferry Commission announced a new era in ferry transportation to fit with the new realities, as the significantly smaller *Dartmouth II* and *Halifax II* went into service. For the first time in 140 years the ferries did not carry vehicles. As one would expect, the bridge radically changed the ferry service. Today, while the ferries no longer carry vehicles, they do carry on a brisk trade in pedestrians travelling from two Dartmouth locations to Halifax.

Not long after the MacDonald Bridge began operating, the dreaming started again. A second bridge? Maybe a tunnel? In 1964 an engineering firm submitted a $37 million proposal for a tunnel across the harbour, not cut through the earth below the bottom of the harbour, but one that would be prefabricated in sections and sit on the harbour floor. An air pumping station on George's Island would provide ventilation. It went nowhere.

The second bridge, named after A Murray MacKay, opened on July 10, 1970. It is a four-lane suspension bridge which carries 55,000 automobiles per day; the weekday traffic for both bridges combined is around 88,000. By comparison, when the MacDonald Bridge opened in 1955, the ferries were carrying approximately 1,830 cars per day.

The bridges have seen much drama over the years. One June morning in 1990, motorists were shocked to find that a group of protesters had attached themselves to the superstructure of the MacDonald Bridge. They were protesting the presence in the harbour of HMS *Ark Royal,* supposedly carrying nuclear weapons. Their unorthodox approach got them the attention they had sought. Across the country, newspaper readers saw pictures of people hanging in hammocks from the upper parts of the bridge, well over sixty metres above the water.

Maintaining the bridges is a local industry in itself. The MacDonald Bridge requires thirty-two tons of paint to keep it looking good. Each summer, a small group of highflying painters takes to the upper reaches of the bridges, twenty-five stories above the water to paint the bridge and the cables, which are the backbone of the structure. A cable on each side is all that keeps the whole thing from falling into the water. The cables are thirty-five centimetres (14 inches) in diameter, composed of sixty-one strands, each strand containing fifty-one wires. When the suspender ropes are included, a bridge contains a total of more than 6,400 kilometres of wire. The cable is surrounded by cedar for protection and the whole bundle is wrapped in wire and heavily painted. They are anchored to two 20,000-ton concrete blocks, one at each end of the bridge.

Under the Bridge

The MacDonald, usually referred to as the "old bridge," is 1,400 metres long and 100 metres high at the towers. The two towers of each bridge sit in the middle of artificial islands of boulders. The deepest island belongs to the MacKay and is in twenty-four metres (80 feet) of water. These islands were added years after the bridges were built and were placed there as a precaution in case a ship should strike one of the towers. There are many rules governing the movements of ships in this area. As a result of the Halifax Explosion, two ships are not permitted in the Narrows at the same time, and the largest ships are accompanied by a tug as they travel through the Narrows.

There was good reason to be cautious, because on May 9, 1980, the 185-metre freighter *Summit Venture* smashed the southbound span of the Sunshine Skyway in Tampa Bay, Florida, taking out a 305-metre section of the bridge and killing more than thirty people. It was the third time the bridge had been struck in four months. A Greyhound Bus plunged forty-two metres into the ocean, taking twenty-three people to their deaths.

The accident was big news in Halifax because it was the kind of incident that could happen here. A lot of the ship traffic regularly goes under both bridges, very close to the towers, so it was decided to place a buffer of stone around the bases of the piers. At the surface, it is shaped like a pyramid with a flat top, but it is oval shaped at the base and covers a very large area. It took me twenty minutes to swim around the deepest one under the MacKay. Each boulder is about the size of a stove.

In 1998 and 1999, with some clever rearranging, a third lane was added to the MacDonald Bridge, along with a new pedestrian lane and a bicycle lane. This was a major undertaking with months of construction. When Greg and I dove in the area under the bridge we found a king's ransom in tools, bolts and other construction paraphernalia that had been lost, dropped, swept and thrown into the water by the construction workers.

Other Harbour Conveyances

Besides the ferries and bridges, there have been other means of moving people around the harbour. The Royal Navy and the Canadian Navy have maintained "duty boats" to ferry staff and workers from one navy location to another, to and from the Dockyard, Eastern Passage, McNab's Island, Dartmouth, and the harbour forts that have existed over the years. John Regan, writing in 1908, says of these boats: "The twelve and sixteen oar man-of-war cutters of bygone days held in readiness at the [Royal Engineers] Yard have been replaced by convenient steam-tugs and launches which make the round of the forts at regular hours daily." (The Royal Engineers Yard was in downtown Halifax across from George's Island. Today it is the site of the Westin Nova Scotian Hotel.)

When a public transit strike visits Halifax, more than the buses are affected. The ferries stop running as well. At such times, enterprising pleasure boaters often provide ferry service across the harbour for a fee. Called "water taxis," these fast speedboats get commuters to work more quickly than the ferries, but at a significantly higher price. Over the years, the harbour has seen increasingly interesting vehicles taking people for pleasure rides. Besides the tour boats operating under power and sail, there have also been seaplanes, helicopters and hovercraft.

The waters of Halifax Harbour considerably complicate the process of getting around, but the harbour is such a fundamental part of the fabric of the area that it is just one more factor in living here. Ferries and bridges are a fact of life for the people who inhabit the harbour.

The Navies of Halifax Harbour

Halifax Harbour drew the Royal Navy across the Atlantic to protect British possessions, and the presence of the Royal Navy in turn shaped the history and culture of the harbour. No other organization influenced the town like His – and later Her – Majesty's Navy. When Cornwallis and company arrived to found Halifax in 1749, Britannia ruled the waves and when the Royal Navy pulled out of Halifax more than 150 years later, Britannia still ruled the waves.

The Royal Navy

Those who served in the Royal Navy at Halifax were assigned to the North America and West Indies Station. The headquarters remained at Halifax until 1819, when it was moved to Bermuda. The great fleets of sailing ships came in the 1700s with d'Anville's French fleet in 1746, Admiral Holburne in 1757, Admiral Boscawen and others in 1758, during the conflicts with the French. One third of the Royal Navy participated in the attack on Quebec in 1759, staged out of Halifax.

Later, when the American colonies rebelled, the harbour was more important than ever to the British. The Royal Navy brought the retreating British armies to Halifax and it became the stronghold against the upstart Americans for a hundred years, requiring a garrison of both soldiers and sailors.

The Royal Navy built the Dockyard to maintain the King's ships; the Victualling Yard, to feed the crews while at sea; the King's Lumber Yard, to provide wood for building and repairing the ships; the King's Ordnance Yard, to arm the ships; and the King's Wharf, where officers and Royalty stepped ashore.

A plate from a Royal Navy ship. From the author's collection.

The legacy of the Royal Navy was fear, respect and admiration — fear of the press gangs and the roving bands of drunken sailors that bullied the locals; respect for the iron discipline of the Navy, maintained through floggings and hangings; and admiration for the competent sailors who ran the fast and powerful ships that maintained Britain's far-flung empire. In the days of sail, ships required very large crews to do the myriad of jobs aboard. Because life was so hard on board the King's ships, captains had a perennial headache keeping enough hands aboard to make things run. The Navy's recruiting methods were not very sophisticated, but they were persuasive and effective. A "press gang" from a ship roamed the town looking for able-bodied males, whom they carted off to the ship, and that was the last anybody saw of them. Fathers, husbands, sons — they did not discriminate in this early form of the draft. Resistance was met with a good clubbing.

This type of recruiting went on anywhere the King's ships landed and Halifax was no exception. It became such a problem that the citizens rioted and in 1779 the Governor required captains and admirals to get a permit that was good for a specified period of time. So, we read of HMS *Alligator* and HMS *Hussar* bringing in captured French ships carrying cargoes valued

151

at £40,000, and, for their trouble, securing permission to "press throughout the town." In April 1802, Captain Bradley of HMS *Cambrian* was fifty men short in his crew and received a "press warrant" good for ten days.

When word got around town that the press gang was loose, their would-be clients headed underground to sweat it out for a few days. As writer Thomas Akins put it, because of the press gangs "many of the idle and worthless vagabonds of the town were happily secured for His Majesty's service, where they would be brought under wholesome restraint." We have no written accounts about whether or not the press gangs' clientele agreed with such a patronizing assessment. But, clearly, not everybody enjoyed the wholesome restraint because desertion from His Majesty's ships was very common.

Once aboard, conditions were barebones and obedience was enforced with the "kiss o' the cat,' the infamous cat o' nine tails, a whip with nine branches, used throughout the British army and navy to keep the rough recruits in line. Some say the maxim "getting the whole nine yards" comes from this whip. Four men who tried to desert from HMS *Columbine* during a mutiny in 1809 received 150 or 300 lashes. As horrible as that sounds, those convicted in the mutiny, if they were not hanged (six were), received 300 and 500 lash sentences. It is difficult to comprehend how anybody could survive such punishment as they were moved from ship to ship to receive a portion of their sentence aboard whatever ships might be in the harbour at the time, in the practice called "flogging around the fleet."

One recruit was unique in the Royal Navy. William Hall, the son of escaped slaves, was one of the first Canadians and the first black person to win the Victoria Cross, the Empire's highest medal for bravery. From Horton's Bluff, Nova Scotia, he joined the RN in 1852 and received his prestigious award in 1857, for bravery under punishing conditions during the Sepoy mutiny in India. He served twenty-four years in the Royal Navy and survived until retirement as a Petty Officer, first class. He lies buried in Hantsport, NS, near his birthplace.

In complete contrast to its brutal side, the RN also brought a level of sophistication through its officers, who represented a segment of British society that always impressed the townspeople. The younger officers also constituted eligible bachelors for the marriageable belles of the town. The Admiral of the station did plenty of entertaining for the appropriate members of society and on summer evenings there was regular movement to and from the ships as guests came and went.

However, nothing could compare with the sight of the fleet coming and going, showing off the latest and the best of the world's leading navy. A study of the paintings and photographs of the harbour through the years is a study in nautical development. From the days of sail, with small cutters to the big first rate 120-gun ships-of-the-line, to the ironclads and iron-hulled ships, paddle-wheeled steamers to propellor-driven steamers, the dreadnoughts to battleships with 30-centimetre-thick iron hulls; they all came and went through Halifax.

Some of the ships stayed forever. The loss of ships in battle against the enemy or the sea has been the legacy of navies throughout history, and Royal Navy ships rest on the bottom of all the world's oceans. So, too, they rest in and about Halifax Harbour. In the spring of 1755, HMS *Mars* struck a rock while entering the harbour. This 64-gun ship had been a part of the French fleet that had sailed into Chebucto nine years earlier under Duc d'Anville, but had since been captured and used in the Royal Navy. Guns and crew were all saved. The rock that she struck now bears the name of the ship and is known as Mars Rock. In December, 1779, His Majesty's sloop of war *North* and the armed sloop *St Helena* were lost while coming into the harbour, with the loss of 170 people. They were en route from Spanish River, which today is called Sydney, on the island of Cape Breton.

Another captured French ship, the 44-gun frigate, HMS *Tribune*, came to grief in the harbour in November of 1797. HMS *Unicorn* had captured the warship from the French on June 8, 1796, off the Scilly Islands. On September 22, 1797, she sailed from England as the escort for the Quebec and Newfoundland convoys. She lost contact with the convoy in mid-Atlantic on October 19. In the early hours of November 23, she approached Halifax. In fair weather, under the direction of an inexperienced pilot, with the captain below deck, she struck the Thrumcap Shoal off McNab's Island and held tight. In an effort to lighten her, the captain ordered all heavy items, including her guns, thrown overboard, with the exception of one that

153

was kept for signaling. All day long, with ships, boats, and sailors in the harbour unable to help, she struggled, waiting for high tide.

That evening, when the tide came in, the ship drifted free, but after grinding against the rocks all day, her hull had endured a beating and she was taking on water. The rudder had also been damaged, making the frigate difficult to maneuver. The enterprising English seafarers were dealing with these problems, when a third more ominous situation faced them. A southeast gale had been brewing and it was blowing them across the harbour mouth towards the cliffs off Herring Cove. They tried everything that their collective ingenuity could concoct, but to no avail. Soon the water was coming in too quickly for the pumps and the ship was moving helplessly towards the cliffs. The hopeless situation soon ended as it appeared it would, with the wreck of the *Tribune*. She sank around 10:30 p.m. and the long and frustrating day ended with the deaths of almost all of the approximately 240 people aboard. This was well before the days of lifeboats.

With the masts sticking out of the water, a few climbed to the top, but the bad weather beat on both them and the rigging. Just a handful made it through the night, in full view of people who stood vigil on the shore. In the morning, with the waves pounding against the rocks, it appeared there was no hope of getting to the few survivors. Thirteen-year-old Joseph Cracker became the hero of the day, when he took his small rowboat into the surf to help the victims, shaming the reluctant spectators into following him. A few were saved because of his efforts, but the total of those saved that morning and those who had managed to get ashore the night before amounted to no more than a dozen.

Local divers found the wreck in 1968 and recovered the rudder. The bell is displayed at the Maritime Museum of the Atlantic in Halifax. Because of the ease of diving this wreck, it never got properly excavated using accepted archaeological methods. Instead, over the years, bits and pieces of the wreck and its artifacts have found their way into lawn displays and souvenir collections.

This is an easy wreck to dive but is of interest only to serious history buffs. Being wooden and old, little of the wreck remains to be seen; a diver could swim past it and notice nothing. For years it was a source of cannon-balls and divers recovered hundreds, but such souvenir collecting has come under severe scrutiny of late. Besides being illegal, it is pointless, for iron objects, impregnated with salt from the ocean, live a very short life after coming out of the water. Unless properly preserved, they simply crumble in a matter of months.

In 1811, the Royal Navy had twenty-one ships stationed at Halifax, ranging from the 74-gun *Swiftsure* to schooners. Included were the 18-gun brig, HMS *Halifax*, the first, and some say, only vessel of war built at the Halifax Dockyard, and the 18-gun brig, HMS *Fantome*. The *Fantome* took a beating in November 1813, when a hurricane struck the harbour and she was beached in the Narrows. She was re-floated and the next year the unlucky ship wrecked for good, after striking the rocks near Prospect, just outside the harbour.

The Royal Navy reduced its permanent presence at Halifax in 1819, when the Admiralty moved the headquarters of the North America and West Indies Station to Bermuda. But Halifax Harbour continued to see plenty of activity from the Royal Navy. Even though Canada became a nation in 1867, the colonial relationship with the Royal Navy did not end as Great Britain continued to maintain the Halifax station, keeping a dozen or so warships stationed there. The last ships stationed at Halifax, in the early years of the twentieth century, consisted of HMS *Diadem*, *Tribune*, *Crescent*, *Psyche*, *Pallas*, *Niobe*, *Proserpine*, and *Indefatigable*. The British have always liked to put imaginative names to their warships. The flagship was HMS *Ariadne*.

At the beginning of the twentieth century, negotiations began for the eventual ending of the Royal Navy's presence. In 1906 Canada assumed control of the facilities at the Dockyard and other Imperial properties in the harbour. The stage was set for the feeble beginnings of what would become the large, world-class Canadian navy.

Canadian Navy

During the early years of nationhood, Canadians and their governments had trouble deciding if they were Canadian or still British. That begged the question of whether they should contribute to the British military or maintain their own. As early as 1877, Britain had told Canada that she would have to defend her own coasts in the event of war but the Canadian government did not react. As a consequence of the national indecision, as naval historian Tony German writes "Response to crisis, rather than strategic vision, became the hallmark of Canadian naval policy for over a hundred years."

The Dominion government finally passed the Naval Service Act on May 4, 1910, setting the wheels in motion for the creation of Canada's navy. Started as the Naval Service of Canada, the name was changed to the Royal Canadian Navy in 1911. The "fleet" was modest, to say the least, consisting of two aging British cruisers, one on each coast. HMCS *Rainbow* was stationed at Esquimault, British Columbia, and HMCS *Niobe* was kept at Halifax.

In the First World War, the Naval Service of Canada made a contribution in personnel, but the early navy of Canada really didn't matter in the grand scheme of events. By the end of that war the regular navy and reserves had reached 9,000, most of whom were attached to the Royal Navy. Canada may have been called an independent nation, but in this most worldly of undertakings, she was very much a novice. By 1922 this so-called navy was back to 366 men and the fleet consisted of two destroyers and four minesweepers, and not a whole lot was going on. Finally, in 1931, the first ships to be commissioned specifically for the Royal Canadian Navy went into service. They were the destroyers *Skeena* and *Saguenay*. British built, these modern warships could attain a speed of thirty-five knots. They were the beginnings of the large navy that Canada built during the next world war, which was already beginning to brew in Europe.

When the Second World War began in 1939, Canada's navy had 1,700 officers and men, 1,800 reservists and a fleet of six destroyers, five minesweepers, and two training vessels. The buildup happened quickly and in

1941, British Rear Admiral S.S. Bonham-Carter dubbed Halifax "probably the most important port in the world." By the war's end in 1945 there were close to 400 ships, another 500 support and miscellaneous vessels, and 95,000 personnel, the majority of them working from the base at Halifax. This fifty-fold increase in size represents, in the words of naval historian Dan van der Vat, "one of the most remarkable (and neglected) stories of high speed mobilisation in military history."

At home, the Navy was called upon to deal with a situation that shocked the Canadian nation. In 1942, German U-boats torpedoed twenty-three ships in the Gulf of St. Lawrence. Included was the Nova Scotia to Newfoundland ferry, SS *Caribou*, sunk by U-69 in the early morning hours of October 14, 1942, with the loss of two-thirds of the 237 passengers and crew. Lives of women and children were being taken in Canadian territorial waters. For the first time since the War of 1812, there was war in Canada.

In the longest battle of the war, the Battle of the Atlantic, which lasted for six years, the Royal Canadian Navy grew up fast, as it slugged it out with German and Italian submarines on the high seas, sending or helping to send fory-nine submarines to the bottom and losing its share of ships and men in the process. Back and forth across the cold and stormy Atlantic, RCN ships escorted convoys to the desperate British Isles, into the Mediterranean, and north to Russia, engaging the enemy over and over again. Canadian warships escorted more than 25,000 ships from North America to Britain. By 1943, Canadians were providing half the escort service across the Atlantic and, by the middle of 1944, the Royal Canadian Navy handled it all. Van der Vat writes: "If there is an injustice or omission in the historiography of the great maritime conflict as published in Britain or the United States, it is the consistent neglect of the Canadian contribution." When the Allies took the offensive in a significant way on D-Day, RCN ships formed a major part of the naval cover needed to get the troops to the beaches of France and established on continental Europe.

The battle in which Canada's navy stood up to be counted took its twenty-fourth and last Royal Canadian Naval vessel within sight of home. The Sambro Light Vessel sat anchored at the outer entrance to the harbour, a beacon to show mariners the way in. U-190 quietly tucked herself under the lightship and waited patiently until the minesweeper HMCS *Esquimault* came within range. On April 16, 1945, a single acoustic torpedo blew the stern off and sent her to the bottom in less than five minutes. Forty-four of her ship's company were lost. U-806 had successfully pulled a similar stunt on *Esquimault's* sister, HMCS *Clayaquot,* the previous Christmas eve, sending her to the bottom and resulting in the loss of eight of her crew. The enemy was cagey and lethal to the end.

It accomplished nothing, however, except perhaps to demonstrate the utter futility of it all, for U-190 surrendered to the Royal Canadian Navy three weeks later because the war was over. She was towed into Bay Bulls, Newfoundland and then to Halifax. She was commissioned into the RCN as HMCS U-190 and toured parts of eastern Canada and the St. Lawrence, where the Navy proudly showed her off. On October 21, 1947, in a well-publicised exercise, Canadian ships and aircraft sank the sub near the spot where she had sunk the *Esquimault*. The periscope from U-190 ended up at the Crow's Nest Officers' Club in St. John's, Newfoundland, where it gave an outside view of downtown Water St. from inside the club. It would be more than fifty years before a German submarine would enter Halifax Harbour. This time, it would be as a ship of an allied nation. On June 10, 1999, two class 206A subs visited Halifax in company with the supply ship *Meersburg*, and tied up at the same Dockyard from which U-boat hunters had been dispatched during the Battle of the Atlantic.

Along with other vessels sunk near the harbour, the Navy lost HMCS *Ypres* on May 12, 1940, when the British battleship HMS *Revenge* ran her down at the entrance to the harbour. *Ypres* was a gate-ship, a 320-ton tender that opened and closed the gate in the anti-submarine net that stretched across the harbour. To minimize the exposure that the harbour experienced when the net was opened, the maneuver had to be carried out at a specific time and under controlled conditions. Somehow the signals got crossed and the big 33,500-ton warship struck the tender a glancing blow and sent her to the bottom near McNab's Island. All eighteen of her crew were successfully recovered from the icy waters. What remains of the little ship lies in about twenty-one metres (70 feet). Launched in July, 1917, she was one of a type with the odd appellation "Battle-class trawler."

Having cut its teeth on chasing submarines, the Canadian Navy has, since the Second World War, evolved to specialize in anti-submarine warfare, which was its contribution to NATO for the remainder of the twentieth century. The need to support the United Nations in Korea and the advent of the Cold War, poignantly played out with the Cuban missile crisis, kept the navy from sinking into its pre-war doldrums. In 1955, HMCS *St Laurent* was the first of a new generation of Canadian designed and constructed ships, built specifically for the North Atlantic that Canada's navy knew so well.

In 1960, the RCN consisted of an aircraft carrier, 25 destroyer escorts, 18 frigates, 10 minesweepers, and 20,000 officers and men. Ten years later, there were less than half as many personnel as in 1960, equipment was getting old, and the navy had become part of the unified Canadian Armed Forces, an undertaking that the army, navy and air force had entered with much less enthusiasm than had Defence Minister Paul Hellyer, the architect of the scheme.

Canada's naval design and engineering talent enjoyed a brief moment of glory in the summer of 1969 when the hydrofoil, HMCS *Bras d'Or*, flew onto the scene in Halifax. It was a small craft of 200 tons designed to chase submarines at the incredible speed of 60 knots, which is faster than the speed limit on our highways. A hydrofoil is a conventional-looking ship or boat when resting that travels at high speed by riding on small skis, which practically eliminate friction from the water. She was based on Alexander Graham Bell's pioneering work on the Bras d'Or Lakes in Cape Breton early in the century. Canadian designed and built, she went down on Federal budget day, the victim of continuing Defence cutbacks. She now rests in a museum on an island in the St. Lawrence River.

One of the first batch of Canadian designed and built warships provides a favourite dive destination for local and visiting divers. The River-class destroyer HMCS *Saguenay* was de-commissioned, after which a local historical group stripped and cleaned her to Environment Canada standards. Then, in June 1994, they scuttled and sank her in twenty-four metres (80 feet) of water outside Lunenburg as the beginning of a marine park for scuba divers. We dove on her a few weeks later. It was fascinating to swim inside the ship and stand on the bridge. Greg and I swam inside the helicopter hangar, where we found an air pocket trapped against the ceiling. We removed our regulators from our mouths and talked to one another inside a sunken ship twenty-four metres below the surface. It was something neither of us had done before. We were interested to find that the air was very stale to the point that it burned our throats.

A second River-class destroyer, HMCS *Fraser,* is tied up in Bridgewater, Nova Scotia, as a floating museum commemorating Canada's first efforts at designing and building her own warships. As these ships have been decommissioned from the fleet, the navy has found itself with a lineup of organisations interested in acquiring them for sinking as artificial reefs. They make for interesting diving because a whole ecosystem builds up around them, much the same way such systems exist around reefs. All that is needed is something for filter feeders to attach themselves to. This attracts fish that eat the filter feeders; then, bigger fish feed on those fish, and so on up the food chain.

Today, Canada's navy has a fleet of new ships and operates its own submarines out of Halifax, having seen its role evolve yet again. With the dissolution of the Soviet Union and the Warsaw Pact, it is engaged more than ever in peacekeeping around the world, as part of United Nations contingents. The attack by suicide bombers on the World Trade Centre on September 11, 2001, affected the Canadian Navy more than any event since the Korean War. In addition to Army personnel, 1,300 sailors embarked for the Mediterranean and Arabian Seas from Halifax and Esquimault to support a multinational force against the terrorist group behind the killing of nearly 3,000 people. When HMCS *Toronto* left Halifax on December 5, she was the sixth Canadian warship to go to the war theatre. At home, the Navy chases away those who try, without permission, to catch increasingly valuable Canadian fish, helps apprehend drug and other smugglers and continues to maintain the sovereignty of the nation with the longest coastline in the world.

The United States Navy

The United States Navy has played and continues to play an important role in the defence of Canada, primarily through Canada's participation in NATO. During the privateering days of the War of 1812, when relations between the two countries were at their all-time low, RN ships out of Halifax had many an altercation with USN ships. Halifax likes to remember the Sunday morning in 1813 when the minister at St. Paul's Church found himself preaching to empty pews while the parishioners ran to the waterfront to see HMS *Shannon* victoriously lead the USS *Chesapeake* up the harbour. The *Shannon* had sailed out of Halifax to Boston and challenged the captain of the *Chesapeake*. In a short and bloody shootout, the 52-gun *Shannon* came out victorious and returned to Halifax with her prize.

In happier times, the United States Navy was instrumental in the beginnings of naval aviation in Halifax, starting the naval air station in Eastern Passage during World War I. The commander of the station was Richard Byrd, the famous aviator who was the first to fly over the South Pole.

The USN was in and out of the harbour regularly during World War II and since, always drawing a crowd with their large and impressive aircraft carriers. In 1995 a big nuclear powered carrier was anchored in the harbour and I decided to take my boat in for a closer look. A large inflatable came barreling towards me, placed its bow against the side of my humble five-metre wooden speedboat and proceeded to push me sideways away from the ship. The humourless crew pointed out that I had crossed the 100-metre barrier they maintain around the vessel and they would help me get back outside. Polite, but firm.

When the nuclear powered submarines come to visit, things are done with far less fanfare than when the surface ships arrive. By definition, submarines hate attention, but on occasion they have received their share at the hands of protesters accusing them of carrying nuclear weapons in supposedly non-nuclear Canadian waters. On a couple of occasions while returning in my boat from a dive offshore I have come across one of these big subs travelling on the surface out of the harbour. They are a sight to behold as the black shape comes looming out of the fog. The words "I surrender" come easily to mind.

The Merchant Navy

To assist prying eyes and ears as little as possible, news dispatches during the Second World War referred to Halifax simply as "an East Coast port." Halifax became famous during the war, so much so that one New York newspaper called it the busiest harbour in the world.

The busyness had most to do with getting goods from the farms and factories of North America to the desperate nations of Europe, principally Great Britain and Russia. German submarines were sinking ships by the dozen, so the Allies decided to send huge convoys of ships across the Atlantic under the protective cover of destroyers and corvettes. Like loyal and self-sacrificing sheep dogs guarding their flock, these fast and nimble little ships fought off, with varying degrees of success, the swarms of U-boats, whose crews liked to refer to themselves as wolf packs.

Halifax was the staging area for the convoys and it was common to see Bedford Basin full of ships laden with the goods of war awaiting their turn to run the gauntlet across the Atlantic. The first convoy, HX-1, left Halifax on September 16, 1939, within days of the war's beginning.

The Merchant Navy's efforts were crucial. A typical 10,000-ton ship could carry enough food to feed 225,000 people for a week. In addition, it carried 2,150 tons of steel bars; enough gun carriers, trucks and motorcycles to equip a battalion of infantry; enough bombs to fill 225 heavy bombers; sufficient lumber and materials to build 90 four-room cottages; two complete bombers; and the aluminum to build 630 fighter aircraft. The ships were loaded in American and Canadian seaports and came primarily to Halifax to await orders. And as fast as the Germans could sink them, North American yards turned them out. For a while at the end of 1942, a new 10,000-ton freighter was going into service every two and a half days.

The harbour was abuzz with activity to keep these ships afloat. The famous oceangoing tug *Foundation Franklin* and her sister tugs were continually answering calls to go to the aid of ships that had been hit but not sunk. They dragged and coaxed these derelicts – some missing bows or sterns or with great gaping holes in them – to the harbour, to be repaired at the Dockyard or at the Halifax Shipyards and pressed back into service.

Many damaged merchant ships came tantalisingly close to making Halifax. In March 1942, the Spanish tanker *Nueva Andalucia* was involved in a collision, caught fire and burned for weeks within sight of the citizens of Halifax. On the night the *Trongate* was sunk in the harbour, the *Nueva Andalucia* had been burning for nineteen days. Her remains went down near the location where HMS *Mars* had supposedly wrecked two hundred years before. Divers from HMCS *Granby* recovered the *Nueva Andalucia's* bell on August 3, 1956, and it became the baptismal font at the Church of the Redeemer at Shannon Park in Dartmouth.

In the fall of 2001, I was involved in a search for HMS *Mars* that ended up in our finding the remains of the *Nueva Andalucia*. I was one of a group of students who had just finished a course in nautical archaeology. Aboard the well-equipped *Divecom III,* a commercial diving vessel complete with remotely controlled underwater video equipment, we surveyed the reef that bears the name of the *Mars*. With giant container ships passing us within hailing distance as they entered and left the harbour, we found a huge debris field of twisted beams, deck and hull plating and other unrecognizable iron in only six to nine metres of water. There was no evidence of the *Mars*, which may well be beneath the *Nueva Andalucia* wreckage.

Other Merchant Navy Losses

In March 1942, at the height of the U-boat menace, the *Clare Lilly*, a British ammunition ship, struck the cliffs of the outer harbour while trying to pick her way through the darkness, snow squalls and U-boats. It was too much to deal with at one time and she ended her days in a brief flurry of excitement that was punctuated with extreme danger and great heroism. With the ship smashing to pieces in the darkness, the lifeboats lost, and men with only minutes to live in the icy, churning sea, a local man plunged into the water from shore and rescued numerous members of the crew, exhausting himself to the point that he needed rescuing himself. But all were saved, including the ship's cat, Toots. The *Clare Lilly*'s remains lie in nine metres (30 feet) of water near the shore of the outer harbour. Although the navy recovered as much of the cargo as they could, what they left behind has provided fodder for souvenir-collecting scuba divers for years.

In the late 1980s, after months of searching, divers found the *Kolkhoznik*. This Russian ship struck a rock in January 1942, while entering Halifax Harbour from Boston. She was destined to join a convoy for Archangelsk in northern Russia. She rests at a depth of forty-five metres (150 feet), with tanks on her deck and ammunition and other materials of war lying around. She is quite spectacular to view.

A few years later, local divers found the *British Freedom* lying in fifty-five metres (180 feet) of water in the mouth of the harbour. She was torpedoed and abandoned in January 1945, but did not sink. The Navy was obliged to sink her as she posed a hazard to navigation. In the same action, another ship from the convoy, *AthelViking,* a tanker loaded with molasses, was torpedoed and sunk. And there were many more. During the Battle of the Atlantic the U-boats sank approximately 2,600 allied merchant ships and themselves lost nearly 800 submarines and crews. Military historians report that the German U-boat service had the highest death rate of any group in the war.

In January 1945, there was a rather bizarre incident that the people of the Sambro area remember with good humour. It started sadly enough, when a U-boat struck a small convoy at the harbour approaches, sinking two ships and scattering the convoy. A few days later, an astonished fisherman found himself in possession of a 10,000-ton freighter carrying 6,000 tons of very useful cargo. While tending his boat, he saw looming out of the fog the massive outline of the American freighter *Martin Van Buren,* named after a U.S. president who took office in 1836. Apparently, on January 14, in the same action that had sunk the *British Freedom*, a torpedo from U-1232 had struck the ship, causing the crew to abandon her. She was taken in tow but broke adrift and became lost in the fog. She had been lost but now she was found, stuck fast on the rocks inside Lobster Claw Reef in reasonably calm weather.

And nobody knew where she was. What a prize!

The ration-weary locals had a field day, making off with boatloads of food, cigarettes, candy, and anything light enough to carry. They couldn't – and didn't want to – do anything about the two locomotives on the ship's deck, however. The authorities soon caught wind of the discovery and quickly took control of the situation, salvaging as much as they could of the $2.5 million dollar cargo, including the locomotives, but not before about 1,500 tons of her cargo made its way into local larders, feeding some families for up to two years.

The men of the merchant marine were unsung heroes. Canada lost 73 merchant ships and 1,500 men from the merchant marine, but the nation's attention – and much of the glory – went to the men in uniform. Since the merchant seamen were not a part of the armed services, the government treated them like ordinary civilians and, while they paid lip service to their contribution to the war effort, they paid little else. More than fifty years after the war ended, with many merchant seamen already gone to their graves, they got the recognition for which they had fought, when they were granted veterans' pension and health coverage. In 1992 they received full veterans' benefits and in 1998 they were officially recognized as full veterans – a fourth arm of Canada's military. And, finally, on February 1, 2000, the federal government allocated $50 million to be apportioned to the remaining merchant mariners.

Under the Warships

Mid October 1999. On a Saturday morning, four of us met at Her Majesty's Canadian Dockyard for a briefing. After years of dreaming about it, we were finally getting to dive the Dockyard, the heartbeat of Halifax Harbour for two and a half centuries. With three destroyers looming above us at dock-side, we listened attentively to Lieutenant Commander Gary Hatton as he gave us very specific instructions on where we could go and where we could not. He was the Queen's Harbourmaster for Halifax. The QHM staff coordinates the movement of all naval ships within Halifax Harbour. He is also the man responsible for our good fortune. A Master Mariner, he navigated our application through the Navy bureaucracy and worked with Greg to bring the project to fruition. Today is the culmination of many hours of effort over many months as Greg worked to convince the wary authorities to support his application that a group of sport divers be permitted to dive this site that is the very reason for the founding of Halifax.

The purpose of our diving project was to report on exactly what was down there. In addition, we were to research the steamship lines that visited the port and to see what evidence of their presence we could find on the bottom. The most common evidence is in the form of dishes and cutlery bearing the names and insignia of the companies, such as White Star Line and Cunard Steamship Co. A portion of the Naval Dockyard now occupies the area where the early steamships docked. A project such as ours would represent a nuisance to the Navy and without their support it could not have happened.

November Juliet

The docks are identified by letters, preceded by the letter "N" for Naval, and always referred to by the pronunciations of the phonetic alphabet. For our first dive, we will check out the area around NJ, or "November Juliet," the last of the big wooden docks built during World War II, now condemned and destined to be replaced by a modern concrete jetty. This is where the aircraft carriers HMCS *Magnificent* and HMCS *Bonaventure*, the "Maggie" and the "Bonnie," berthed while in port during the 1950s and '60s. Greg, Dana and I are joined by Jim Camano, now retired from the Navy after a career serving on five of Canada's warships.

In this area, there is so much to see on the bottom that it is impossible to take it all in. Your eyes can only focus on one area at a time, so it quickly becomes overwhelming. The bank drops from twelve metres (40 feet) at the base of the jetty to twenty-one metres (70 feet) within a short distance and it is on the incline that most of the artifacts lie.

Predominant are empty brass shell casings, pop bottles from the mid-twentieth century and Navy dishes and cutlery. Plates, bowls, cups and saucers bearing insignia from different periods of the Canadian, British and American Navies are scattered throughout the area. In one place I found a pile of brass instruments from a ship – round dials with the faces long gone, perhaps clocks or engine gauges to indicate steam pressure or fuel levels on an early Canadian warship. I was pleased to add several new bottles to my collection and one of our number found an old Dutch crock from the early 1800s. It was sad to think that this area would soon be sealed forever under a big new concrete jetty, without first being systematically sifted through for what it could tell us about harbour history.

To the north lie several areas of rocky ledges that appear as steps leading to the harbour bottom. They have acted as catchalls and accumulated great mounds of machinery, cable and other items that are slowly deteriorating. Swimming among this debris reminds me of other similar places in the harbour – under the harbour tugs, at Piers 20 and 21, and near the Bedford Institute of Oceanography.

Dana just surfacing from a dive near the Dockyard.

The latter ranks among what I consider the spookiest areas in which to dive. The main dock at the B.I.O. is in twenty-four metres (80 feet) of water, which means that it sits ten stories high before it breaks the surface. Presumably because of the depth, the engineers found it necessary to build up the bottom with great blocks of concrete and stone, surrounded and held together by large beams covered with heavy equipment tires and arranged like giant games of jacks. The solid docks block the light on two sides and with the accumulations of black silt in the area, there is very little to reflect the light that remains.

I wandered into the area on a dive one evening just as the sun was settling over the western side of the Basin. I decided to come up and found myself encountering these long wooden beams jutting out of the gloom. It is very unsettling to be ascending in poor visibility and to run across something above you, where you thought there was only water and eventually the surface. You find yourself wondering if your way up has been blocked, which can set off a whole chain of irrational thinking. I eventually found my way to the surface and was happy and relieved to be there.

As I lay on the bottom at twelve metres (40 feet) near November Juliet and looked up and through the big dock towards the low afternoon sun, the picture was one of an immense structure literally on its last legs. This dock is fenced off on the surface with signs warning against stepping on it. Through the water under the dock, I could see the afternoon sun, a pale and faint ball when viewed through the reduced light, silhouetting a jumble of crisscrossed beams, some of which had let go but could not escape through the tangled mass of wood and iron. Though it looked unsteady, it had the support of the water, so it was not about to fall in a heap. These docks were well designed and constructed to last a long time.

November Golf

We were back on the next weekend to dive "November Golf," in a raging autumn storm that had everything in the harbour shut down. With howling southeast gales and sheets of rain, Greg and I did the first set of dives south of the jetty. To our disappointment, this area had been dredged (in 1985, as it turned out), so the bottom had nothing to tell us. The overburden containing the artifacts had been scooped up by large shovels, placed on a barge and dumped elsewhere, so the area now presented only a sterile, gravel bottom, somewhat like the bottom of a river. Several years earlier Greg had talked to a construction foreman who had supervised a dredging operation at the Dockyard; perhaps this was the area. The dredge spoils had contained so many artifacts that it attracted the attention of the workers, who took every available opportunity to wade into them to retrieve the bottles, crocks, dishes and other items. The foreman decreed that such scavenging had to stop because it was interfering with getting the job done.

Finding a dredged area is always disappointing. The bottom of Halifax Harbour is so interesting because most of it has not been dredged. Many of the world's major harbours are at the mouths of rivers, which annually dump tons of silt, or they are naturally shallower than Halifax. When they were established, they were deep enough for the ships of the day, but to accommodate the increasingly larger vessels that have come into use, these harbours have been dredged to increase the depth. The sad thing is that the hundreds of years of historical artifacts contained in as little as one scoop of material is often put on a barge and dumped out to sea, or used to provide fill for a new parking lot. Most of Halifax Harbour has been spared the ravages of dredging, except in contained areas such as this one. Unfortunately, this is also one of the most historic areas of the harbour, so its story has been lost forever.

Our second dive, north of the jetty, was a more complex undertaking. We were advised beforehand that HMCS *Anticosti* would be returning from a tour of duty. We waited until she tied up and the crew disembarked, and when we got the okay from the duty officer, we checked out this area.

This was one of the most confined dives I have ever done; it was no place for a claustrophobic. The space between the two jetties is the width of two ships. With the *Anticosti* at one dock and a barge at the other dock alongside, it was crowded on the surface, but the bottom was equally challenging because the hulls above seemed to be bearing down on us. A set of tracks extended from a dry-dock on the shore and down an underwater incline to nine metres (30 feet). It cut the remainder of the area in two, which meant the rest of this small space was like two deep holes. Because it was such a stormy and dark day, there was little light on the surface, let alone down where we were. There were docks looming up on three sides, and we had the ship and barge above us, so our field of vision was severely diminished. Despite that, we found out what we wanted to know – that this area had nothing to tell us. After it was all over, somebody pronounced the benediction that usually follows such dives: "Well, it had to be done. We would have always wondered what was down there." The rest of us nodded philosophically.

But we were not through with the area around the Dockyard.

The Beginnings of the Dockyard

Halifax was founded during a time of intense naval activity between the French and the British. The struggle for North America involved numerous engagements off the East Coast. But the harsh winters made life difficult for sailors and their ships, so the combatants were forced to do their fighting in the summer. The long voyage across the Atlantic from the bases in Europe had always presented complications and shortened the season during which they could batter one another's ships. In the early years after the founding of Halifax there was a town and a good harbour, which helped sustain the British, but there were no facilities to repair and maintain warships.

However, the presence of the town made it possible to over-winter. To be ready for a spring offensive, four Royal Navy warships (HMS *Fougeux, Litchfield, Centurion* and *Norwich*) and two sloops (*Success* and *Vulture*) spent the winter in Halifax and got the jump on the enemy in the spring. They repeated the strategy the next year, and this convinced the Lords of the Admiralty in London to build a naval base at Halifax and eliminate the need to return to Portsmouth in the fall. Eight warships over-wintered in 1757-58 in preparation for an attack on Louisbourg and the next year the careening wharf was built. This was a significant achievement because it meant that a ship could be hove down on its sides so that work such as repairing leaks and replacing planks could be done on its sides and bottom. The next year, 1759, is officially recognized as the date that His Majesty's Dockyard was established at Halifax. It was built to the north of the town but today it is completely surrounded by the city of Halifax.

In the following years, the yard was expanded, with the addition of support facilities, such as the Capstan House, Hawser Stores, Mast House, and Oil Stores. A hospital was built in 1784. Then, with all this naval activity, it became necessary to document the features of the harbour. The Royal Navy called on its premier surveyor, Captain James Cook, to survey and map the harbour, which he declared to be one of the finest in North America, capable of holding all the ships of the Royal Navy at the same time. After this work, Cook went on to his famous voyages of discovery in the Pacific.

Now in its third century, the yard has continuously expanded. It reached its peak of activity in the later years of World War II when the Canadian Navy was responsible for convoy escort services across the North Atlantic to Europe. Early in the 1900s, when the future of the harbour was being evaluated and there was a search on for new dock facilities, authorities gave brief consideration to ending naval activity in Halifax. A 1913 consultant's study recommended four sites for the new Ocean Terminals docks that were being planned. In describing the necessity to remove the facilities that existed to make way for the new docks, one proposal called for removal from Halifax of HMC Dockyard. It then followed up with the monumental understatement that the Dockyard "may become vitally necessary at any period in the history of the country." In the following thirty-two years, it certainly did become vitally necessary as it kept hundreds of ships floating and fighting, and itself underwent a huge expansion.

The Discovery Nobody Wanted to Make

On a dive in the late fall of 2000, Dana found what none of us ever wanted to run into – a human body. With a harbour the size of Halifax, surrounded by a large population, it has always been a fact that people have ended up dead in the harbour, through accidents, murder and suicide – the latter particularly associated with jumping from one of the two suspension bridges. I have been asked many times if I have ever made such a grisly discovery and every time I get asked, my mind goes back to a day many years ago when Greg and I had come close.

We stood on a wharf in Dartmouth looking down at the water considering where to dive. The spot looked inviting, but we decided that it would be too difficult to get out after the dive, there being no convenient set of stairs close by. Instead we went down the shore a couple of hundred metres. When we came out of the water, we noticed ambulance and police vehicles at the very place that we had stood an hour earlier. Upon inquiring, we discovered that they were in the process of fishing out the body of a man.

The day of Dana's discovery had started as a routine dive. Greg, Dana and I launched Dana's boat about a kilometre away at Seaview Park at 9 a.m. on a sunny, calm and cold Saturday morning, December 2, 2000. The cold weather necessitated that we wear our drysuits, which we put on before getting into the boat. We headed out the harbour under the MacKay Bridge and observed a crew working on one of the two huge abutments that support the bridge's weight. Passing the Nova Scotia Power generating station, and the Halifax Shipyards, with a couple of big ships high in the air above us on floating drydocks, we soon arrived at the Dockyard. The MacDonald Bridge loomed high above our heads and its structure caused the traffic noises to be amplified as we tied up directly below.

Since we already knew what the area around the dock was like from previous dives, the goal was to swim out into the channel, so we made sure there were no scheduled ship movements for the next couple of hours. In we went. I took a compass bearing and headed directly out from shore into twenty-one metres (70 feet) but to my disappointment the bottom was very silty. As is the case in this area, the site was shadowy with big shapes looming up from the bottom here and there, covered by a coating of light silt and vegetation.

Off to my right, Dana was on the same bearing, although we could not see one another. He came to an area of old cables and metal objects. As he was looking around he saw what he first thought were the two feet of a mannequin, but soon realized he was dreadfully wrong. It was the almost completely decomposed body of a young man, clad in a sweater and jeans. Dana attached a line to a piece of nearby cable and shot his lift bag to the surface to mark the spot. He then headed back to the boat. Greg and I came out shortly afterwards and we called Halifax Traffic to report what had been found. The Military Police arrived within minutes, followed by the Halifax Regional Police.

The RCMP dive team recovered the remains about four hours later, after thoroughly searching and videotaping the area. The area was treated as a crime scene. The search did not unearth any clues as to the identity of the person or how the individual had died. The next day, an autopsy revealed the body to be that of a white male aged 18 to 24. He had been in the water for at least six months. Two days later, they announced that they had identified the remains as being a 23-year-old Dartmouth native who had last been seen at 3:30 a.m. on May 29, 2000. There was no evidence of foul play. On the following Friday, amid the farewells of family and friends, he was laid to his eternal rest.

About a year and a half before this incident, two of our diving friends were involved in the recovery of a body. A man and his daughter were watching the surf pound onto the rocks at Herring Cove, not far from where HMS *Tribune* had wrecked in 1797. They were swept off the rocks and drowned. Shortly afterwards, the Coast Guard were in the process of trying to recover the man's body when they were assisted by a group returning from a dive nearby. Two of the divers re-entered the water and helped get the man's body into the Coast Guard launch.

Success at Last

Our enthusiasm for diving at the Dockyard did not diminish and within a few weeks we were back at it. But we were hitting disappointment after disappointment as we systematically checked between the long piers, descending into the eighteen-metre (60-foot) depths only to find waves of silt, reminiscent of the pictures we see of desert sand dunes. At one site was evidence of the destruction of a previous dock, as the bottom was covered with large concrete slabs that had once covered the dock's surface. Within my memory I could recall the destruction and rebuilding of the wharf. Intentionally or accidentally, the construction company had left much of the earlier dock on the bottom.

Throughout the winter and spring of 2001, we covered much of the area that makes up the Dockyard, going farther out into the shipping channel to get away from the silt. Instead of tying up at the Dockyard and swimming out, we would commence the dive from Dana's boat in mid-channel. The boatman would then closely follow the buoy that the diver was carrying. Even though we confirmed with Halifax Traffic Control that there would be no large vessel movements during our dives, the boat carried explosive cartridges that could be used to signal a diver to surface immediately. In the channel between the bridges, there is simply no room for a large vessel to maneuver. Even if there were room, the pilots of the container ships that go through the Narrows are so high up that they would not see our little boat. It still would take several kilometres to stop the ship if they did see us. Hoping that the big ships would or could avoid us was just not an option. Only on one occasion that winter did we have to call a diver up, necessitated by the impending arrival of a container ship.

In the channel, where the currents sweep the bottom, we began to find evidence of the Royal Navy presence, in the form of broken china bearing RN regalia such as White Ensigns and Mess numbers. Then our patience paid off, ironically back where we had started. In the traffic lanes out from dock NJ, the site of our first dive, we found the elusive "clean" bottom – free of silt – and found torpedo and Codd-stoppered bottles from the glory days of the Royal Navy, from haunts like Bermuda, Malta, Gibraltar, and Trinidad. There were Royal Navy dishes from the mid-1800s; wide, squat free-blown bottles from the 1700s, and crockery from the late 1700s and early 1800s. There were long clay tobacco pipes embossed with anchors and

Crocks for ink, boot blacking and table salt. From the author's collection.

medicine bottles embossed with the broad arrow of the Royal Navy. Of course, this was interspersed with bottles and other castoffs going right up to modern beer and pop bottles.

This is the oldest part of the Naval Dockyards, where the Royal Navy began careening and repairing ships in 1759. It is also the location of what used to be coaling dock No. 4, significant as the site where the Halifax ships involved in the recovery of bodies from the RMS *Titanic* disaster brought their unfortunate cargo ashore in 1912.

We continued to dive throughout the winter and spring of 2001, working our way north to the Halifax Shipyards, but were eventually blocked by the two large floating dry-docks. Without a doubt, the diving was the most challenging we had done in the inner harbour. Carrying lift bags and lights, dragging a buoy and reel, handling precise navigation, dealing with strong currents, and worrying about boat traffic left minimal time for observation and searching for artifacts.

Several times, while acting as boatman, I was obliged to get on the radio and direct the movements of vessels away from the divers below. On another day, while I was down and Dana was boatman, I got several strong tugs on the line. I knew instantly what it meant. It was the signal that a scheduled ship movement was happening as anticipated. I came up as quickly as I safely could, to see a 40,000-ton ship accompanied by two tugs and the Pilot boat heading towards us. Dana was already on the radio with

No time to be in the water. MSC *Pamela* and tug, *Point Halifax*, in the Narrows.

Halifax Traffic Control, as planned. I got into the boat, we got out of the way and the four vessels went by within a stone's throw. On many occasions, we have had to make last minute changes to dive plans because of movements of ships in the area.

Our explorations at the Dockyard came to an abrupt end in the fall of 2001, when terrorists destroyed the twin towers of the World Trade Centre in New York, taking the lives of close to 3,000 people. Military establishments throughout North America went on alert as personnel and equipment got sent to the Middle East to hunt for those responsible. Four ships and crews left Halifax for the Persian Gulf soon after the event, and the erstwhile easygoing security at the Dockyard underwent a radical change. Patrol boats with armed guards appeared near the docks and the area was out of bounds for such activities as ours. Throughout the harbour, we were subjected to scrutiny as we prepared to dive and we began to fear that the adventure of diving Her Majesty's Canadian Dockyard was over.

But even though security remained tight, we became familiar and, though they kept an eye on us, we were essentially left alone. During the winter of 2002 we moved our diving activities outside the perimeter that the

Navy had established and continued to enjoy ourselves, discovering that there were pockets of artifacts spread around the area. We concluded that they came from anchorage areas. When the fleet was in port, ships anchored in the area off the Dockyard and proceeded, as usual, to use the harbour as the dumping ground, leaving an interesting history of the Royal Navy. We were impressed by the elaborate patterns inscribed on dishes used by the RN in the last century. For years, Greg had been working with many local divers documenting the patterns and crests used by shipping organizations visiting the harbour, and this area yielded such a rich harvest that he prepared a new report specifically covering the Royal Navy. Dana, John, Dwayne and I kept a steady stream of pieces coming that he researched and documented.

Even though what we accomplished is a far cry from a scientific survey, it is better than the alternative – the slow destruction of the harbour's history. As time marches on, it is getting covered up or dug up or destroyed in some other way and any small contribution we can make to preserving at least some of that history is important.

The Coast Guard

On the Dartmouth side of the harbour are the familiar red ships of the Canadian Coast Guard. Unlike the United States Coast Guard, which does coastal patrol and policing, the Canadian Coast Guard's primary role is to support shipping and boating activities. This includes maintaining a wide network of lighthouses, lights and buoys along the coast; keeping the shipping channels open in winter; and providing search and rescue coordination for ships in distress far out to sea.

The Coast Guard is part of the Department – now the Ministry – of Transport, which was formed in 1936. It grew out of the Department of Marine and Fisheries and the Department of Railways and Canals, both of which had been formed in 1867 at Confederation, when the provincial departments were absorbed by the new Dominion government. The title Canadian Coast Guard was introduced in 1962.

Coast Guard Ships

Coast Guard ships work in and around many Canadian ports but our context is Halifax. In the early days the *Druid* supplied the lights of Nova Scotia in the service of the Provincial Board of Works. She was an iron side-wheel paddler built in Scotland by Todd & McGregor in 1856. She was replaced by the *Lady Head* – named after Maria Head, wife of Sir Edmund Walker Head, Governor in Chief of Canada and the man who recommended Ottawa as the capital when the new country came into being. Of the many duties which this ship performed, one of the saddest was in transporting several bodies of the SS *Atlantic* shipwreck victims from the wreck site off Terence Bay to Halifax.

At that time, Nova Scotia used schooners for fisheries patrol. The colony commissioned the schooners *Daring* and *La Canadienne* and many more were subsequently built or chartered for this work. The *Daring* was wrecked in a snowstorm at Herring Cove in December 1867. The last fishery protection schooner to be purchased for use in Nova Scotia was the *Kingfisher*.

The Department of Marine and Fisheries was briefly in the warship business. The first major warship to be owned by the Dominion of Canada was HMS *Charybdis*. Canada had no navy at the time, so the Department of Marine and Fisheries commissioned her in 1881. Launched in 1859, she was a full-rigged ship of 2,250 tons with a steam engine and had been used by the Royal Navy on the China station. After an inauspicious year in Canadian hands, she was towed to Halifax from Saint John, New Brunswick, and disposed of at the Dockyard. She was followed by CGS *Canada*, built in England by Vickers at Barrow-in-Furness in 1904. This vessel was sixty-one metres long and could steam at twenty-two knots, was armed with four small quick-firing guns, and carried seventy-five officers and men.

Some of the wood from the *Charybdis* ended up being used to build the gates of the Scott Manor house in Bedford. This house, which dates from the 1770s, is the oldest residence in the metro area and is on the site where Fort Sackville stood to guard the historic route from Chebucto to Windsor, the Annapolis Valley and, ultimately, to the English fort at Annapolis Royal.

During my trips past the Coast Guard base in my boat, I have often seen a ship with the unusual name of *Provo Wallis*. She is named after one of the great sons of the harbour, who rose to become an Admiral in the Royal Navy. As a young Second Lieutenant in the War of 1812, Provo Wallis had taken command of HMS *Shannon* after Captain Broke was severely wounded and the First Lieutenant killed, and had taken the captive USS *Chesapeake* from Boston to Halifax.

Icebreakers

Canadian waters spend a large part of the year covered in ice, so there has always been the need to create open channels through the ice and to keep them open during the winter. The first effective icebreaker in Canada was the CGS *Stanley*, built in 1888 by the Fairfield Shipbuilding and Engineering Co. in Scotland. Named after the same Lord Stanley who gave us the Stanley Cup, the symbol of supremacy in the National Hockey League, she was built to provide a winter passenger and mail service to Prince Edward Island in accordance with the terms by which the Island had joined the Canadian Confederation. Several ships had proved unsuccessful and were icebreakers in name only, spending much of the winter frozen into the ice of the Northumberland Strait. The *Stanley* ran between Charlottetown, Prince Edward Island, and Pictou, Nova Scotia. The *Minto* joined her in 1900. The *Stanley* lasted until 1936, although she was not in service in her later years.

CCGS *Champlain* and CCGS *Montcalm* were ordered in 1904 to keep the St. Lawrence clear. Others followed. Halifax contributed a significant addition to the fleet in 1930 when the *N.B. McLean* was launched from Halifax Shipyards. At 3,254 tons, she was the second biggest icebreaker in the world. She served until 1979 and was scrapped in 1988. The next big development was after World War II, when Canada needed to maintain a presence in the north and supply the Distant Early Warning line of radar sites. The *d'Iberville* was built in 1952 for the Department of Transport, followed by HMCS *Labrador* for the navy in 1953. The first large ship to go through the Northwest Passage, the *Labrador* was only the second vessel to circumnavigate North America. She was turned over to the Department of Transport in 1958.

The first ship to go completely around North America was the RCMP supply auxiliary schooner *St. Roch,* which navigated the Northwest Passage from west to east between 1940 and 1942, becoming the first ship to do so, and only the second ship ever to navigate the Passage. In 1944, she went through from east to west, becoming the first ship to travel the Northwest Passage in both directions. After twenty years of service, she was retired in

1948 and was sent to Halifax by way of the Panama Canal in 1950. This voyage made *St. Roch* the first ship to circumnavigate North America. This historic vessel has been preserved and is now the centrepiece of the Vancouver Maritime Museum.

The *John A. MacDonald* came in 1960 and today the biggest icebreaker is the *Louis S. St. Laurent,* conspicuous by her size as she sits at the dock in Dartmouth next to the other Coast Guard vessels. The *MacDonald* became famous when she guided the American supertanker *Manhattan* through the Northwest Passage in 1969.

Icebreakers are interesting vessels which play an important role in Canadian waters. Most do not cut through ice as one might suppose, but break the ice by ramming it or crushing it. Instead of being slender and fast, they are stout, bulky vessels with a bow that enables them to slide up on the ice, the weight of the ship then causing the ice to break.

Weight and power are the two most important factors needed in breaking heavy ice. The effective use of this power calls for ships that can be thrust up on the ice without losing their stability and can work themselves free when they get in a jam. Modern icebreakers have tanks within the hull arranged so that very large capacity pumps can transfer water from one side of the vessel to the other, or from a stern trimming tank to a forward one. This causes the ship to roll about until the surrounding ice is fractured sufficiently to enable the propellors to be effective. The hull of such a ship must be well rounded under water and deep enough to provide good immersion for the propellors which are placed as low as possible, both to avoid damage from the ice and to give them water to bite into.

Lighthouses and Lightships

The oldest danger to ships has been running into the land at night or having nothing by which to mark their location in the darkness. For this reason, lighthouses were built to reveal the first point of land a ship was likely to encounter, usually on an island or a point of land called a cape or head.

The Lighthouse Board was founded in February, 1904, to administer the existing lighthouses of Canada and to build new ones. As a result, the ensuing two decades saw a boom in lighthouse construction in Canada, with approximately forty new lights coming on stream.

The first lighthouse north of the Caribbean was at Boston in 1716 while the first in Canada was built at Louisbourg in 1734. It was lit by a circle of thirty-six oil-fed wicks on a column twenty metres high and could be seen twenty-nine kilometres out to sea. It burned down and was re-built two years later. During the second and final siege of Louisbourg in the summer of 1758, the British set up a battery at this location to bombard the French harbour defences and the lighthouse was again destroyed. A 1798 chart shows it as being in ruins. The ruins are still there and the area has been designated a national historic site. The British built a new light in 1842 and it burned in 1922. It was re-built and still stands today.

The Sambro light – guiding ships to Halifax for almost 250 years.

Halifax Harbour got the third light in North America, when the Sambro light was built. It started operating in 1760 and still stands, making it the oldest operating lighthouse in Canada. For nearly a hundred years it was the first light that ships travelling from Europe to North America sighted, before Cape Race, in southern Newfoundland, got a light late in 1856. Interestingly, the decision to build the Sambro light was taken just two months after the fall of Louisbourg. The French light in North America had been extinguished and that of the British shone forth, guiding ships into the new stronghold of Halifax.

Halifax Harbour has been served by at least six lighthouses over the years. Today there are five lighthouses that guide vessels into the harbour, as there have been for more than a hundred years. In fact, when Halifax Harbour got its fifth light – on Devil's island in 1877 – the whole of British Columbia had only three. At that time, Nova Scotia was served by at least fifty-five lights. In 1835 there were eighteen lighthouses on the Nova Scotia coastline, compared to only one in Newfoundland and ten in the entire Gulf of St. Lawrence and St. Lawrence River.

Four of the five harbour lights are located on islands. They started operating in the following years: Sambro Island 1760; Maugher's Beach (McNab's Island) 1815; Chebucto Head 1872; George's Island 1876; and Devil's Island 1877.

Until 1966, there was also a ship carrying a light and serving as a lighthouse. Called the Sambro lightship, she was put into position eight kilometres southeast of Sambro Island in November of 1872 to warn ships away from the Sambro Ledges, a treacherous area of rocks and reefs on one side of the harbour entrance. It was a floating lighthouse, placed in an area where a light was needed but where there was no firm location on which to build one. With no means of propulsion, she almost foundered in a gale and had to be towed into Halifax for repairs. But she survived, along with her crew, which makes them more fortunate than those aboard a new lightship being delivered from England in 1914. It overturned at Liscombe on the Eastern Shore of Nova Scotia, with the loss of all hands.

For almost a century the first Sambro lightship and her successors provided incoming ships with a guide to line up with the harbour approaches. The last lightship was removed in 1966 when more modern navigation techniques made it unnecessary. This 37-metre vessel had a steel hull, painted red, with a tower in the centre topped by the light. Winds of 160 kilometres an hour and 15-metre waves could not move her from her anchorage. In addition to the light, she carried a foghorn (imagine being a member of the crew as the foghorn blared out its mournful drone hour after hour in the fog) and radio equipment that sent out a signal on which an incoming ship could get a navigation fix. The ship's crews were assigned for three-month tours and were then relieved for three months, while another crew took over. Considering her location and the weather that hits the area, it's a wonder that she never got run into. At the time of Confederation, there were about a dozen lightships operating in Canada, in areas where a lighthouse just didn't work. The last lightship in Canada was on the Lurcher Shoal at the entrance to the Bay of Fundy.

The light at Maugher's Beach on McNab's Island has an interesting history. It is built on the site of Sherbrooke Tower, an early fortification of the harbour. This was one of several short, round towers called Martello Towers, used as part of the harbour defences. The last surviving example stands in Point Pleasant Park. At the time the Maugher's Beach light was built, lighthouses were illuminated by burning whale oil or seal oil. Dr. Abraham Gesner (1797-1864), a country doctor from Cornwallis in the Annapolis Valley of Nova Scotia, invented a new substance called coal oil or kerosene, and by 1846 it was illuminating the lighthouse at Maugher's Beach. Dr. Gesner was the first to extract oil from Nova Scotia coal. He grew rich from the North American Kerosene Gas and Light Company.

Search and Rescue

As long as there have been ships, there has been a need to rescue drowning seamen and passengers. Unfortunately, in the past, there have been dreadful shipwrecks resulting in huge loss of life, but there have also been people who have worked to save lives.

Today there is a large and sophisticated system of search and rescue in Canada, which includes the Coast Guard, Canadian Armed Forces and other agencies. Because of its vast distances, wild terrain and harsh climate, Canada has become a world leader in search and rescue. While other countries boast of their war heroes, many of Canada's heroes wear medals won for extraordinary feats of courage in plucking sailors from the pitching decks of half-sunken ships; parachuting into the night to bring first aid and sustenance to a downed aircraft crew in the north; or rescuing somebody trapped underwater.

There are three Rescue Coordination Centres in Canada – at Halifax, Trenton (Ontario) and Vancouver. The centre in Halifax coordinates ships, helicopters, airplanes, and fast rescue craft throughout eastern Canada. Like most things Canadian, search and rescue had humble beginnings. A "life saving station" consisted of a rowboat and local fishermen to crew it when called upon. In 1914, the lifesaving service had forty stations, of which there were four in New Brunswick, sixteen in Nova Scotia, five in Prince Edward Island, eleven on the Great Lakes, and four in British Columbia. Again, because of its traffic volume and strategic location, Halifax Harbour warranted three stations: at Devil's Island, Herring Cove and Duncan's Cove, near Chebucto Head.

Diving Near the Coast Guard Base

The bottom around the Coast Guard base is fairly flat and shallow. Since this area served as anchorage for ships in the early days of Halifax there is evidence of artifacts probably lost or thrown from vessels. Unfortunately, the mud is deep in this area and has swallowed up anything that went into it. Just south of the base is one of the last remaining pieces of original shoreline left in the harbour. This area has an interesting and strange assortment of bottles, iron, wreckage, wharves, and other paraphernalia that washes in or becomes exposed when winter storms stir up the bottom. When Transport Canada built a parking and storage area in the late 1980s, they covered a large part of this shoreline. I was saddened to see this happen, because I had seen many old artifacts in this area and now they are gone, buried under many tons of rock.

Samuel Cunard

Of all the sons of the harbour, one name has endured through time above the others. That is because the company he founded close to two hundred years ago bears his name, as have some of the world's most famous ships, such as the *Queen Mary* and the *Queen Elizabeth*.

Ambitious, energetic, wily, loyal, Samuel Cunard was one of the great men of the harbour and a man who had a significant influence on one of the harbour's major activities – commercial shipping. His New England ancestors had grown prosperous from shipping, but when the American Revolution came, they had to choose between their king or their possessions, for Loyalists were lucky to get out of the rebel colonies with their lives. His grandfather, Robert, chose for the King and arrived in New Brunswick penniless. Robert's son, Abraham, headed for Halifax in 1784, where he went to work in the King's Lumber Yard. He stayed and soon married Samuel's mother, Margaret. Samuel was the second of their nine children and when he was born on November 21, 1787, his diligent father was already laying the modest foundation on which his energetic son would build.

Samuel Cubard attended the Halifax Grammar School, which is still going strong, but his real education took place around the Halifax docks. While he was still young, he was working deals on cargoes, buying what he could afford and reselling it from door to door at a profit. In March, 1813, the firm of A. Cunard and Son bought the square-rigged ship *White Oak* from the Vice-Admiralty court. This was the time of the War of 1812, when

England was at war with the United States and the Vice-Admiralty Court sold American prize ships that Halifax privateers captured on the high seas. No doubt Abraham savoured the bargain and saw some justice in recouping at least some of what his family had been forced to leave behind in the United States. This vessel supplemented the two little coasting schooners they already owned and their transatlantic shipping business was off and running.

As one of the most successful traders and businessmen in Halifax by 1825, Samuel Cunard was invited to take part in the formation of what was to become an icon in Canadian banking – the Halifax Banking Company, which ultimately merged with the Canadian Bank of Commerce in 1901. Until then, Halifax business was transacted in cash and Samuel probably welcomed the change from having to carry a bag of Spanish and American coins in the company of a club-wielding clerk as he conducted business on the waterfront.

But he was more than a businessman; he was a visionary who saw the potential for a new technology that would revolutionize travel. The technology was steam. Samuel Cunard saw the possibilities in having a regular, predictable passenger and freight service across the Atlantic at a time when ships came and went subject to the vagaries of the weather, the whims of the captain and a hundred other factors. A voyage that was supposed to take weeks could take months as the sails went limp from lack of wind, or worse, the ship got blown back towards its point of origin by contrary winds.

This age-old reliance on natural forces to facilitate travel had bred a casual attitude towards schedules and routes. We take such things for granted today, but in Samuel Cunard's time travel routes, and arrival and departure times were vague and general because everybody knew you could neither plan your arrival time nor travel in a straight line to your destination. The Black Ball Line of sailing ships had advertised scheduled departure times from New York since 1817, but they were still victims of the tyranny of the wind and really had no control over when their ships would reach their destinations.

The very significant invention of the steam engine changed travel forever, for it freed us from dependence on the elements or other living creatures to get us about. For thousands of years, sails and oars had moved boats; horses and oxen moved wagons; and dogs moved carts and sleighs. Steam changed all that; it fired the Industrial Revolution, made railroads possible and led to self-propelled ships. John Molson, the founder of the famous brewing empire, was the first to run a steam-operated vessel in Canada. He launched the *Accommodation* in 1809 to provide passenger service between Montreal and Quebec City.

Cunard saw the opportunity to take the technology further than Molson had. His first steamship, the *Royal William*, crossed to England in August 1833, with seven brave passengers and a crew of thirty-six. This eighteen-and-a half-day voyage from Pictou to Cowes is believed by many to have been the first transatlantic crossing of a steam-driven ship. The 49-metre long wooden side-wheeler, built at Quebec and named after William IV, the first member of the royal family to visit there in 1787, belonged to the Quebec and Halifax Steam Navigation Company, which Cunard and others had formed in 1825. She carried a full complement of sails, as steamships would do for another half-century. In a discipline as traditional as the sailing of ships, change came slowly and with much debate. The *Royal William* was eventually sold to Spain and renamed the *Isabella Segunda*. Three years after her historic voyage, she achieved another first on May 5, 1836, when she became the first steam-driven warship to fire a shot in action.

Amid ridicule that it was impossible to carry enough coal to get a steamer across the Atlantic – some argued that you simply had to do the mathematics to see it – Samuel Cunard planned, schemed, cajoled, wheeled and dealed a line of steamers into existence that proved not only that it was possible, but also that it was very desirable. The world was ready for sea travel that featured a predictable departure and arrival time. Steamships became known as "ocean liners" because, for the first time, a ship could now follow a prescribed course in almost any weather. The winds might have blown sailing ships around but a steam-driven ship could stay on a course, thus following a straight line that the navigator had drawn on a chart.

Passengers were ready for the benefits that steam might bring but they were reluctant to, as they saw it, risk their lives by crossing the Atlantic in one of these new-fangled things. With good reason, for in the beginning there was a distinct element of danger to both passengers and crew, as the first steam engines, with their high pressure boilers, had an annoying habit of blowing up and killing all within reach. Steamships were also involved in more than their share of collisions, especially at night. So Cunard put a heavy emphasis on safety and in so doing he earned the confidence of the travelling public. His ships were the first to use the now universal system of displaying red and green running lights at night to indicate to other vessels the direction in which a ship is travelling.

Understanding that the public's confidence was of paramount importance, Cunard pursued other ways to ensure safer shipping. In his early years as a ship owner and trader in Halifax, he served for twenty years as chairman of the Lighthouse Commission of Nova Scotia. Under his energetic leadership, new lighthouses were built and by 1835 Nova Scotia boasted more navigation aids than anywhere in British North America. The system of painting lighthouses with horizontal and vertical stripes for easy identification during daylight is believed to have originated with him.

As soon as he got involved in steam, he went after the plum he knew he would need to ensure success. With his usual thoroughness and persistence he landed the contract to carry the Royal Mail between England and North America, and his future was secure. In 1839, with English partners, he formed the British and North American Royal Mail Steam Packet Company. It wasn't long before it became known as "Cunard's." When the company's first mail ship, SS *Unicorn*, arrived at Halifax on June 1, 1840, it was the first of what would become thousands of transatlantic steamers to call at Halifax Harbour. Those of us who have been to the bottom of the harbour have seen the evidence of the huge numbers of coal-burning steamers that have come to Halifax, for the harbour floor has hundreds of tons of coal scattered around.

Six weeks after the *Unicorn's* arrival, Cunard's second ship, the *Britannia,* steamed into Halifax after a lightning fast crossing of twelve days from Liverpool. At sixty-three metres long, this was a bigger ship and required from four to six men just to handle the steering wheel. She even carried cows for fresh milk. Cunard arrived at Halifax aboard the *Britannia* to a hero's welcome. Two years later, the famous English novelist Charles Dickens visited Halifax aboard the same ship and even mentioned a cow in his description of the voyage. By 1848, Cunard's had nine large steamships plying the Atlantic, and Halifax Harbour was becoming the hub of North American steam travel, but Boston and New York, serving much larger populations, would soon eclipse Halifax.

Samuel Cunard was also the driving force behind the first railway in Atlantic Canada — ten kilometres long from the Albion Coal Mine to the docks at Pictou. The impressive Museum of Industry has been built on the site of this early coal mine. Among its many displays, it houses the oldest locomotive in Canada, which would have belonged to Cunard and his partners. Being in the coal business then was like being in the oil business today. With forty wagons and seventy-five horses, S. Cunard and Company was a major supplier of coal to the businesses and households of Halifax and to Cunard ships.

The Cunard family lived on Brunswick Street overlooking their waterfront holdings. From their window, they could see their three docks on what is now the south part of the Dockyard. Harbour charts show that by 1878 the site had expanded to six wharves. The Deep Water Terminus eventually replaced these wharves in the 1880s, to be replaced in turn by Pier 2 in 1913. Pier 2 was absorbed into the Naval Dockyard in 1971 and replaced by a new jetty in 1996.

Steam travel also revolutionized journalism and propagated an atmosphere of cutthroat competition among newspapers. The idea of scheduled crossings meant that the news from Europe arrived at a predictable time, so the newspapers of Boston and New York were forever concocting ways to outwit one another in the race to get the news dispatches on paper and into the hands of readers. They kept correspondents in Halifax to sort through the dispatches, prepare the copy and fire it off to the newspaper via pony express, carrier pigeon, chartered vessels across the Bay of Fundy, and eventually by telegraph. No scheme was too outrageous if the competition was lurking about.

Samuel's wife, Susan, died ten days after the birth of their ninth child on January 23, 1827. She lies in the Old Burying Ground in Halifax, which is a National Historic Site. Cunard was always careful to look to the welfare of his children, but as they grew older and the years progressed, he spent more and more time in England. He became Sir Samuel Cunard in 1859 in recognition of his ready willingness to put his ships at the disposal of the war effort in the Crimea. He had fourteen vessels converted to transport troops to the war theatre and for moving the wounded to hospital, where Florence Nightingale and her little group of nurses laboured to ease their suffering.

On the road to revolutionizing transatlantic travel, he and his partners had to battle competitors every step of the way. Other lines came and went but Cunard, although he was a visionary and pacesetter, was also conservative. He managed to steer a profitable course among them all, not losing a single passenger during a period when loss of life from shipwrecks was all too common.

The SS Humboldt

Several competitors lost ships on Cunard's doorstep. The SS *Humboldt* of the New York and Havre Line wrecked while entering Halifax Harbour on December 6, 1853, apparently without loss of life. The *Humboldt* was a steamship driven by paddlewheels. Called a side-wheeler, she had a paddlewheel ten metres in diameter on each side. These paddles turned at fifteen revolutions per minute giving her an operational speed of ten and a half knots. She struck a reef on the rocky area known as the Sambro Ledges, and the captain, knowing his ship was doomed, grounded the vessel near Portuguese Cove where passengers and crew managed to get ashore.

There is little discernible wreckage at the wreck site today but it is an interesting dive nonetheless. The water in this exposed area is from nine to fifteen metres deep and the open ocean has pounded the site for 150 years, so the debris has scattered. More interesting is the way the wood has decayed, turning into a black coal-like substance and settling among the crevices of the rocky bottom. Thin, grey and very subtle plant growth has disguised the wreck so that it is very hard to make out. Even while looking at it from a metre it is difficult to distinguish rock from wreckage. While diving the area a few years ago I came upon a two-metre-long Atlantic Torpedo Ray, a large and wide member of the shark family. This bottom-dweller, which ranges from North Carolina to Nova Scotia, blended in well with the grey rocks. I was close to touching it before I saw it, which was fortunate for me since it packed a charge of 220 volts.

The *Humboldt* was carrying a large cargo of watches, medallions, buttons and other jewelry items. Although attempts were made to salvage the cargo at the time, much of it went to the bottom and spread among the wreckage, making it extremely difficult to see, now that the ship has deteriorated so much. For years, divers have visited the site and patiently dug among the crevices to recover pieces of the jewelry.

More Wrecks Near Halifax

As competition heated up, Samuel Cunard's insistence on safety continued to pay off. Other lines were obsessed with speed and took risks that made Cunard's look stodgy by comparison. They paid with lost ships and lives. He did not live to see several more spectacular losses occur near his home port.

On January 28, 1870, the *City of Boston*, belonging to the Inman Line, left Seeton's Wharf in Halifax and sailed out the harbour. That was the last anybody ever saw of the ship and her 207 passengers and crew. Halifax shipowner James Farquhar, writing fifty years later, commented: "A great many Halifax families had representatives in her. To this day, although it happened more than half a century ago, you will hear Nova Scotians speak of prominent persons who sailed in the *City of Boston* and so dropped from sight. In its time, her loss was like that of the *Titanic* or of the *Lusitania*."

Three years later, on March 31, 1873, the luxurious new White Star liner SS *Atlantic*, travelling between Liverpool and New York, decided to put in to Halifax for additional fuel. At 3 o'clock the next morning, while searching for the Sambro light, she struck the rocks at the entrance to Halifax Harbour near Terence Bay, eventually turning on her side and sinking. Between 550 and 600 people perished by drowning, exposure or exhaustion. All the women and all the children but one were lost.

This is the wreck of a large ship, which lies in twelve to twenty-four metres (40 to 80 feet) of water. All that is left standing are the steam boilers at the bottom of the slope in twenty-four metres, and they are disintegrating rapidly. The balance of the wreckage is strewn along the bank with very little of it discernible. Like the *Humboldt*, much of it has taken on the appearance of the rocky bottom, but the shafts, huge propellor blades and hull plating are all clearly visible, along with the boilers. People who have not dived on the wrecks off Eastern Canada often have a mental picture of a submerged ship sitting on the bottom of the ocean. Bearing in mind that these ships are *wrecks*, there is usually very little left to see and what is there has often been smashed beyond recognition. Most accessible wrecks have been commercially salvaged by blowing them asunder to get at their brass fittings and anything of value. What the salvers have not scrounged, the weather often works to reduce to twisted metal and rusting iron.

The Company After Cunard

Sir Samuel Cunard died on April 28, 1865, in England, rich but not excessively so. He had always been generous to his nine children and horde of grandchildren, on whom he doted. The company lived on, prospered, fought it out with its competitors during the golden age of ocean liners, survived the decline brought about by the jet airplane, and managed to find a place in the cruise market of the 1980s and '90s. In the process it has forgotten and rediscovered its links to Halifax several times.

In the late 1920s, when Cunard ships were reaching their zenith in size, speed and luxury the Halifax Board of Trade could boast, "Thirty-six lines of steamships, some of them the largest in the North Atlantic service, make this port their terminal or port of call and some fifteen coastal services their headquarters." These companies and their ships are all gone, but as the stately *Queen Elizabeth 2* enters Halifax Harbour at the beginning of the twenty-first century, there is still the reminder of her glorious heritage printed in large, red letters across her side – Cunard. Historian John Maxtone-Graham has written of this ship, the only north Atlantic express liner left, "what Cunard started, Cunard will finish."

Steamships of Halifax -
The Red Cross Line

Commercial shipping has naturally been attracted to the spacious and deep harbour at Halifax, discharging and picking up passengers and cargo. Boston, New York, the West Indies, South America, the Orient and, of course, Europe exchanged and continue to exchange their ships with Halifax on a regular basis. The Red Cross Line was typical of the early passenger steamship companies and their ships were a familiar sight in the late 1800s and early 1900s .

The name had nothing to do with the organization known as the Red Cross. The symbol was more like a red "X," painted on the large smokestacks common to early steamers. The ships docked south of the Plant Line wharf near the Brewery Market on the old waterfront. They ran a regular passenger and freight service from St. John's to Halifax and New York and at least two of their ships met their demise on Nova Scotia's shores.

Their Halifax location has been easy to identify because of the preponderance of Red Cross Line china that lies concentrated in a small area, most of it broken, with many pieces bearing the pennant and name of the line. In the area we have seen the occasional bottle from St. John's or New York, dating from the time that Red Cross Line ships called at Halifax. There is also clear evidence of the presence of two of their ships. Cutlery bearing the names of the SS *Stephano* and SS *Florizel* has been found at the same site.

SS *Stephano* and SS *Florizel* were their best-known ships in the twentieth century. Author David Kerr writes that the Red Cross Line "made its St. John's, Halifax and New York run one of the most romantic along the North American seaboard. *Stephano*, for instance, could carry 180 first

Two patterns of dinnerware from the Red Cross Line. From the author's collection.

class passengers in deluxe cabins and two berth rooms, and 60 passengers in the second class. The passengers were accommodated on two decks, and took their meals in a spacious dining saloon which extended the full width of the ship, while music and other recreations could be enjoyed in a saloon in the fore part of the shelter deck house. Both ships enjoyed remarkable success. They carried not only business men and freight but also American tourists in search of comfort, relaxation, entertainment aboard and expeditions ashore."

The Red Cross Line's roots go back to 1811 when Benjamin Bowring came from England and set up as a merchant in St. John's, Newfoundland. To make it easier to transport his goods from England, he bought the little 44-ton schooner *Charlotte* in 1823, followed by the purchase of the *Eagle* and the *Dove*, built in Prince Edward Island in the same year. Things went so well that Benjamin eventually returned to England and established Bowring's in Liverpool to handle the purchase of goods for shipping to the St. John's operation.

After his death, his sons took over the firm. In Liverpool, they operated as C.T. Bowring and Co. (after Charles Tricks Bowring, Benjamin's eldest son). The St. John's branch operated under the name Bowring Brothers. By

the time they bought their first steamers in the 1870s they had accumulated thirty-six sailing ships, moving cargoes and passengers all over the world.

Established in 1884, the Red Cross Line marked Bowrings' commitment to scheduled passenger service. Like most shipping lines, it is associated with adventure and tragedy. In 1899, the SS *Portia* sank at the entrance to Halifax Harbour in an area that has claimed many ships. It was the line's third loss in five years. This iron steamer was travelling on her regular run from New York to Halifax when she struck Big Fish Shoal near Sambro Island *inside* the Sambro light.

Today her bones rest on a sandy bottom in twenty-five metres of water and the site is a popular destination for local scuba divers. This part of the harbour entrance has claimed countless ships because of the many reefs and shoals, the stormy weather and, of course, the fog. The storms have played havoc with this wreck by keeping the bottom sands forever shifting. For a diver, the sandy bottom presents a measure of frustration because, even at this depth, the sands move around and much of the wreck has been buried as a consequence. Straight out to sea from here is the graveyard of the Atlantic, Sable Island, whose sands have consumed literally hundreds of ships, leaving not a trace. Sometimes parts of old wrecks eerily appear out of the sands of Sable Island, only to be swallowed again with the next storm.

Diving the Portia

My first visit to the *Portia* had its share of frustration. We had a fisherman take us out to the site, which is in a wide passage between two islands; we located the site by use of a navigation system called Loran C. But it was very windy and our boat captain was not experienced with the precision of keeping the boat above a shipwreck. The boat kept blowing about as we tried to get a navigation fix on the wreck. We finally got above it and threw the anchor over. I was elected to go down and confirm that we were indeed on the wreck before anybody else wasted air and bottom time. I went twenty-five metres (80 feet) down the anchor line and arrived on a flat sandy bottom, with no wreck to be seen. I was concerned that the anchor was dragging, thanks to the high winds above. As I swam around looking for the wreck, I kept an eye on the anchor to make sure it didn't get away from me.

Suddenly, the wreck appeared out of the gloom directly in the path of the moving anchor. Excited but concerned about getting the anchor set, I swam ahead of it and we both bore down on the wreck. I thought I would be able to hook it to a piece of wreckage. As the heavy anchor came alongside, I struggled to lift it and hooked it to a piece of the *Portia*'s railing. It simply slid off and proceeded on its way. I grabbed it again and, to keep it from getting away, hung on to the wreck with my other hand. I felt ridiculous, twenty-five metres down, with a shipwreck in one hand and an anchor in the other, about to be slowly split down the middle if I continued to hold on to both. I had to let go and headed up the anchor line. The nearly two minutes it took me to surface meant we had blown far from the wreck site

197

and, try as we might, that was the only sighting any of us got of the *Portia* that day. Such are the vagaries of wreck diving.

Stephano and Florizel

After losing many vessels, things were looking bad for the Red Cross Line, which, incidentally, named its ships after characters in Shakespeare's plays. But the introduction of *Florizel* and *Stephano* to the fleet gave the company the injection it needed. Both had ice-breaking hulls and were successful sealing ships making extremely profitable sealing voyages for their owners.

Unfortunately, both ships met an untimely end. A German submarine torpedoed the *Stephano* off Nantucket on October 8, 1916, with no loss of life. But the most harrowing loss of a Red Cross Line ship was the *Florizel,* which wrecked on February 23, 1918, while en route from St. John's to Halifax. Ninety-four people died, including 11-year-old Blanche Beaumont, who was on her way to attend the School for the Blind in Halifax; 7-year-old Clarence Moulton, going to the School for the Deaf and Dumb in Halifax; and 4-year-old Betty Munn, daughter of the Managing Director of the Red Cross Line. The inrushing waters tore her from her father's arms as they both perished. Her mother had undergone surgery in New York and Betty and her father were on their way to visit her. In her memory, Bowrings erected a large statue of Peter Pan in Bowring Park in St. John's.

In 1929, Bowrings sold the line to the Bermuda and West Indies Steamship Co., a subsidiary of Furness Withy, a British ship owner and another important shipper in and out of Halifax. Their docks were situated farther in the harbour, close to where the Purdy's Wharf office towers are located. The Furness Red Cross Line continued to call at Halifax into the 1960s.

Other Notable Red Cross Line Ships

Bowring's was a very diverse company and had a number of ships in their fleet that were involved in many adventurous undertakings. They participated actively in whaling in the Arctic and sealing in the Gulf of St. Lawrence and off Newfoundland in late winter. Bowring's was the first major firm to conduct the seal hunt in Newfoundland and Canadian waters and did so for more than a century. As its sturdy ships and tough crews were experienced at working in the extremely dangerous business of navigating through heavy pack ice, several of the company's sealing ships were used in significant Arctic and Antarctic expeditions in the late 1800s and early 1900s. This was a period of feverish attempts by adventurers and nations to be the first to reach the North and South Poles.

In one of her three trips to the Antarctic, the barque-rigged steamer, SS *Terra Nova*, took the British explorer Robert Falcon Scott on the voyage in which he reached the South Pole. But this 1912 expedition cost Scott and his team their lives, bringing sadness to the whole British nation. During this frantic period of Antarctic exploration these wooden ships and iron men were in demand. The SS *Aurora* also made several Antarctic trips. On one, she accompanied the brand new British vessel SS *Endurance*, which took Ernest Shackleton to the Antarctic in 1914. The *Endurance* was crushed in the ice and went to the bottom in pieces, leaving Shackleton and his crew to live through what many consider to be the most remarkable story of survival ever. On that trip, the *Aurora* spent a year stuck in the ice and out of reach of Shackleton, but managed to survive.

The SS *Algerine* was another interesting vessel. Built in Belfast as a British gunboat for use against the Barbary pirates on the North African coast, she was acquired by Bowring's for use as a sealer. After several Arctic trips involving dramatic rescues of Polar expeditions, she was used in the search for victims of the *Titanic* disaster. Just two months later, on June 26, 1912, she left Sydney, Nova Scotia, and herself fell victim to the ice as she was lost off Baffin Island.

The man who is generally recognized as Canada's greatest Arctic explorer, Bob Bartlett, had commanded the *Algerine* during part of her long and adventurous career. He had been her captain in 1905 and had served as first mate when his uncle took the ship into Hudson Bay. Captain Bartlett was celebrated throughout the United States after he rammed the SS *Roosevelt* through the Arctic ice and clawed his way to within sledding distance of the North Pole in 1909, thereby setting the stage for Commander Robert Peary of the United States to became credited as the first white man to make it to the Pole. Prior to that momentous occasion, Peary had sailed on two other Bowring ships – SS *Kite* in 1891 and SS *Falcon* in 1893. Both trips were to explore northern Greenland, where Peary named Falcon Bay in honour of the ship that had taken him there. Unfortunately, the *Falcon* was lost shortly thereafter. Having survived the Arctic, she was lost with all hands after dropping Peary and family safely at Philadelphia in 1894.

Yet another Bowring sealing ship, the SS *Viking*, caught worldwide attention in 1931 when, on March 15, she blew up near the Horse Islands off northern Newfoundland while engaged in the making of an American motion picture about the seal hunt. Sealing ships of the day carried large amounts of explosive to blast their way through the heavy ice encountered at the sealing front. The *Viking* carried extra for the scenes that were planned and it proved to be her undoing. Twenty-seven men, including the director and cameraman and a 14-year-old stowaway, were killed when the stern blew off the 50-year old Norwegian-built ship. My next door neighbour during my childhood had been a stowaway on the *Viking* and he survived that fateful trip. He was eleven years old at the time. The desire to travel on sealing vessels was so strong among some Newfoundland youth that stowaways were common as they sought a taste of adventure. Sometimes they got more than they bargained for.

The film, called *The Viking,* had been forgotten (It was a forgettable film!) and disappeared until 1950, when one of Job Brothers and Co.'s fish storage sheds was being torn down to make way for a new harbour development in St. John's. A copy was found buried in the dust of an abandoned shelf. The highly flammable nitrate film was transferred to modern film at the National Film Board and the movie was released in 1996 to commemorate the fiftieth anniversary of Bob Bartlett's death. What it lacked in plot and acting, it more than compensated for as a documentary about the early seal hunt and the awful struggles of those involved. Bartlett, who was a friend of the American Director, Varick Frissell, played the role of a sealing captain in the movie. Bob Bartlett's father, William, had skippered the *Viking* for many years.

After the *Portia*, the second Bowring ship to wreck in Nova Scotia was the SS *Imogene*, which grounded on a reef off Canso on September 22, 1940. She was carrying a cargo of salt from Turks Island in the Caribbean to Gaspé, Quebec. In the same month, Bowring's SS *Urla* sailed with the first World War II convoy – HX72 from Halifax – to be mauled by the German U-boats at the beginning of the Battle of the Atlantic. The convoy was so severely pounded by a wolf pack in September 1940, that the Royal Navy was obliged to come to terms with the significance of the U-boat force. The *Urla* survived that trip, but sank just four months later after being torpedoed by an Italian submarine. The SS *Plover*, another Bowring ship, had also been lost at sea after departing from Sydney in 1890. Bowrings continued their involvement in Nova Scotia shipping into the 1950s through the *Cape Breton*, which transported coal to the steel plant at Sydney.

In 1979 the great-great-great-great grandson of Benjamin Bowring was in Halifax looking for a ship to be part of the first surface expedition to circumnavigate the globe through both the North and South Poles. The expedition needed a ship and Antony Bowring, having applied to join the crew, was accepted on the condition that he come up with a suitable vessel. With a family history so closely linked to polar expeditions, he approached C. T. Bowring & Company in London. By then it had become a large insurance brokerage business with just a few modern bulk carriers. It was a publicly traded company, but a few members of the family were still employed by the firm, including his father, Peter Bowring, who was chairman.

Bowring found in Halifax a 27-year-old ship that by coincidence had just finished work at the Labrador seal fishery – a modern day equivalent to the *Terra Nova*, *Aurora*, and their sisters. The *Martin Karlsen*, built in 1952, was a 1,200-ton ice-strengthened ship of sixty-four metres and owned by the Karlsen Shipping Company in Halifax.

Bowring's agreed to buy her on behalf of the Transglobe Expedition and renamed her *Benjamin Bowring*, after the clock and watchmaker in Exeter who had set off for Newfoundland in 1811 at the age of thrity-three. The *Charlotte* was the first of the Bowring fleet and the *Benjamin Bowring* would become the last. While she was at sea during the expedition, C. T.

Bowring & Co. Ltd. was taken over by the American firm Marsh & McLennan, who sold all the remaining ships except the *Benjamin Bowring*.

The expedition was a success. The leader, Ranulph Fiennes, and his colleague, Charlie Burton, established a number of firsts including being the first to circumnavigate the world on land, sea, and ice via both Poles. Ranulph Fiennes's wife, Virginia, who was responsible for the expedition's communications links and ran the mobile base camps, was the first woman to visit both Poles, and their Jack Russell dog, Bothy, was the first animal to visit both Poles. In August 1982, having completed over 100,000 sea miles, the *Benjamin Bowring* sailed up the Thames to Greenwich with Prince Charles, the expedition's Patron, at the helm.

The Bowring name continues to have a presence in Canada through a chain of gift stores in many large Canadian cities. The profile of the SS *Terra Nova* serves as their corporate logo. In the meantime, ownership of the stores has passed to Canadian interests and is no longer connected with the Bowring family.

Doing the Bohemian

Bob, it's Dwayne. We're doin' the Bohemian tomorrow.
Are you interested?"

It is not an invitation to learn a new dance; it's an invitation to go diving on the wreck of the SS *Bohemian*.

"Absolutely! I'm interested."

"The boat leaves from Gray's Boatyard at 2."

The point of departure consists of a few houses in Sambro Harbour, facing the open Atlantic just south of Halifax Harbour. With a load of six enthusiastic divers aboard, the 10-metre fishing boat pulls away from the dock at 2:10 and heads out towards the open Atlantic. When we get outside Sambro Harbour and are far enough from shore, Dave Gray, the owner, turns the boat left and heads towards Halifax Harbour, seven or eight kilometres away.

After about fifteen minutes of steaming, we see off to our left in the distance the great yawning entrance to Halifax Harbour, stretching across ten kilometres from Chebucto Head to Hartlen Point. Our destination is just outside the harbour, near the approaches. We are travelling through an area of low islands, rocks and reefs. Off to the right is Outer Sambro Island, which hosts the historic Sambro lighthouse. The 28-metre high granite structure holds the light for which captains have searched for close to two and a half centuries, as they sought the shelter of Halifax Harbour. We are diving here today because some of them, including the *Bohemian*'s, found it too late or didn't find it at all.

The harbour entrance is wide but the safe shipping lane is only a fraction of that width. In order to avoid the shoals farther in, the recommended approach goes in a straight line along the extreme left side of the outer harbour, close to Chebucto Head. Deviating from that prescribed route has meant destruction and death for many ships and crews. The 5,500-ton iron steamer *Bohemian*, owned by Leyland and Co. of Liverpool, was one of them. In the pre-dawn hours of an early March morning in 1920, she was heading from Boston to Liverpool with a planned stop at Halifax for coal. Contending with snow squalls and darkness, the captain had slowed to a crawl as he tried to get on the harbour approaches, which was normally done by taking a bearing on the Sambro lightship. The *Bohemian* gently struck a rock called Broad Breaker. She did not sink but held fast to the granite reef.

Up to this point, the incident lacked the drama normally associated with wrecks of ships at sea. The passengers slept through the incident and the stewards had to call them, telling them to dress and report to the deck. As a precaution, the crew lowered the boats and put the passengers aboard. But the land was a long way off, so the boats stood by the ship, the dark, cold loneliness punctuated only by the occasional glimpse of the light on Sambro Island as it wound out its monotonous circuits. Tugs from Halifax arrived three or four hours later to take the passengers ashore. They eventually completed their journey to Liverpool aboard the SS *Canada*.

But the story continued for the crew, seven of whom would shortly perish. Because the ship was still holding to the rocks, surrounded by deep water, it was believed that she could be saved. The next day, the crew went to work jettisoning the 7,000-ton cargo of meat, grain and cotton. Salvage tugs and a barge were brought alongside and hopes ran high that they might still make the most of a bad situation. But after midnight things went terribly wrong. As one surviving member of the crew described it, "stanchions were falling and rivets drawing out of the plates with a noise like machine guns. The vibration was tremendous. . . ." The ship was beginning to break up. The tugs had returned to Halifax and, before one could get back, the *Bohemian,* which had survived three submarine attacks during

World War I, would be in two pieces on the bottom and seven men would be dead.

The two sections of the ship lie so far apart on the bottom that they constitute two different dives. Today we are going to dive on the bow section. My buddy for the dive is a 64-year-old grandmother, who took up diving with her teenage grandson. She does between fifty and sixty dives during the six-month period from April to November. One of the unwritten rules of diving is that you must be able to deal with your own gear – no gentlemen, please – but this doesn't alarm Jane, as she quickly dons her suit, tank and weight belt. Her slightly more than 45-kilogram frame is one of the first over the side. What she lacks in size and strength, she more than compensates for in skill and enthusiasm.

It's a warm, sunny day in August, shorts and T-shirt weather, and very different from the night that the ship was lost. People are swimming at the beaches ashore, so our diving suits are more than adequate on the surface. I'm wearing my wetsuit, which I normally use between May and November. It will be essential when we get to the bottom where the summer sun's heat does not penetrate. After going over the side, I am careful to keep some distance from the boat, which is bobbing and lurching around and looks a lot bigger from down here. I recall a dive eighty kilometres off the North Carolina coast when a diver next to me got a bloodied head after taking a whack from the fifteen-metre dive boat that was pitching in very heavy seas. He was lucky it didn't kill him.

Jane and I descend by pulling ourselves down the anchor line for the first few feet; then comes the familiar heaviness as the water pressure compresses my suit. It's the signal to let some air into my buoyancy vest to keep from becoming too heavy. My weight belt also starts to loosen as my suit compresses, so I tighten it. I also need to compensate for the pressure on my ears and mask. A quick snort of air through my nostrils relieves the pressure of the mask pushing in against my face. At the same time, I do a little contraction in my throat, which lets air go inside my eardrums to equalize the pressure. Some people hold their nose and blow.

There is a definite change in water temperature, called a thermocline, at six metres (20 feet). Brrrr! Down we go into the void and, at twelve me-

205

tres (40 feet) the wreck comes into view. We level off at eighteen metres (60 feet). It's a predictable sight for wrecks in this area – smashed almost beyond recognition. What seems like acres of iron hull plates, gears, and machinery lies strewn around. The bottom is extremely rough, rolling rock with pinnacles sticking up and waiting for an unsuspecting ship to happen by. The bow is still intact, rising from the bottom with the hawseholes, through which the anchor chain passed, clearly recognizable. There's the anchor. There is a fair amount of growth on everything – sponges, anemones, kelp. A large school of juvenile pollock swims by, splitting to go around the divers and moving at a speed that makes me dizzy. Whenever I see a school of fish coming towards me I can't help wondering if there is something bigger following them.

Because the ship has been torn apart and the metal cracked and twisted, this wreck, like others in the area, has many sharp edges sticking up. Even though it is a calm day, there is still a noticeable amount of surge, as the water seems to slop back and forth around the wreck. Watching the constant sway of the long, thick kelp leaves can make a diver dizzy or sick in no time. It is actually possible to get seasick while under the water. It is easy to counteract, however, by looking at something firm such as the bottom or a part of the wreck. It's the same trick we use to avoid seasickness on a boat; in that case, you fix your eyes on the horizon, which is stable, instead of on the water, which is moving. But worse than making you seasick, the surge can put you onto one of the sharp edges of the wreck. This heightens the challenge involved in swimming in close quarters among the wreckage.

It's particularly risky trying to see under things, when you need to poke your head in for a closer look. There are times when the surge is so strong and the edges so sharp that sticking your head into a hole exposes you to unnecessary peril. On one occasion, I was pulling my head out of a hole in the wreckage, when the mouthpiece of my regulator got snagged. After a few tense moments, I managed to get it free, but I came close to having it torn out of my mouth. And sometimes there are critters such as wolf fish or big lobsters in these confined spaces, and they don't like surprises any more than we do.

After forty minutes, I'm beginning to get chilly. Jane went up about five minutes ago, but I decide to take a last swim around. The other divers have gone up, with the possible exception of Dwayne, whom I have not seen throughout the dive; he is wearing his double tanks and is usually one of the last out of the water. With the other four divers gone, the commotion has disappeared and all is peace and serenity. It's a chance to reflect on the significance of where I am and on the events that led to the unfortunate and dramatic loss of a big ship.

I return to the anchor line that will guide me back to the boat and start my slow ascent, giving my body and equipment lots of time to adjust to the reduced water pressure. The air inside my mask expands, causing my mask to loosen, and my ears crack several times. My weight belt tightens and I also become buoyant with the expanding air in my buoyancy vest. All these things need attention as I keep a keen eye on my depth gauge. Holding the line enables me to keep tight control on my rate of ascent without having to worry about drifting away from the boat. It's comforting to know exactly where I am.

I start to think about the fact that there have been a number of shark sightings lately. There are many kinds of sharks in Nova Scotia waters, but during August and September, as the water warms up, there are visitors from down south including more varieties of sharks. Seeing a shark or barracuda is a thrill but thinking about it, alone on the anchor line, is not. As I slowly come up, I turn 360 degrees just to be sure and to get away from the cloud of air bubbles surrounding my head. As it turns out, there are no sharks today.

After the dive, while standing on the deck of the sturdy fishing boat, I look around in the beautiful sunshine across the blue waters and see the water breaking on the reefs and rocks that pepper the area. Once a ship wandered off course into this area it would be practically impossible to extricate it safely. We're anchored near Broad Breaker about three kilometres from shore. There are five known shipwrecks behind us, and we passed three on the way out. Ahead of us is a reef called The Sisters, and beyond that is the shipping channel and the harbour. The Sisters has claimed at least seven ships. If we were to travel forward we would go near at least twenty more wrecks before we rounded Chebucto Head and went into the harbour, following a stream of wrecks all the way.

This area has claimed too many ships to name. In his 1987 chart, Greg has identified more than a hundred wrecks at the approaches and in the harbour. There are many times that number that never got documented in the days before newspapers, when fishing schooners came and went by the dozen every day. Most wrecks occurred here because of a tiny error in navigation, but not always. Sometimes it was from a strong current.

Currents are insidious. They must be taken into consideration when navigating, but that is asking a lot when they change speed and direction with the tides and seasons. On one trip a captain could be dealing with a current that is moving him to the left while, on another trip and in the same location, a current may be moving him in the opposite direction. Add to the mix a soupy fog that sits for days at a time and you have a recipe for disaster. And, to top it off, combine high winds and driving snow in winter, or ice forming on the hull from the spray and making the ship top-heavy and in danger of flipping over. No wonder so many vessels ended their days so tragically, and yet so close to refuge.

But on a day like today, with calm winds and a hot sun, it is difficult to picture such conditions. We all relax with a cold drink to wash away the salty taste, and chatter about the dive, as the boat leisurely winds its way among the reefs and back to shore.

More Interesting Wreck Dives

E ven though it's a long way from the city and many residents have never visited it, Chebucto Head is the beginning of Halifax Harbour. It is the corner around which a boat goes to move along the coast and the last land that a ship passes when heading out of the harbour to the open sea. It lines up with Ketch Head, Hartlen Point and Osborne Head to form part of the Nova Scotia coastline.

During the wild winter storms, a few brave souls make their way along the narrow road that leads to the head, so they can watch the spectacular seas rolling in and pounding against the granite cliffs below. Their visit is usually tempered by the deafening blare of the foghorn, which kicks in whenever snow, rain or fog hampers the visibility. The cliffs on this striking piece of shore are dotted with the concrete remains of World War II gun batteries. One enterprising builder has cleverly integrated one of them into the construction of his home. There are a few houses perched on the rocks, looking bravely out towards the horizon.

Isleworth and Perry

Not surprisingly, Chebucto Head has a couple of shipwrecks to attract divers. Two large steamships ended their days on these rocks early in the twentieth century. The first was the *Isleworth*, a 3,000-ton ship that ran into the cliffs in foggy weather on March 12, 1912. Just eight months old, she was en route from Boston to Louisbourg when she started having problems with her propellor and the captain decided to put into Halifax for repairs. She now lies in reasonably deep water with the bottom up. The second wreck is that of the *A.W. Perry*, which struck in almost the same spot three years later, on June 15, 1915. In a second irony, she was also travelling from Boston and struck the head in dense fog. Interestingly, both ships wrecked below the lighthouse.

While talking diving with a friend visiting from the United States, who regularly dives many of the major locations around the world, we asked him to tell us about his favourite dive. He thought for a few minutes and responded that it would be a toss-up between the Red Sea and Chebucto Head. There are two things that make Chebucto Head an attractive dive. The first is the awe-inspiring sight of the large wreck of the *Isleworth* nestled at the base of the formidable underwater cliffs. The second is the very attractive swim to the wreck. Either is a dive in itself.

Many people dive the *Isleworth* from a boat. That's a much easier approach, but when they do, they miss the dive "down through the gut." This is a twelve- to fifteen-metre (40- to 50-foot) descent between two cliffs and must be tackled from the shore. When you dive the wreck from the shore, you must first enter a little lagoon that is about three metres (10 feet) deep. On the outer side of the lagoon, there is a narrow opening between two rocks leading to the open ocean. It is a cut in the cliff that drops straight down for twelve metres (40 feet) and then leads farther down an incline. There is a granite wall on both sides as you descend through a feast of colour. The ocean's waters pound through here, feeding a jungle of plant and animal life and making for a very exciting diving experience. The heavy surge of the water, the wildness of the rocks and the vibrant beauty of the plants and fish provide a real treat for the senses.

On one dive there on a summer's day, Pete Hicklenton and I returned from the wreck and, for a few minutes, reverted to our boyish ways. As a precaution, when returning from deep dives many divers do an extra stop in shallow water over and above the decompression time required by the dive tables. With the strong surge passing through the narrow opening in the gut, we couldn't resist playing for a few minutes. At a depth of three to four metres (10 to 15 feet) we positioned ourselves on the outside and waited for the next wave to crash in. It hurled us through the gut and into the lagoon. Then we flipped over and let the undertow pull us back out. Another flip and back into the lagoon, and then back out again. This was definitely more fun that a typical decompression stop, which usually consists of hovering below the surface and staring at nothing.

A few weeks later we repeated the dive. This experience reminded me of how quickly conditions change and how this area is affected by events we may not experience. Even though we had had a period of unprecedented weather – calm and sunny – for weeks, the visibility was very poor. Several hurricanes in the Caribbean had headed out to sea and their effects had been visited upon the Nova Scotia shore. Even though the weather had been calm for the previous week, huge waves had been flung against the coast, caused by the hurricane thousands of kilometres away. Just down the shore from us, at Herring Cove, a man and his eight-year-old daughter had been swept off the rocks to their deaths the previous weekend, the same two whose bodies our club members had helped to recover.

But despite the ravages of the storm, the water was teeming with life. Schools of herring, pollock, and mackerel provided easy pickings for a group of seals. We encountered the seals at a depth of twenty-seven metres (90 feet) as they darted from the gloom in and out of the top of the wreck. There were several females, one of which nipped at the ends of my brightly coloured fins. I was a little unnerved by the appearance of the bull, who wanted us to know we were unwelcome. As he came towards me and then swung upwards, I got a good view of his 3-metre length. As with other experiences I have had with bull grey seals, he made an interesting display of aggression, but that was all. His bark seemed to be worse than his bite, which was fine with me.

Less than a stone's throw from the *Isleworth* is the wreck of the *A.W. Perry*. This, too, is a scenic wreck as it lies on a steep incline. It was on this wreck many years ago that I saw my first shark. Greg and I were buddies but we were separated for a few minutes by a large piece of wreckage. While swimming along alone, I glanced up and saw the shark moving leisurely about seven metres above me. I stopped and watched as it swam out of sight. While this was early in my diving years, I knew enough to realize that seeing a shark is more of a treat than a threat, but I was still relieved when Greg rounded the corner. On the boat, our first words to one another were "Did you see what I just saw?"

In this area, I have seen other interesting sea life, including schools of dogfish, which are small sharks; a torpedo ray, sunfish, seals, whales and many other kinds of fish which range north to Nova Scotia in late summer.

The SS Atlantic

When I first started diving, I had the good fortune to be invited to join the Underwater Adventurers, a dive club of experienced and somewhat imaginative wreck divers. They had several longstanding traditions, including a dive at noon on New Year's Day and a dive on April 1 on the wreck of the SS *Atlantic*. April 1 is the anniversary of the loss of this fine ocean liner. On April 15, 1912, the White Star Line lost the RMS *Titanic*, but in an equally tragic incident thirty-two years earlier, the same line lost the SS *Atlantic*. In the early morning hours of April 1, 1873, it plowed into the rocks near Lower Prospect about thirty kilometres outside Halifax Harbour with the loss, by some estimates, of nearly six hundred victims.

One of the worst transatlantic disasters of the nineteenth century, the *Atlantic's* fate grabbed headlines across North America. She had left Liverpool for New York on March 20, 1873. It was the nineteenth ocean crossing

Brass key tags from the SS *Atlantic*. From the collection of Greg Cochkanoff.

for the 2-year-old vessel, commanded by Captain James Williams. Built in Belfast by Harland and Wolff, the yard that would later build the *Titanic*, the *Atlantic* was a state of the art iron steamer, 128 metres long, with four masts and six watertight bulkheads. Her first class passengers enjoyed piano music, a library, barbershop, and smoking room and could relax on the finest of velvet

212

upholstered furniture. They might enjoy such things, but even a state of the art ship like the *Atlantic* did not have private bath facilities, so first class passengers were obliged to share with other passengers of their class. There were close to a thousand people aboard, more than half of whom were crammed in the steerage area – emigrants from Germany, Italy and Ireland.

As is common in the north Atlantic, the crossing was stormy and the ship burned a lot of coal. After eleven days the Chief Engineer calculated that if the ship's rate of coal consumption did not decline, they would run out of fuel before arriving at New York. Captain Williams made the decision that eventually led to disaster as he ordered the ship to head northeast to Halifax for additional coal.

It was a clear night, so, after ordering that a lookout be kept for icebergs and the Sambro lighthouse and that he be called at 20 minutes before 3 a.m., Williams retired around midnight to get some sleep. Of those standing the watch, only the Third Officer had been to Halifax but he was unfamiliar with the coast and the rocky approaches to the big harbour. There was also concern among some of the crew who had been there before, as the ship barreled along at eleven to twelve knots into the darkness. They had reason for concern because, in the early morning hours of April 1, the ship ran full speed into the rocks at the tip of Mosher Island. Within minutes, the decks were awash.

It was 3:20 a.m. The crash woke the captain, who ordered the crew to help the passengers abandon ship, but the high seas swept away most of the ten lifeboats. The water rushed in so fast that many were drowned in their beds. One passenger, who survived by climbing into the rigging, later described the scene to a Halifax reporter: "I heard a dismal wail, which was fearful to listen to. It proceeded from the steerage passengers below who were then smothering. It did not last more than two minutes when all was still as death."

The survivors struggled to get ashore through the icy waters or clung to the rigging throughout the night, hoping for rescue at dawn. When the light finally came, it revealed a pathetic scene. People, some of them barely alive, were sprawled on the rocks or staggering in search of help. Fortunately, the word got out quickly and local people were soon rallying to help those in the rigging get ashore and to revive those who had, with Herculean effort, managed to claw their way out of the water and up over the rocks. Only one child survived, a boy named John Hindley. He had made it through the night in the rigging. None of the women survived and few, if any, married men.

The wreck received a high profile in newspapers and magazines in the United States and England. Photographers and artists from magazines such as *Harpers Weekly* descended on the community to capture the full extent of the tragedy. Currier and Ives later issued a lithograph depicting the sinking, and the great American artist Winslow Homer created a wood engraving.

Carriages from Halifax drove out to see the site firsthand and a tug gave tours along the coast for $2 per person. Divers soon arrived from the New York Wrecking Company and offered to retrieve the bodies still trapped in the wreck at $50 per cabin passenger and $20 for each steerage passenger. Even in death, the poorest of the passengers were worth less. Many of the dead could not be identified and eventually 277 Protestants were buried in a mass grave on the shores of Terence Bay. A simple memorial marks the spot. On several occasions in the past, the sea has eroded the area where the dead lie, as though it were still trying to reclaim its victims.

The inquiry report concluded that it was only a question of time before the *Atlantic* struck somewhere along the coast, because of the excessive speed and lack of vigilance on the part of the ship's officers. When she struck, the captain was absent from the bridge – not a good situation– and as a consequence of the loss of his ship, his mariner's certificate was suspended for two years. As the report stated: "She was run at full speed, engines and boilers all in perfect order, upon well known rocks in fine weather." The report concluded that a strong current had taken the ship off course without the captain's knowledge. Then, to add insult to injury, a further investigation found that Chief Engineer Foxley had miscalculated the amount of coal – there had been sufficient to take the *Atlantic* to New York, after all.

Today the remains of this fine ship lie in twelve to twenty-four metres (40 to 80 feet) of water, strewn down a very steep series of granite cliffs and boulders. Photographs taken within days of the wreck show her lying on her side with the decks facing outward. She would have disgorged much of her contents before finally going to the bottom. Several times over the past century and a quarter, the ship's remains have been commercially salvaged for anything of value. Even though what is left does not remotely resemble a ship, this is still a popular dive

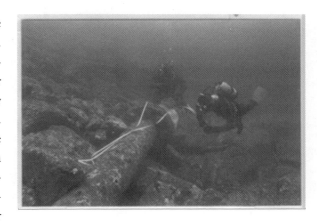

Grant MacLeod and the author taking measurements on the wreck of the *Atlantic*. Photo by Dwayne McLaughlin.

destination because it carries so much drama and tragedy.

The boilers and most of the ribs lie at the bottom of the incline, twenty-four metres (80 feet) deep. Not far away are parts of the propellor shaft. A large pile of broken dishes, probably from the cargo, is scattered among the boulders. For hundreds of metres in all directions are the flattened remains of the ship, consisting of iron hull plates and shafts, decayed wood, gears, pieces of brass and lead.

In the fifteen years that I have visited this wreck, I have seen significant change in its character. It is very exposed to the open ocean and because of its location among the rocks, about one in four dives must be cancelled because of weather. The weather also exacts an enormous toll on what remains. Sometimes, even at a depth of twenty-one metres (70 feet), it is necessary to hold on to the wreck because of the heavy surge. There is a great deal to see, including several of the boilers, some blades from the propeller, and the iron plates of the hull but seeing things on the wreck of the *Atlantic* requires some learning. As one diver put it, "You have to push your face into the bottom" to see most of it.

Several local divers have impressive collections of artifacts from this wreck and many hope that they will find their way into a museum someday. The people of Terence Bay have been working to establish such a museum and interpretation centre to keep the memory of this sad and unnecessary wreck alive. Their efforts are beginning to bear fruit as knowledge of the wreck grows.

In late April of 2001, the *Titanic* Historical Society met in Halifax. The organization, which has more than five thousand members, is committed to recording and preserving the history of the White Star Line and its ships. In what was billed as the first public presentation on the loss of the *Atlantic*, Greg told the audience from around the world about this previously unknown wreck and its notorious history. The Canadian Broadcasting Corporation filmed part of the event for public presentation to the people of Canada. The story of the *Atlantic* is finally being told.

Diving the Havana and Gertrude de Costa

On the second level of the Maritime Museum of the Atlantic in Halifax stands a bust of Captain James Farquhar, who was a ship-owner, sealer, diver, and salvage master. Shortly after returning from a sealing voyage in the spring of 1906, he learned of the sinking of the schooner *Alexander R* in the shipping channel between Point Pleasant and McNab's Island. The 74-ton schooner, just a year old, was beating in the harbour in the early hours of April 2, 1906, when the Boston passenger steamer *Aranmore*, owned by the Plant Line and also coming in the harbour, struck her. In the twenty minutes that it took the vessel to sink, the crew of four was saved.

Smelling an opportunity, Farquhar went to work to recover the cargo of the *Alexander R*. He took his salvage steamer, *Havana,* to the spot where the schooner had gone down. But an unpleasant surprise was in store for the crew of the salvage vessel. At 10:30 p.m. on April 26, while anchored over the spot where the schooner had been sunk, the *Havana* was cut down by the SS *Strathcona* of the Halifax and Canso Steamship Co. and sent to the bottom. In this second sinking, the crew of twelve was also saved.

As far as I know, the *Alexander R* has never been found, but the *Havana* was located in the mid-1990s. Few people have dove this wreck so I was pleased to get an opportunity in the fall of 1998. With seven other divers from the Aqualantics Dive Club, we hired a boat and went to the spot. Within a short time, we picked up a large anomaly on the depth sounder. It would be a big rock or a wreck. Events would soon show it to be the wreck of the *Havana*.

The water was warm, which always makes for a pleasant dive. But it was also dark. Thirty metres (100 feet) down, we came upon the wreck, lying on its side. It was a spooky dive because of the darkness caused by the muddy bottom, which absorbs the light. The wreck was completely covered in large sea anemones. Among other interesting things, we saw a large pile of bullets, probably used to shoot seals, and several rifles encrusted together in a mass. At least two bottles were recovered, complete with contents, with the words "A. Keith and Sons, Brewers, Halifax NS" written on the corks. Alexander Keith started a brewery in Halifax in 1820; Labatt Breweries now owns the name under which it markets the popular brand.

After a two-hour surface interval, we were ready for another dive. The target this time was the wreck of another schooner, *Gertrude de Costa*. The 35-metre fishing schooner was struck aft of amidships on the starboard side by the ship *Island Connector*. The latter was coming from the Imperial Oil refinery heading outbound, while the *Gertrude de Costa* was coming in the harbour. The collision happened at 2 a.m. on March 18, 1950. The *Gertrude de Costa* was swept under the bow of the *Island Connector* and sank in the incredibly short space of fifteen to twenty seconds, according to the testimony of survivors. Eleven of her crew were lost.

Survivors from the *Gertrude de Costa* said the freighter struck after their young captain made a futile attempt to alter course and avoid the collision. The big steel freighter knifed into the frail wooden hull, completely wrecking the wheelhouse and blocking all means of escape for sleeping crewmembers on the starboard side.

These events had followed two days of tragedy and ill luck for the schooner on the high seas. As she neared home port and subsequent disaster her flag was already flying at half mast. Two days before, a member of the crew had lost his life when his dory capsized. The dead man's dory mate was hauled to safety, only to perish in the collision with the *Island Connector*. The day following that loss, the *Gertrude de Costa* collided with a dory from the Lunenburg vessel *Alcala*, throwing its two occupants into the water; they were quickly rescued by the schooner's crew. Poor fishing also jinxed the trip and the vessel put for port with her holds only half full of fish. Families came from Canso and Lunenburg, the lucky to be reunited with loved ones after nearly losing them; the less fortunate to identify the bodies of loved ones they had lost.

The *Gertrude de Costa* was owned by Lawrence Sweeney of Yarmouth and was operated out of Halifax by a subsidiary company of the Sweeney shipping company. (There is an excellent little museum about the Sweeney fishing and shipping interests in Yarmouth.) The *Island Connector* belonged to Clarke Steamship Company, Montreal.

The wreck lies on her starboard side with the bow pointing toward McNab's Island, thirty metres (100 feet) down. The scene is similar to the wreck of the *Havana*, except that it is in better condition. It, too, is spooky because of the darkness and the sad knowledge that eleven men lost their lives there not so very long ago.

We revisited the *Havana* several times and always found the dive to be very dark, often requiring lights. Each time we have done so, directly in the traffic lanes of so busy a harbour, I have always had in my mind that first the *Alexander R* was struck and sunk, then the *Havana* and then the *Gertrude de Costa*. It would indeed be ironic if our dive boat were to suffer the same fate.

The Hunt for the Odysseus

You never know what will wash up on the beach. During a walk on a lonely stretch of coastline near Halifax in the winter of 1999, Greg came across a piece of iron. It was puzzling that it should be there in the middle of nowhere. He reasoned that it must have come from a shipwreck. We talked about the find off and on for a year or so and concluded that, if it were from a wreck, it would be that of the World War II iron freighter *Odysseus*.

In the summer of 2000, we decided to take my small boat to the lonely and wild stretch of shore and do an exploration dive. We waited for what looked like a reasonable day and on a Saturday morning we loaded up my 4-metre aluminum boat and engine. The boat was small and light enough to carry over the rocks and launch at Ketch Harbour. After dragging it down over the bank and loading our dive gear aboard, we gingerly poked the boat's nose out of Ketch Harbour and into the open Atlantic. We had to stay a distance offshore in order to escape the groundswell. The restless Atlantic outside Halifax is never calm like a lake. The moving of the tides and the aftermath of two-day-old winds or a storm hundreds of kilometres away keep the waters constantly in motion. There is always surf on the shore, which means turbulence, so we stayed out for safety. We motored for about a kilometre outside the harbour, with Greg scrutinising the shore until he found the area.

The boat was too small to dive from so it would have to be beached, even though there was no beach – only rocks and cliffs. We knew it would be a challenge getting ashore so we planned how we would handle it. We found a safe looking nook between two rocks and carefully pointed the boat in its direction. As we got closer we could feel the ocean rising beneath us and were soon surfing. As we got to the shore, the waves started tossing us around and Greg had no option but to jump, fully clothed, into the water to hold the boat. Two or three waves broke over the stern and in a second we had fifteen centimetres of water aboard. I gave the order to push off, Greg clambered aboard and we knew there would be no getting ashore that day. After a couple of minutes of frantic bailing, we were stable again and spent the next hour peering down into the water trying to see something, anything that resembled a wreck. We saw nothing.

Greg continued to walk the shore in the winter of 2000-01, finding more clues and becoming more convinced that there was a wreck lying just offshore. On June 24, he and I walked to the place where he suspected it might lie. It was too far to carry our dive gear, so we decided that we would try our luck at snorkeling, since the water was not deep. We drove to the end of a narrow road which led to the shore and there we put our wetsuits on. The intent was to walk along the shore carrying only our masks and fins.

While we were suiting up, Greg began to reminisce about the search and discovery of the *Petra*, an iron-hulled barque of Norwegian registry, which was lost not far from this spot just before Christmas in 1910. En route from Rio de Janeiro to Halifax, she was driven ashore in a gale. The crew was saved thanks to the heroism of a local fisherman and his son, but the ship, aground on a reef, was destroyed. Through patient research, Greg deduced the location of the ship's remains and went searching with four other divers in 1984. Their efforts were rewarded as they found what was left of the ill-fated ship. Perhaps we might have similar luck today.

It was a very difficult walk of about a kilometre that required climbing up and down huge rocks or carefully walking across beaches of round, rolling granite rocks about the size of grapefruit. When we got to the suspected place, Greg produced the evidence: several large pieces of hull plating up in the woods, about sixty metres from the water and at least six metres above the high water mark. There was also a solid iron ball the size of a basketball with two rings to which a rope or chain could attach. I could not imagine what kind of storm would have hurled these heavy iron objects so far. What were they doing there if not from a wrecked ship?

In a few moments we were in the water, moving in a pre-arranged pattern to cover the area. While snorkeling, face down and straining to see the kelp-covered bottom six metres below, I heard a crash that made me whip my head up and frantically look around. I didn't know what to expect when I looked around, but all I saw was ocean, with rocks behind me. It was noisy from the waves breaking against the cliffs on the shore, but what my ears picked up was unlike any sound of water I had ever heard. I looked around and about twelve metres away, I saw the fluorescent red tip of Greg's snorkel, with an occasional jet of water shooting skywards as he expelled water from the waves breaking over his head. It appeared that he had heard nothing. I continued searching.

Then I saw below me a kelp-covered finger of something pointing up at me from the bottom. It rose about two metres and was perfectly straight – too straight and too slender to be a rock. It had to be an iron beam and if it was, then it must have come from a wreck. I signaled Greg, who came alongside, looked down and immediately dove, a difficult undertaking in a wetsuit with no weight belt. He struggled, but managed to get to it. He looked up at me and gave the two thumbs up signal. It was wreckage.

Then I heard the mysterious noise again. Greg had heard it as well. We bobbed on the surface, discussing what we had found and what we had just heard. I was scanning the surface, when I noticed a strange sight away to the south, behind Greg's shoulder. He knew I had seen something and he turned to look. About 150 metres behind him was a series of pipes sticking up out of the water like the snorkels of several submarines.

We set out to investigate. As we got closer to the mysterious object, sure enough, the strange sounds that I had heard became louder and more frequent, to the point that they were almost deafening. We soon saw that, just breaking the surface, was the giant boiler of a steamship. It was shaped like a tin can on its end, with the pipes we had seen sticking out of the top. Because the tide was falling, the flat top was just breaking the surface. On the portion that touched the bottom it was teetering as the waves moved it, creating the crashing and grinding noises. This, surely, was the wreck of the *Odysseus*.

More than a month would pass before we could return, but on August 4, 2001, we were finally going to dive the wreck. Again, we used my little 4-metre boat for the same reasons; it was light and portable and easy to launch in an area that had no boat launch. This time we were better prepared and more determined. In the early morning, ahead of the winds, with calm seas, wearing our wetsuits in case we swamped the boat again, we once more edged out of Ketch Harbour into the open Atlantic. We stayed offshore as before and took note of the rumbling of thunderstorms in the distance. A local breeze shivered across the surface and light rain started to fall. But it was warm and the conditions were acceptable, despite the imminent thunderstorm. We motored for about a kilometre and found the familiar rocks down which we had slithered like seals short weeks before.

We knew we faced the same challenge getting ashore so we planned how we would handle it. We found a likely looking target between two rocks and pointed the boat in its direction. As we got closer there was the familiar feel of the ocean rising beneath us and we were soon at the point of no return as the waves carried us in. At just the right moment Greg jumped over the side, found the bottom under his feet and held the boat from pounding onto the rocks. I quickly got the heavy gear such as tanks and weight belts out and we hauled the boat up on a convenient bed of kelp. As we did so, the inevitable wave came in over the stern and we had a boat half full of water but we held it in place as the wave receded and we managed to pull it a few feet farther along. We drained the water out and hauled the boat well away from the shore. How we were going to get it back in without swamping was another matter, but right now all we were thinking about was the dive that awaited us.

In a few moments we were in full gear and looking for a way to get into the water without taking too much of a pounding on the rocks. With just a suit and fins on it's fun slithering down over the slippery sluices that the ocean has worn in the rocks, but with tanks, buoyancy compensator and weight belt, things are much more complicated. We got in and were met by an extremely strong surge that was to accompany us throughout the dive and make the whole experience exhausting. The current would pull us a couple of metres in one direction and then send us right back. This is not uncommon when there are heavy seas rolling, but it caught us unawares because the surface conditions seemed so benign. The kelp was quite thick and it, of course, waved back and forth in the surge, so the effect made us dizzy in short order.

We headed in the direction of the first wreckage we had seen previously and soon located it. There were structural pieces and hull plating scattered among the boulders. We did a quick survey of the area but were soon forced to pack it in, because of the heavy surge that was wearing us out. The next weekend, five of us went to the site in a proper dive boat, a rigid-bottomed inflatable, and did a thorough investigation of the wreck. We found a second large boiler, along with a large debris field, but the shallow water (about 7 metres or 25 feet) and very rough bottom covered with large boulders had conspired to reduce the wreck to a mass of flattened and twisted iron. We thoroughly covered the site, noting areas of particular interest and then relaxed on the boat. After a second dive, we concluded that the wreck's significance was minimal and headed back to the port of Sambro, satisfied with an enjoyable day of diving.

But we remained curious about the large iron ball with the two loops, which had been washed upon the shore and had originally caught Greg's attention a couple of years before. Upon further investigation, we learned that on a ship it would be attached to the end of the anchor chain. In the event that all the anchor chain went out, it would keep the end of the chain from going out through the hawseholes in the ship's bow and being lost. It is called the "bitter end," and is, no doubt, the source of the term that refers to using up all of one's resources.

Harvesting the Sea
from Halifax Harbour

The first Europeans to use Halifax Harbour were people in search of safe anchorage for their fishing boats and a place to dry their fish. It was a convenient destination long before the founding of the town. In 1701, John Alden of Boston claimed to have been coming to Halifax for thirty years. Malachi Salter, an early settler and town leader, after whom a downtown street was named, was trading here five years before the founding of the town. There are many accounts of those who harvested the sea from Halifax Harbour.

Whaling

The first major industry in Dartmouth was a whaling company that came from Massachusetts and set up in Dartmouth Cove in 1785, providing employment for hundreds. It was started by Loyalists from Nantucket, who came north after the American War of Independence. Being non-violent Quakers, they were not fiercely loyal to the British crown, as were some Loyalists, but neither were they interested in the rebellion going on in the British colonies. However, it was just as difficult for them to remain neutral during such a period of tumult in the colonies. They managed to get by, but they ultimately ended up moving as much for business reasons as any other.

When the British imposed tariffs on American products, the oil, whalebone and other products they produced became expensive and uncompetitive in England. The practical response was to move to British territory, and Halifax Harbour was a logical choice.

About forty families moved in, building houses, a large wharf, warehouses and workshops in Dartmouth Cove. At least ten ships sailed from Dartmouth in 1786 to participate in the whale fishery, mostly in the southern Atlantic off the coasts of Africa and South America, but to other parts of the world as well. In the fall of 1786 they started exporting products such as whale oil and bone to the British market. They prospered and in 1790 needed twenty-eight vessels to handle the cargo, as the annual value of their hard work exceeded £20,000.

But with prosperity was bound to come the ire of the British, who liked to have colonies but only so long as they provided raw materials and did not compete with British industry. They decided that this fishery must be conducted from Britain and took steps to ensure that it happened. The Nantucket whalers were forced to move again. In 1792 six ships sailed out of Halifax Harbour to move the whaling community to Milford Haven in Wales.

Today there is no discernible underwater evidence of the presence of this company. If Dartmouth Cove holds any it is guarding it jealously under four or five metres of sludge from the years of heavy industrial and sewage dumping. In the summer of 1997, the sewage dumping was diverted so it became safe to enter the water – which Greg and I did the following winter – but we found the cove to be like a desert. The water is relatively clean now, but the bottom has been obliterated and will probably never recover without dredging.

There are the remains of a large wharf on the edge of the cove outside of the existing shipyard. Judging by its flattened appearance, this is an old and large dock, but there is no way of telling if it belonged to the Nantucket Whalers. Based on an 1898 photograph, I suspect it is Evans's wharf. Historians generally accept that the site of the Nantucket Whaling company lies beneath the shipyard itself. What does remain nearby, though, is the house of a member of the group. It dates from 1786, making it the second oldest residence on Halifax Harbour. It has been restored to its original condition in downtown Dartmouth and now serves as a museum about the Nantucket whalers. (The oldest house on the harbour, as already mentioned, is that of Joseph Scott, built in 1770 in the upper part of the Basin in present day Bedford. The oldest building is St. Paul's Anglican Church, built in 1750 and still housing a sizable congregation.)

Being a major seaport, Halifax continued to play a role in whaling. There are many individual stories of local people's involvement, such as that of 17-year-old Tom Creighton, who left Dartmouth on January 15, 1843, for a three-year whaling voyage to the Pacific aboard the barque *Rose*. He returned in March 1846, a notable achievement in itself. The vessel on which he sailed belonged to Samuel Cunard and this was her last voyage under Cunard's ownership. She returned with a full load.

Cunard had dreamed of building up a whaling fleet out of Halifax but it never came to be. He had started with the brig *Rachel*, which he had sent to the Strait of Belle Isle in 1817. This area is near the most northerly tip of Newfoundland and had been a traditional whaling area for three hundred years before that. On the bottom of the harbour at nearby Red Bay in Labrador sits what is purported to be the oldest shipwreck in North America, the *San Juan*. This Basque whaler sat at anchor fully loaded with whale oil and was about to depart for Europe in the autumn of 1565 when a hurricane came up and sank her, along with several other vessels. Like the *San Juan*, the *Rachel* was lost on the return voyage from the whaling grounds to Halifax, the difference being that the *Rachel* went down with a paltry ninety barrels of oil aboard.

I dove on the *San Juan* in 1996. Like other vessels of this period, it makes for a rather unspectacular dive, as all that remains visible is the stone she carried for ballast and some nondescript pieces of wood. From an archaeological point of view, the wreck is, of course, priceless because of what it can tell us about the ships and people of the period. Red Bay gets its name from the red clay tiles that abound on the beach and in the cove, left from the Spanish whaling station.

Sealing

In an all too common story, the Halifax *Evening Mail* reported in July 1908 that "The sealing schooner *Alice Gertrude* hauled into the wharf to-day. She lost three of her crew on April 11ᵗʰ in the South Atlantic. The boat in which they were never returned." The *Alice Gertrude* belonged to the Halifax Sealing Company and had been engaged in the seal hunt. The newspaper also noted that "This year there will be two schooners less in the fleet, as the *Edith R. Balcom* and the *Baden Powell* were wrecked last year."

Before the widespread use of petroleum products, whale and seal oil were the most common sources of oil for lighting and lubrication. Halifax sealers sailed to such far-flung places as Antarctica, as well as the Canadian Arctic, in what today is the equivalent of the search for oil.

For two hundred years the fishermen of Newfoundland hunted seals in March and April as millions of seals, swimming north, encountered the Arctic ice drifting south and stopped to give birth to their young. In the 1700s and first half of the nineteenth century, they engaged in this very dangerous industry from small sailing vessels such as schooners, dodging the massive ice floes and icebergs and often becoming stuck and crushed by the rafting ice. Although St. John's companies controlled the hunt almost exclusively, Nova Scotia vessels participated, especially in the Gulf of St. Lawrence. In March 1833 a Halifax newspaper reported that Halifax Harbour was frozen in and that two sealing vessels were unable to get out – not an auspicious start, considering that they were headed for conditions much worse than the harbour had to offer.

In the second half of the nineteenth century, the Newfoundland firms upgraded from sail and started using wooden steamers for the hunt. With thick hulls of oak and greenheart, sheathed in iron, they could ram their way into the ice packs in search of their valuable prey. Eventually these ships gave way, in turn, to iron-hulled steamers, like the *Florizel* and *Stephano*.

As time passed, Halifax companies became more and more involved in the hunt. In 1893, James Farquhar of Halifax purchased the SS *Newfoundland*, a wooden steamer that had provided mail service between Halifax and St. John's for several years. She had been built in Montreal in 1872 as a private yacht for Andrew Allan, the owner of the Allan Line, the main Canadian transatlantic steamship company whose ships called regularly at Halifax. To the dismay of the St. John's companies, Halifax now began to play a role in this large and lucrative harvest. By the 1950s Halifax had a bigger sealing fleet than all Newfoundland ports combined. In 1957, as the hunt declined, eleven Halifax ships "went to the ice" compared to only five Newfoundland vessels.

The SS *Newfoundland* had an interesting history. After using the vessel as a blockade-runner to Cuba during the Spanish-American War of 1898, during which time she was arrested by the Americans, Farquhar sold the ship to a St. John's firm in 1904. He later acquired the SS *Seal*. Ten years later, while engaged in the 1914 seal hunt, the *Newfoundland* gained notoriety when, because of a miscommunication with the SS *Stephano*, more than a hundred men and teenage boys were left on the ice for two nights during a blizzard. Seventy-seven of them drowned or froze to death because the captains of the two ships thought the other had picked them up.

Resting on the bottom of Halifax Harbour near downtown Dartmouth is a stout wooden ship, which has been ice strengthened and may well be a sealing vessel. It has an iron-clad bow and has two wooden fenders running along the sides of the vessel as protection, probably against ice. One source identifies it as the *Arctic Prince*, which sailed out of Halifax for Shaw Steamships in the 1940s and '50s. It supposedly sank at the dock in the late 1960s.

Fishing

For hundreds of years, the fishing industry of what is now eastern Canada produced salt fish for the Roman Catholics of Europe and also provided a cheap means of feeding the slaves in the Caribbean. Slaves worked on the sugar plantations that became such an important part of the economy of the New World. There grew up an extensive trade in salt fish from Nova Scotia and Newfoundland, with ships travelling south loaded with fish and returning with molasses and rum from the Caribbean. Old photographs of the Halifax waterfront show the names of fish exporters and salt merchants, such as George E. Boak, Nathaniel and Martin Smith and others.

Fishing and its supporting industries constitute the biggest component in the harvest of the ocean from Halifax Harbour. The Portuguese probably started the whole thing, with some reports dating their arrival as early as 1520. The whole east coast was a fishing gold mine, so Chebucto would have played an important part. French explorer, Samuel de Champlain's log book of 1607 mentions the fishermen of St. Malo naming the islands near Chebucto, which would indicate that there was activity at that time. There are other records of the fishing industry in the area, including a report by the French Governor Villebon that English fishermen had been ordered out of the harbour, which was French territory, in 1698. In the same year, the Sedentary Fishing Company of Acadia attempted to form an establishment, even bringing over a missionary from the Penobscot in what is modern day Maine.

The interesting name of this company might refer to the fact that it represented an attempt to set up a more permanent presence for fishing, as opposed to the migratory fishing industry that prevailed then. Fishermen came annually from Europe in the spring and went back in the fall, so perhaps the backers of this venture saw value in having a permanent establishment. However, when a M. Diereville visited in 1699 it was gone. More likely, though, the name derives from the general term the French used for their inshore fishing activities – "la peche sedentaire."

"A right sturdy set of men are the fishermen of Halifax!" gushed a 1903 publication extolling the virtues of Halifax and everything about the place. At that time, they sold their catch at the fish market next door to the ferry terminal in downtown Halifax, as generations of fishermen before them had done. What is now the famous Historic Properties area had fish flakes to dry cod in the early years after the founding of Halifax. Well into the twentieth century it was common to see fish drying in the sun atop downtown waterfront buildings.

Fishermen and their families normally resided near the outside of the harbour to be nearer the fishing grounds, but sometimes the fish were uncommonly cooperative. In 1827 an indignant ferry passenger wrote a letter to the *Acadian Recorder,* complaining that during a trip across the harbour there was a group of enthusiastic mackerel fishermen aboard, and that the deck had been "covered with fish and splitting and salting carried on with as much facility as at any fishing establishment along the shore."

Many residents still enjoy fishing for mackerel in the harbour. On any day in late summer, they are along the beaches, parking lots, and docks that skirt the harbour, catching the mackerel that come to Nova Scotia each summer.

The Halifax *Mail Star*, in an article on July 27, 1960, reported an uncommonly plentiful herring fishery in the harbour. Twenty-two fishing boats, each crewed by two men, were each taking up to 6,000 pounds (2,720 kilograms) of herring per day near the main Halifax docks. In addition, National Sea Products, a local fishing company of national significance, were taking 10,000 to 15,000 pounds (4,540 to 6,800 kilograms) of herring per day in front of their plant near Ocean Terminals. There was so much activity that the National Harbours Board became concerned that a fishing boat or two would get run over by a large ship coming or going in the harbour so the National Harbours Board police had to put a stop to it. No wonder we once thought the ocean's resources were limitless.

In the summer the harbour fills with herring boats, or seiners, following the schools of herring that come north along the coast. These vessels, which look like very large toy boats, measure their catch in hundreds of tons for a night's fishing. Unlike the boats in the summer of 1960, they fish outside the harbour but they often unload their catches at the Halifax docks for trucking to fish plants elsewhere in the province.

Fishermen harvest lobster from the harbour and Bedford Basin and, in season, they set herring nets in the harbour. Not all harbour fishing is done legally, however. Lobster poachers have a handy way of capturing and storing their clandestine catch. To keep their illegal delicacies away from prying eyes until the time comes to sell or consume them, they must keep the lobsters alive and what better place than leaving them in the ocean from whence they came? But if they mark the location of the booty with a buoy, they risk getting caught or having their treasure stolen. So they join two lobster traps with about sixty metres of rope, toss one trap over the side in about six metres (20 feet) of water, travel until the line comes tight and throw the other overboard.

Now the traps are on the bottom, sixty metres apart and joined by a piece of rope. There is no evidence that there are two traps illegally filling with lobsters on the bottom. And they will fill, for there are plenty of lobsters in the harbour. When the owner of the traps wants to retrieve some, he simply drags a hook from a boat along the bottom in the vicinity of the traps until he hooks the line. Up it comes, he takes out a few and returns the remainder to the ocean for safekeeping. He is unaware that, to a scuba diver, such activities are quite obvious and public.

Scuba diving has made harvesting of some ocean creatures much easier. It is illegal to dive for lobsters, but divers may obtain a license for scallops and other shellfish. Commercial harvesting of sea urchins is quite common as well; it is also difficult and uncomfortable. A sea urchin is a living pin cushion, a shellfish about five to seven sentimetres in diameter, round and somewhat flat, and covered in bristling spines. The Japanese love them and will pay a premium for them. Urchin divers work many hours a day in the dead of winter, picking them up one at a time with diving mitts that have been coated in liquid plastic. Otherwise, the spines would easily penetrate their mitts and go into the diver's fingers and hands. Once they have become embedded, they are practically impossible to remove. I have had my share of them in my fingers and knuckles.

Sea urchins eat kelp, which grows on bare rock — and they are ravenous. When an infestation of urchins begins to devour a kelp bed, it is reminiscent of a scene from a movie, where the young military recruit, having just arrived at boot camp, gets his hair cut by the unsympathetic barber. Picture a longhaired person after the barber has cut the first swathe across the top of his head and you are close to visualising a partially consumed kelp bed.

Not surprisingly, the harbour bottom has some things – such as fishing vessels – that the owners would have preferred had stayed on the surface. On March 16, 1929, the liner *Stavenjerfjord* rammed the National Fish Company trawler *Good Hope*, sending her to the bottom near McNab's Island. The crew got off safely.

As already noted, the crew of the fishing schooner *Gertrude de Costa* were not so fortunate. Rammed by the steel freighter *Island Connector* on March 18, 1950, between George's and McNab's Islands, eleven of her crew were lost, while six survived. On January 6, 1956, the *Cape Agulhas*, returning from a fishing trip, suffered a malfunction in her navigation systems and drove ashore in the fog at the harbour entrance. And four years later the *Gloucester*, with twenty tons of fish aboard, was lost in a storm while entering the harbour.

February of 1967 brought another misfortune with the loss of the *Cape Bonnie*. This 400-ton National Sea Products trawler was returning from the Grand Banks of Newfoundland after a successful fishing trip, when she got ensnarled in one of the winter storms that pound the area. Even modern facilities such as helicopter search and rescue could not save her crew of eighteen, all of whom perished.

On a happier and more colourful note, in August, the harbour is visited by an armada of more than a hundred tuna boats from as far away as Quebec. They come for what must be the shortest fishery of all. It is almost like a lottery, for the winners win big and there are lots of losers. Each boat is licensed to catch just two fish but they are very valuable fish. A single tuna brings from $10,000 to $20,000, so it can be a very lucrative trip out the harbour. Some of the boats are even trucked in, which is quite an undertaking for a 12-metre boat. The method of catching these 300- to 500-kilogram fish is very traditional – a rod and reel.

A harbour diver regularly witnesses the results of fishing activity. Many sites around the harbour have scallop shells, which stay around for many years, if not indefinitely. I have picked up the occasional sword from a swordfish. The innards of a catch of haddock or cod sometimes sit on the bottom of the surrounding fishing communities, but they do not last long. The local scavengers, such as gulls, crab and lobster usually consume every scrap. Nature ensures that everything is used.

Recovering the Lost

One of the most distressing jobs for those who sail from Halifax Harbour has been the unhappy task of searching for the dead and missing. While many Search and Rescue personnel have the arduous but ultimately fulfilling job of rescuing the living from danger and distress, others have the grim chore of recovering those who have died at sea. There have been many individual cases of ships and boats coming into the harbour carrying their dead, but two catastrophes stand out because of the sheer magnitude of the recovery effort. One of those catastrophes was a ship and the other was an airplane.

Royal Mail Steamer Titanic

White Star Line, the owners of the *Titanic*, chartered the cable-laying ship *MacKay-Bennett* to search for and recover the 1,523 bodies in the aftermath of the sinking after the great liner was lost on April 15, 1912. The *MacKay-Bennett* sailed under the command of Captain Lardner. Her crew recovered 306 bodies from the area of the wreck. One hundred and sixteen were buried at sea and the remaining 190 returned to Halifax for burial or forwarding to relatives. Later, another Halifax vessel, the *Minia,* joined the *MacKay-Bennett* in the effort.

The SS *Carpathia* had picked up 705 survivors and as she headed for Pier 54 in New York, to reunite them with their loved ones, the Commercial

Cable Company's vessel, with an all-volunteer crew, headed toward the scene of the disaster. She left Halifax in the evening of April 17, with a supply of ice, embalmer's tools, canvas and burlap bags, and a large number of coffins aboard. Along with the crew, there was an embalmer and a clergyman. Additional embalmers waited in Halifax for the returning cargo. As they approached the disaster site, a crewmember reported in his diary, "The Embalmer becomes more and more cheerful as we approach the scene of his future professional activities, to-morrow will be a good day for him."

The next day, he recorded, "The ocean is strewn with a litter of woodwork, chairs, and bodies. . . . The cutter lowered, and work commenced and kept up continuously all day, picking up bodies. Hauling the soaked remains in saturated clothing over the side of the cutter is no light task. Fifty-one we have taken on board to-day, two children, three women, and forty-six men, and still the sea seems strewn."

As each body came aboard, a member of the recovery team attached a square of canvas with a stenciled number on it. They placed personal property in canvas bags bearing the same number. For each body, a full description of the victim including hair colour, height, weight, age, birthmarks and scars were carefully entered into a ledger, on the corresponding page number. They hoped that this information would help in the identification of the remains.

As the search continued, the diary records, "All round is splintered woodwork, cabin fittings, mahogany fronts of drawers, carvings, all wrenched away from their fastenings, deck chairs, and then more bodies."

After the first day of the body retrieval, all assembled for burial services as thirty bodies wrapped in canvas and weighted down with iron weights were recommitted to the sea. For nearly an hour the doleful words "For as much as it hath pleased . . . we therefore commit his body to the deep," rang out. But not all went back to the ocean. The bodies of the first-class passengers were embalmed and each placed in a coffin for the return to Halifax. The names of the bodies that could be identified were wired ashore, while the others would require a family member or loved one to make a positive identification.

Captain Lardner had realized that there were more bodies than his ship could handle and contacted White Star Line. On April 21, the company's Halifax agents chartered the *Minia*, a cable ship owned by the Anglo-American Telegraph Company Ltd. Stocked with ice, iron weights, coffins, and embalming supplies, *Minia* left Halifax at midnight on April 22 to participate in the taxing venture.

By April 23, the *Mackay-Bennett* had eighty bodies on board. After fourteen straight hours of searching, the crew recovered an additional eighty-seven victims, which they then searched and tagged. Another burial took place that night and at noon on the 24th, seventy-seven more bodies followed the others. By Friday, April 26, with the *Minia's* assistance, the *Mackay-Bennett* had recovered a full load. Her crew had found 306 bodies, including the 116, which had been buried at sea. She returned to Halifax with 190 victims on board, 100 filling the available coffins and the rest in canvas bags on her deck. The *Minia* continued to search, but bad weather and high winds made retrieval of additional bodies almost impossible. The captain advised White Star Line that the gales had swept the remaining corpses into the Gulf Stream, where they would be dispersed. The *Minia* managed to recover fifteen more, which she brought in to Halifax on May 6.

As the *Minia* left for Halifax a third ship had been dispatched by the White Star Line to continue the search. The Canadian Ministry of Marine and Fisheries ship *Montmagny* arrived from Sorel, Quebec. She recovered only four additional corpses, which were landed at Louisbourg for shipment to Halifax. And then, in a final effort to locate additional victims, White Star chartered Bowring Brothers' sealing vessel *Algerine*, which departed from St. John's, Newfoundland, one day later. She found one body, that of saloon steward James McGrady.

The *Mackay-Bennett* arrived back in Halifax on April 30, 1912. The crew off-loaded the bodies at the Naval Dockyard, north coaling wharf number 4, the area that we would dive so thoroughly during the winter of 2001. Close by were twenty sailors from the Canadian warship *Niobe*. Their job was to keep the curious and photographers from interfering with the dismal task. The first of the bodies to be taken ashore were the *Titanic's* crew members for whom there had been no embalming or other preparation, followed by the second- and third-class passengers wrapped in canvas bags. Then came the embalmed bodies of the first-class passengers, each in a coffin. Horse-drawn hearses pulled up to take one of the wrapped bodies or coffins, which was then transported to the Mayflower Curling Rink in Halifax. The curling rink had been turned into a temporary morgue for the embalming, storage and identification of the bodies.

Then came the job of burying the victims. The burials began on Friday, May 3, 1912. During the days of denominational cemeteries, it was difficult to determine where they should be buried. Some of the decisions were based solely on the victim's last name. Catholics were to be buried at the Mount Olivet Cemetery, Jews at the Baron de Hirsch Cemetery and the remainder at the non-sectarian Fairview Cemetery. At Fairview, 121 were laid to rest in long trenches. Individual graves were dug at the other two cemeteries where an additional twenty-nine were interred.

The six weeks of searching by four ships had recovered 328 bodies, of which 119 had been buried at sea. Of the 209 returned to Halifax, 59 were claimed and shipped to other locations, and 150 were buried in the city's three cemeteries. Of all the 328 recovered, 128 remained unidentified.

Swissair Flight 111

At 10:30 on the evening of Wednesday, September 2, 1998, the people living around St. Margaret's Bay near Halifax had their normal late summer tranquility shattered by a loud bang over the ocean. They knew something terrible had happened. Instinctively, fishermen took to their boats and headed in the direction from which the noise had come.

Air traffic controllers in Moncton had already suspected the worst. They had been guiding Swissair Flight 111 towards an emergency landing at Halifax International Airport when they lost all contact with the airplane. The pilot of the New York-Geneva flight had radioed that there was smoke in the cockpit and declared an emergency. He needed to get rid of some fuel before attempting a landing, so the air traffic control centre ordered the pilot to jettison his fuel over the water. Six minutes after losing contact with Moncton, with a complete loss of electrical power and a suspected fire in the cockpit, the MD-11 aircraft flew into the water eight kilometres from the popular and picturesque village of Peggy's Cove.

The plane and its contents, including 229 passengers and crew, shattered upon impact with the water and settled to the bottom, fifty-five metres (180 feet) below. The search for survivors began almost immediately but it became painfully apparent that there were none. Debris from the crash was spread over a huge area and, over the weeks following, covered dozens of square kilometres. Thousands of volunteers and RCMP, Armed Forces, Coast Guard and other personnel went to work, picking up debris, dealing with victims' families, and trying to locate the crash site.

The Navy brought in remote controlled underwater cameras, and sonar sensing equipment, and they finally pinpointed where the shattered aircraft lay on the bottom. Then, to the more than two hundred divers of the Navy, Army and RCMP, fell the tiring and dangerous task of recovering the wreckage. While one group of divers scoured the shallow waters of the bay, more than a hundred Canadian and US Navy divers engaged in the deep-water recovery of human remains and anything else associated with the aircraft and its occupants. Day after day, week after week, they tramped the bottom of St. Margaret's Bay. It was hurricane season farther south and that meant bad weather along the Nova Scotia coast. In addition to the physical dangers, the work was tedious and emotionally draining.

A 150-person team worked to identify the remains. Under the direction of the Chief Medical Examiner of the Province of Nova Scotia, Dr. John Butt, they worked in B Hanger at the Shearwater air base near the shores of the harbour, south of Dartmouth and overlooking the place where the CSS *Tallahassee* had slipped out of the harbour and eluded the Union gunboats 135 years earlier. There were more than three hundred people involved in the process. The destruction of the aircraft had been so complete that human remains had to be measured, not by the body but by the kilogram. Two weeks after the crash, they had recovered two tons of remains, but had succeeded in identifying only eight persons by using dental records and fingerprints. A week later, they had identified twenty-three people. Two hundred soldiers, after three weeks of combing the beaches of the mainland and islands of St. Margaret's Bay, determined there was nothing else to find and they returned to their base in New Brunswick, leaving 1,200 military personnel still engaged in search and recovery.

By October 20, six weeks after the crash, they had succeeded in identifying the one hundredth victim. The remains were so badly damaged that investigators were now using DNA sampling and matching it with living relatives. Only one person had been visually identified by family members. The recovery team had brought up less than 30 percent of the aircraft more than a month and a half after the crash.

What remained of the aircraft at the wreck site below the water was described as looking the way a floor would look with a smashed pop bottle spread around. The big jet was broken so badly that one diver likened handling the small, sharp pieces to dealing with handfuls of razor blades. A few round windows were the only indication that the jumbled mass was an airplane. Early in the process, a diver nearly lost his life when he tore his suit and was obliged to make a rapid ascent out of the frigid waters.

This was the most technical of diving, with twenty-eight minutes of bottom time, followed by nearly three hours in a decompression chamber. The divers reverted to a more modern version of the traditional "hard hat" method of diving, wearing helmets – made of fiberglass instead of brass – with full face masks, breathing gasses supplied from the surface, shod in weighted boots and walking around on the bottom like the first divers had done two centuries before. Each wore a video camera on his helmet, attached to monitors aboard a ship on the surface. Investigators watching on the screen could direct the diver to specific areas of the wreckage.

The Halifax *Mail Star* reported on October 1, "Divers described a surreal underwater world of jagged twisted metal stacked five metres high and dotted with human remains. Their lifelines, which ran along the ocean bottom and up to the surface 19 stories above, were constantly getting snagged in wreckage, threatening their every movement." By October 27, 60 percent of Swissair Flight 111 had been recovered. The recovery team switched from the barge they had been using and started using a scallop dragger because the rest of the wreckage was so small.

By Christmas, all 229 victims had been identified and there were five hundred boxes of wreckage at Shearwater holding more than a million pieces. But there was still 19,000 kilograms on the bottom. The recovery process was maddeningly slow. Forty percent of the front fuselage, essential for the investigation, was still underwater. In early November, the RCMP had cautiously declared the recovery process almost complete, but ten months later, it would still be going on.

Early in September of 1999, the remains of the victims were finally laid to rest, near the crash site in Bayswater, across the bay from Peggy's Cove. In the meantime, researchers were conducting tests of the aircraft's wiring and the insulation that covered it, suspecting that the insulation had deteriorated to the point that current flowing through the wires had arced and caused the fire that the pilots had reported sixteen minutes before the crash occurred. With 90 percent of the aircraft recovered, workers began to use a suction dredge to vacuum up the last bits of the plane, in their efforts to piece the puzzle together and determine what had happened. They were still missing important parts from the nose and cockpit. It would take only a few days to scrounge these last important pieces.

The work and dedication of the people involved received official recognition. On the following May 28, Government House in Ottawa announced that six navy divers had been awarded the Meritorious Service Medal for their contribution to the investigation and recovery. The citation noted, "With the ever-present danger of entrapment and life-threatening damage to their equipment, these divers were directly responsible for the recovery of the flight data recorder and of human remains from the seabed."

And on the anniversary of the crash, many family members of the victims returned to the place that had taken their loved ones from them in an effort to bring closure to the sad affair. Unidentified remains were laid to rest at Bayswater and the Prime Minister of Canada hosted a reception with family members and those who had participated in the search and had helped in other ways.

At the beginning of November 1999, the recovery effort was finally completed. The police and other investigative agencies lifted the exclusion order on the area and permitted fishermen and other boaters back into the area in St. Margaret's Bay that had been sealed off for fourteen months.

Within days of the crash, the speculating had begun as to what might have been the cause. The focus went to the hundreds of kilometres of wiring in the aircraft and especially the wiring in the cockpit. The pilots had reported smoke; smoke comes from fire; a fire would probably be electrical in nature. The first bits and pieces that came up indicated that some wiring insulation was chafed and cracked. Investigators found that the insulation used inside the bulkheads of the aircraft to keep heat in and noise out had spread the fire. This did not point to the cause of the fire, but it was a contributing factor in the disaster. On August 11, 1999, the US Federal Aviation Administration ordered the replacement of metallized mylar insulation blankets on 693 US-registered aircraft. The order would ripple to a total of 1,230 aircraft worldwide. It had helped spread the fire, but what had caused the fire? They still struggled to find the answer.

On December 15, 1999, the Transportation Safety Board of Canada officially announced that it had completed the recovery effort. The suction dredge had brought the total recovered portion of the aircraft to 98 percent, adding significantly to the estimated one million pieces already being sifted through. They did not say if the aircraft's valuables had been recovered. Among other things, there had been bank notes, watches, jewelry, and a kilogram of diamonds worth millions of dollars. More than a year later, when an insurance company applied to undertake a recovery effort to search for the lost diamonds, the government of Nova Scotia turned them down on the grounds that the area was a burial site.

The search for the cause went on, as patient investigators pieced the aircraft together and used computer modeling to simulate the workings of the tiny electronic components and wires and to re-enact how the events of that evening had unfolded to lead to the tragedy. It was clear from the recovered pieces that there had been a fire and its effects had been worked out, leading ultimately to the electrical failure that had brought the plane down.

Regulatory agencies around the world had learned from the crash and had implemented the safety recommendations in the bulletins issued as a result of the investigation. At the beginning of December 2000, the Transportation Safety Board of Canada released a third set of recommendations stemming from its investigations. But, after two years of searching, they were still unable to say definitively why the fire had started. They did know that it had originated in the dropped ceiling above the cockpit.

For the first time, the TSB admitted that, even though the investigation had cost $50 to $60 million and was the most complex ever undertaken in the history of aviation, there was a good chance that they would never know for sure what had caused the fire. There was evidence of arcing among the wires above the cockpit; the wiring insulation was suspect and they knew that the insulation had

The Swissair 111 memorial. The Peggy's Cove lighthouse is on the left.

spread the fire, but that was it. In the TSB's words, "It has not been determined whether the arcing was the origin of the heat that resulted in the fire or whether arcing was the secondary result of a fire that originated elsewhere and damaged the wiring insulation to the extent that arcing occurred."

On December 15, the investigators left what turned out to be more than two million pieces of wreckage at the Shearwater hangar and took the next phase of the probe to Ottawa. Three months later, in March of 2001, they announced that the final report was being drafted. It was now two and a half years since the crash had occurred. The final report would be a composite of eleven separate reports created by different groups and submitted to a team of senior investigators for analysis. It was evident to those following the investigation that there would be no further revelations.

The world moved on, new crises filled the news and the sad story of Swissair Flight 111 drifted into memory. It has now become another of the stories of local folklore and takes its place with the many incidents of human loss along the Nova Scotia coast. On any day, at the Swissair Flight 111 Memorial near Peggy's Cove, you can see a person or two, more when the weather is fine, solemnly looking out to sea as generations of Nova Scotians have done before them, over the horizon from where so many have never returned.

The Harbour as Heritage

Underwater heritage sites are a rich source of information about the past. A shipwreck can represent the next best thing to a moment in time, and the information about its structure, cargo and the personal effects of the passengers and crew can embody a wealth of information about the period in which the ship sailed. A harbour such as Halifax is a collection of such wreck sites, along with other sites similar to what would be found on the land. There are isolated wrecks in the approaches and outer harbour, but there are also significant areas associated with historic sites on land, such as the Dockyard. Some have been lost, but there is still much to learn about underwater Halifax.

There are very few such places in the world and probably none in Canada. Yes, there are older harbours but most have been dredged as the ships using them have gotten bigger and bigger. There is no other harbour in Canada with such magnitude, great depth and long history. The depth is a key factor because up to now, there has been no need to dredge most of the harbour — it is deep enough, which means that the harbour floor has been left relatively untouched. Many areas of the harbour floor contain artifacts from the first visitors to Halifax.

Filling in the Harbour

When Halifax native Sara Yablon lived at the corner of Inglis and Barrington Streets in the early 1920s, there were three large houses on the harbour side of Barrington Street. Behind those houses was the harbour. She and her friends crossed Barrington Street, passed the houses and went swimming at the beach nearby. The houses are gone now, replaced by a shopping centre. If Sara went in the same direction to swim today, she would first have to cross dozens of railway tracks, walk past the railway station, maybe dodge a train or two, cross a busy street, duck through a large freight shed, and walk across a dock before leaping into the water six metres below.

In this area the harbour has been filled in on an impressive scale.

When Sara finally got to the water, if she did not encounter an ocean liner from Bermuda or the Bahamas, she would be swimming in water that is close to fifteen metres (50 feet) deep at the Ocean Terminals docks. These docks opened in 1928, in what was the second of four major harbour developments that have occurred in the race to keep Halifax in the forefront as a major Canadian port of entry. The first was the building of the Deep Water Terminus in the late 1800s in an area now occupied by the Halifax Dockyard. The third was the opening in the 1960s of the Halterm container terminals near Point Pleasant, and the fourth was the construction of the Fairview Cove container terminals in the Bedford Basin during the 1980s and 1990s.

If Sara were a scuba diver and she descended to the bottom below the Ocean Terminals, she would be greeted by a somewhat spooky scenario. It always seems to be dingy below these docks, with their immense granite blocks rising from the bottom and going up out of sight, gloomy and showing the havoc that big ships and their tugs wreak on the bottom. From here the *Queen Mary* and the *Queen Elizabeth* took troops to Europe in World War II and brought at least some of them back, along with their new brides.

And the world's biggest ships also delivered 1.25 million new Canadians to Pier 21 between 1928 and 1971.

This area begins at the site of John E. Fairbanks's wharf inside George's Island. In 1816 he and James McNab of McNab's Island formed Fairbanks and McNab's, dealers in "Port and Madeira, Teas, Sugar, Coffee, Chocolate, Spices." It extends more than 1.5 kilometres towards Point Pleasant and has been filled out from shore close to 400 metres. From the end of the filled-in area the docks push out even farther into the harbour. Parents of one hundred years ago would have been alarmed to see their 12- or 13-year-old this far from shore in a rowboat. Halterm occupies an area of twenty-four hectares (60 acres). The other container terminal in Fairview Cove is more than twenty-one hectares (52 acres).

On the bottom, the evidence of enormous power is overwhelming. Modern ocean liners are equipped with bow thrusters, huge propellors that are used to push the front of the ship from the dock. In the process a massive volume of water strikes the dock face and is deflected downward, pounding the bottom with enough force to dig great trenches, exposing dishes, cabling, machine gun ammunition, and the usual assortment of rusting objects that have gone over the sides of the ships that have tied up here. Globules of oil have collected in the bottom of some of these trenches and fill many of the containers such as the bottles that inhabit the site.

As with most ports, mankind's influence in Halifax is everywhere to be seen. If you walked around the harbour from Point Pleasant to Eastern Passage, you would be hard pressed to set your foot upon original shoreline. There is very little natural shore left in this area, for it has been covered by stone, concrete and asphalt. In some places on the waterfront, the drop from the water's surface to the harbour bottom is equivalent to the height of a seven-story building. Yet the slope of the bottom is very gradual, which indicates that it has been filled out a long distance from the original shore.

A 1913 report to the Department of Railways and Canals of Canada made sweeping recommendations for the development of the harbour to accommodate the next generation of shipping. As a result, the shore from George's Island to Point Pleasant was changed forever. The report called for the building of a system of large world-class docks to accommodate the bigger ships that were coming on stream. The message was the same one we hear today and applies to all ports involved in the cutthroat business of transportation: upgrade the port facilities or lose out to New York, Philadelphia, Montreal, and other such places. Those ports would make the same recommendations to compete against Halifax.

Author Archibald MacMechan wrote enthusiastically about the 1913 proposals, stating: "A plot of ground, nearly two miles long, extending from Point Pleasant Park to the heart of Irishtown, will be needed for the improvements proposed. Many buildings must be razed to make room for the huge new stations. Steele's Pond, where young Halifax skated and played hockey, must be filled in. Green Bank, where happy bathers took refreshing plunges in the brine on summer mornings, must be merged in flat level piers. Dynamite and steam shovels will plow their way through the fine old properties bordering the Arm – which is a pity. But you cannot make an omelet without breaking eggs."

As a consequence of the report, the mammoth development took place in the very centre of what would have become a major recreational area of the harbour. A huge swath got cut through the rock across peninsular Halifax to bring double track railway service to the new docks. The millions of tons of stone that came out of the ground went to build the Ocean Terminals docks. By 1930 the world's biggest ocean liners were tying up at the modern facilities in fifteen metres (50 feet) of water, close to a kilometre from the original shoreline. A further development took place in 1970 with the building of the Halterm Container Terminal next door to Ocean Terminals, covering up the historic anchorage of the Royal Nova Scotia Yacht Squadron, the oldest yacht club in North America.

This type of activity is not unusual in ports like Halifax. Major buildings and parking lots downtown sit on what was once water. The original shoreline of downtown Halifax was gone by 1830 and, in some ways, has been moving out into the harbour ever since. As recently as 1998, the parking lot adjacent to The Brewery Market has been extended farther out into the harbour. In July 1998, municipal council approved the building of two new apartment buildings on Lower Water Street to exist entirely on land that came from filling in the harbour and covering up where ships had docked for two hundred years. This came about in spite of a 1975 recommendation that this area, where the famous schooner, *Bluenose II*, docked in the 1960s, be used for small scale recreational boating.

Travel around the harbour and it is the same story. Dredging here, filling in there, blasting somewhere else. We think of history as having happened on land and have preserved places where our history has been made. But we need to change our thinking and realize how much history has happened in the waters of Halifax Harbour, think of it as a single location and stop the heedless changes without prior consideration of the history that we are destroying.

Across the harbour from Halifax is the old Dartmouth City Hall and adjacent buildings, a park and parking lot. All are on reclaimed land that housed shipyards and other industries associated with the history of the harbour. Next door to it, the Coast Guard base sits on an area that was filled in during the 1980s. This could well be the area where, in 1758, General Wolfe trained his troops in preparation for the assault of Louisbourg and Quebec, which changed the character of Canada forever. Many old paintings and sketches show the Royal Navy ships anchored off this area, sheltered from southeasterly storms by the Dartmouth shore.

The bottom in this area shows evidence of very early visitors from the mid to late 1700s. At least it did until the early 1990s, when bulldozers moved in and dropped several thousand tons of rock to make still another parking lot and storage yard. This intrusion altered the characteristics of the shoreline and the ensuing changes in the current flow resulted in the formation of great dunes of silt on the bottom.

Let's return to the Halifax shore. In the last century, the biggest commercial ships landed in the area between Historic Properties and the Naval Dockyard. The Intercolonial Railway built the Deep Water Terminus to handle cargoes from up to twelve steamships at a time. The early Cunard ships landed in this area, as did the Furness Line. All those docks are gone now, in part to allow the Naval Dockyard to expand during wartime. Later, additional filling-in took place and more of the area was buried to make way for a casino in 1998.

The Cunard location could have been made into a national historic site. If we try to remember those people who have made contributions that changed our lives, Samuel Cunard surely was one such person. But the present geography of the area displays no memory of this pioneer of modern travel. His stone buildings, his large house on Brunswick Street and the docks are gone without so much as a plaque. In fact, most Canadians who have heard of Samuel Cunard probably think he was an Englishman.

When you travel along the Bedford highway from Halifax to Bedford the railway tracks are on your right. They skirt around the western side of the Bedford Basin all the way through Bedford, from where they head north to Truro. At some places along this road, the water is twelve metres (40 feet) deep, indicating that these tracks, too, run over an area that was once occupied by water.

They cover some very historic shoreline, for the western side of the Basin around Birch Cove is generally recognized as the area where Duc d'Anville's fleet spent several weeks in the fall of 1746. It is believed that as many as 1,100 men died and were buried in this area. But the railway and the highway cover it all and even the cove has yet another parking lot intruding on its waters. Many local historians fear that sunken ships from the d'Anville expedition have been buried here.

At one end of this historic area is Fairview Cove, tucked in behind the Halifax peninsula. It was filled in during the 1980s to build a container terminal. At the other end is the Round House, a tiny reminder of Governor John Wentworth's estate that housed the father of yet unborn Queen Victoria when he resided in Halifax. The Duke of Kent was commander of the British Army forces in Nova Scotia at the beginning of the nineteenth century.

Another big change has occurred on the inner part of the Bedford Basin, where, in a manner of speaking, the harbour has had to move over to provide for a shopping centre, movie threatres, roads, apartment buildings, a sewer treatment plant, houses, parkland, and more railway tracks. Kilometres of waterfront have been lost to the bulldozer and pile driver, without any apparent thought being given to what was being buried under the tons of stone and gravel.

There's more. On the Dartmouth side of the Narrows and visible from practically anywhere in the city are the three towers of the Tuft's Cove power generating station. To accommodate its fuel tanks and storage yard, much of the cove had to be filled in. It covers the remains of a traditional Mi'kmaq living area. Those of its inhabitants who were not killed in the 1917 explosion moved away shortly after the explosion took place.

Farther out the harbour, south of the MacDonald Bridge, a long stone structure that looks somewhat like a dock sticks out, cutting the Dartmouth shore in two. The way this dock's demise was handled is a good example of the lack of regard for the harbour. It was called the Dartmouth Pier where Canadian Northern Steamships, Canadian National Steamships and others tied up, often loading lumber. When it began to deteriorate the most expedient but environmentally foolish of all alternatives was taken. Instead of removing the dilapidated quay, the authorities dumped rock on top of it. Now we have a long and useless finger of boulders protruding into nowhere. Judging by the bottom in this area, it was dredged as part of the pier's construction early in the twentieth century.

Eastern Passage runs between Lawlor Island and the mainland and was once wide and deep enough to accommodate a sixty-one metre (200-foot) ship. Today it can barely accommodate a fishing boat because so much sand and mud have accumulated between the island and the mainland. During the Wars, piles were driven and a net placed across the passage as part of the system of defences against German submarines, which lurked at the harbour gates, hoping to get loose in the harbour. Certainly, under the circumstances, nobody would argue against such measures. After the war, though, the nets were removed but the wooden posts are still there, collecting mud and sand from the tides. Today only the narrowest of passages keeps Lawlor Island adrift from the mainland.

Farther out the harbour from Eastern Passage, human activity has had a different effect. This case involves the removal of material from the harbour. After the great explosion of 1917, the government created the Halifax

Relief Commission to rebuild the devastated north end of Halifax. The building material they chose for housing construction was a type of concrete called hydrostone. These hydrostone blocks were made from sand and gravel from Barrie's Beach, which stretched between Lawlor and Devil's Islands. So big was the undertaking that a railway line was built to the area to transport concrete products for years afterwards. The sandy beach that was a favourite bathing area for local people is only a memory now.

We cannot expect to live in the harbour without influencing it. But during these times, when as a nation we are becoming more conscious of our environment and more carefully considering the long-term impact of changes that we make, it is time that we stopped filling in so much and forever changing the natural beauty of Halifax Harbour. During the 1960s, it appeared that Halifax had turned its back on the ocean and had forgotten its historic waterfront. But the waterfront has undergone a facelift and it has gone from being a place to avoid to being an award-winning place to be. Because the harbour is so big and comes under so many conflicting jurisdictions and interests, there are many parts that are suffering and the historical heritage is slowly eroding.

Working with the Museum

And somewhere out there lie the remains of the French ships from 1746. They may already be buried but we really don't know. Because these ships are so historically important, the archaeological community and the Maritime Museum of the Atlantic have lived with the fear that they will be found and picked over before a professional excavation can be done. But the Museum and those who administer the laws that try to protect heritage sites have found themselves in a dilemma. They must contend with budget cuts that prevent them from doing any significant study, while, at the same time, there is a growing community of divers, who could provide a ready resource for checking out potentially historic sites. Some in the sport diving community would like to work closer with the Museum in what they see as a mutually beneficial relationship.

After many years of distrust, the first attempts at a dialogue between divers and those tasked with preserving historical sites started crawling slowly in the late 1990s. There had been sporadic attempts at cooperation in the past. I was part of a dive group that checked out Brister's wrecking yard in the Arm, looking for the remains of the World War I submarine that was scrapped there. Then, in the fall of 1998, the Narrows north of the MacKay Bridge was being dredged to make the shipping channel deeper. Greg challenged the Maritime Museum to sponsor a dive trip to recover artifacts before the dredging company destroyed the bottom in the area. They responded and a group of us presented them with a large assortment of crockery, china, bottles and other items up to two hundred years old, opening their eyes to the extent to which the harbour bottom is littered with items of historical interest. For us, it was a rare opportunity to have access to their expertise in identifying china, stoneware and the colours and patterns used throughout the decades. Everybody got something.

In the summer of 1999, the Museum made an exception to a long-standing policy of refusing to accept artifacts that had not been recovered using accepted archaeological methods. A member of our dive club had died in a non-diving related accident. Many years previously, he had recovered the bell from the SS *City of Vienna*, which had sunk on the Sambro Ledges in the summer of 1918. The Museum accepted the bell from his estate and placed it on display, to the great delight of many local divers. This was followed, in the summer of 2001, by the opening of a shipwreck exhibit at the Maritime Museum. It told about Nova Scotia's wrecks and attempted to include the role – both positive and negative – that sport scuba divers have played in the discovery of shipwrecks and the recovery of artifacts.

Policing the underwater heritage is next to impossible. The debate is very complex and, like all such issues, will never be resolved to the satisfaction of everyone. First of all, there are apparently conflicting laws pertaining to the recovery of artifacts from the ocean. Then, there are many diverse groups, especially among those with the easiest access to the resource – the diving community. They represent all parts of the spectrum, from those who can barely tolerate having a diver swim by a shipwreck to those who advocate a free-for-all. The community includes those who have completely different motives for entering the water, from salvage operators, to treasure hunters, to souvenir collectors, to photographers.

The debate simmers quietly – and boils over occasionally – within this small community of people. The public at large neither understands the issues nor seems to care a great deal about them. The financial rewards are not significant in the grand scheme of things, but the "resource," as some refer to our underwater heritage, is being slowly eroded and can never be replaced.

Select Bibliography

Akins, Thomas Beamish, *History of Halifax City*, Halifax, Nova Scotia Historical Society Collections, 1895.

Andrieux, J.P., *East Coast Panorama*, W.F. Rainnie, Lincoln, Ontario, 1984.

Appleton, Thomas E., *Ravenscrag The Allan Royal Mail Line*, McClelland and Stewart, Toronto, 1974.

Appleton, Thomas E., *Usque Ad Mare A History of the Canadian Coast Guard and Marine Services*, The Queen's Printer, Ottawa, 1969.

Barratt, Glynn R. deV., "Halifax through Russian Eyes: Fleet Lieutenant Iurii Lisianskii's Notes of 1794-96", *Nova Scotia Historical Review*, Vol. 12, No. 2, 1992.

Barron, David N., *Atlantic Diver Guide, Volume II Nova Scotia*, Atlantic Diver, St. John's, 1988.

Blakeley, Phyllis R., *Glimpses of Halifax 1867-1900*, Public Archives of Nova Scotia, Halifax, 1949.

Brown, Joe, *The View From Here, An Oral History of Eastern Passage, 1864-1945*, Shearwater Development Corp., Dartmouth, 1998.

Borrett, William C., *East Coast Port and Other Tales Told Under the Old Town Clock*, Imperial Publishing Company, Halifax, 1944.

Borrett, William C., *Down East*, Imperial Publishing Company, Halifax, 1945.

Brown, Cassie, *A Winter's Tale*, Doubleday Canada Ltd., Toronto, 1976.

Byers, Mary and McBurney, Margaret, *Atlantic Hearth Early Homes and Families of Nova Scotia*, Toronto, University of Toronto Press, 1994.

Candow, James E., *Of Men and Seals: A History of the Newfoundland Seal Hunt*, Canadian Parks Service, Ottawa 1989.

Cahill, Robert Ellis, *New England's Naughty Navy*, Chandler-Smith Publishing House Collectibles Classics, Number 11, 1987.

Chapman, Harry, *White Shirts with Blue Collars, Industry in Dartmouth, Nova Scotia 1785–1995*, The Dartmouth Historical Association, 1995.

Churchill, Winston Spencer, *A History of the English Speaking Peoples*, Dodd, Mead & Company, New York, 1958.

Cochkanoff, Greg, *Shipwrecks of Halifax Harbour*, Chart, 1987.

Cochkanoff, Greg, *Steamship China From Halifax Harbour*, Unpublished.

Collins, Louis W., *In Halifax Town*, Halcraft Printing Limited, Halifax, 1975.

Cousteau, J.Y., *The Silent World*, Harper and Row, New York, 1953.

Cowie, Frederick W., *Report to the Honourable Frank Cochrane on Halifax Harbour*, Dept. of Railways and Canals of Canada, 1913.

Cranston, Robert D., *75th Anniversary Naval Service of Canada A Pictorial History*, The 75th Anniversary Publishing Company, Halifax, 1985.

Crawford, Steve, *Battleships and Carriers*, Prospero Books, Toronto, 1999.

Davis, Stephen A, Cottreau, Catherine, Niven, Laird, *Artifacts from 18th Century Halifax*, St. Mary's University Archaeology Laboratory, 1987.

Doane, Benjamin, *Following the Sea*, Nimbus Publishing Limited and the Nova Scotia Museum, Halifax, 1987.

Duivenvoorden Mitic, Trudy and Leblanc, J.P., *Pier 21, The Gateway that Changed Canada*, Lancelot Press, Hantsport, N.S., 1988.

Earle, Sylvia A. and Giddings, Al, *Exploring the Deep Frontier*, National Geographic Society, Washington.

England, George Allan, *The Greatest Hunt in the World*, Tundra Books, Montreal, 1969.

Elliot, Shirley B., *Nova Scotia Book of Days*, N.S. Communications & Information Centre, 1979.

Erhard, Nancie, *First in Its Class The Story of the Royal Nova Scotia Yacht Squadron*, Nimbus Publishing Limited, Halifax, 1986.

Erickson, Paul A., *Halifax's Other Hill*, St. Mary's University Dept of Anthropology, Halifax, 1984.

Erickson, Paul A., *Halifax's North End*, Lancelot Press.

Farquhar, James A., *Farquhar's Luck*, Petheric Press Limited, Halifax 1980.

Feltham, John, *Sealing Steamers*, Harry Cuff Publications, St. John's, 1995.

Fingard, Judith, *The Dark Side of Life in Victorian Halifax,* Pottersfield Press, 1989.

Fingard, Judith, Guildford, Janet and Sutherland, David, *Halifax, the First 250 Years*, Formac Publishing Company Limited, Halifax, 1999.

German, Tony, *The Sea is at Our Gates*, McClelland and Stewart, Toronto, 1990.

Grant, Kay, *Samuel Cunard Pioneer of the Atlantic Steamship*, Abelard-Schuman, London, 1967.

Gurney Smith, Marilyn, *The King's Yard, An Illustrated History of the Halifax Dockyard*, Nimbus Publishing, Halifax, 1985.

Gwyn, Julian, "French and British Naval Power at the Two Sieges of Louisbourg: 1745 and 1758", *Nova Scotia Historical Review*, Vol. 10, No. 2, 1990.

Hanington, Felicity, *The Lady Boats*, Canadian Marine Transportation Centre, Dalhousie University, Halifax, 1980.

Harris, W.F. , *Nova Scotia's Pops & Crocks*, Private Publishing, Halifax, 1977.

Harvey, D.C., "Halifax 1749–1949", *Canadian Geographical Journal*, January, 1949.

Hatchard, Keith A., *The Two Atlantics*, Nimbus Publishing Limited, Halifax, 1981.

Hopkins, H.W., *City Atlas of Halifax*, Provincial Surveying and Publishing Co., Halifax, 1878.

Horwood, Harold, *Bartlett The Great Explorer*, Doubleday Canada Ltd., Toronto, 1989.

Johnston, A.J.B. *Defending Halifax: Ordnance, 1825-1906*, Minister of Supply and Services Canada, 1981.

Keir, David, *The Bowring Story*, William Clowes and Sons Ltd., Beccles, 1962.

Kemp, Peter, *The Oxford Companion to Ships and the Sea*, Oxford University Press, 1976.

Kemp, Peter, *The History of Ships,* Orbus Publishing, London, 1978.

Ketchum, William C. Jr., *A Treasury of American Bottles*, A & W Visual Library, New York, 1975.

Kimber, Stephen, *Net Profits The Story of National Sea*, Nimbus Publishing Limited, Halifax, 1989.

Kitz, Janet, Survivors, *Children of the Halifax Explosion*, Nimbus Publishing, Halifax, 1992.

Leacock, Stephen, *Canada and the Sea*, Alvah M. Beatty Publications (1943) Limited, Montreal, 1944.

MacLaren, George, *Nova Scotia Glass*, Nova Scotia Museum 1974.

MacMechan, Archibald, *Old Province Tales,* McClelland & Stewart, Toronto, 1924.

Major, Marjorie, "Melville Island", *Nova Scotia Historical Quarterly,* September, 1974, Petheric Press, Halifax, 1974.

Martin, John Patrick, *The Story of Dartmouth*, Privately published, Dartmouth, 1957.

Martin, John Patrick, *Our Storied Harbour: The Haven of Halifax where D'Anville's Fleet Assembled two centuries ago*, Tourist and Travel Department of the City of Halifax, 1948.

Marx, Robert F., *Into the Deep The History of Man's Underwater Exploration*, VAN Nostrand Reinhold Company, New York, 1978.

Maxtone-Graham, John, *Cunard 150 Glorious Years*, David & Charles, London, 1989.

McLennan, J.S., *Louisbourg From its Foundation to its Fall*, The Book Room Limited, Halifax, 1979.

Metson, Graham, *An East Coast Port...Halifax at War 1939-1945*, McGraw-Hill Ryerson Limited, Toronto, 1981.

Millington, Elsie, *Purcell's Cove,* Copyright 2000 by Elsie Millington.

Molloy, David J., *The First Landfall Historic Lighthouses of Newfoundland and Labrador*, Breakwater, St. John's, 1994.

Mosher, Edith, *From Howe to Now*, Lancelot Press, Hantsport, 1981.

Nolan, Brian & Street, Brian Jeffrey, *Champagne Navy*, Random House, Toronto, 1991.

O'Brien, David, *HX72: The First Convoy to Die*, Nimbus Publishing Limited, Halifax, 1999.

Pacey, Elizabeth, *Georgian Halifax*, Lancelot Press, Hantsport, 1987.

Parkman, Francis, *A Half-Century of Conflict*, George N. Morang and Co. Limited, Toronto, 1906.

Payzant, Joan M., *Halifax, Cornerstone of Canada*, Windsor Publications Inc., 1985.

Pritchard, James, *Anatomy of a Naval Disaster*, Montreal, McGill-Queen's University Press, 1995.

Pullen, H.F., "The Attempted Mutiny Onboard HM Sloop Columbine on 1 August, 1809," *Nova Scotia Historical Quarterly,* December, 1978, Petheric Press, Halifax, 1978.

Pullen, H.F., "The Loss of HMS Tribune off Herring Cove, 23 November, 1797," *Nova Scotia Historical Quarterly*, December, 1975, Petheric Press, Halifax, 1975.

Regan, John W., *Sketches and Traditions of the Northwest Arm*, Hounslow Press, 1908.

Ryan, Shannon, *Seals and Sealers*, Breakwater Books, St. John's, 1987.

Ryan, Shannon, *The Ice Hunters*, Breakwater Books, St. John's, 1994.

Sandberg. L. Anders and Deborah Trask, "The Glass-Workers of Pictou County, Nova Scotia 1881-1917," *Nova Scotia Historical Review*, Vol. 11, No. 2, 1991.

Sawyer, L.A. and Mitchell, W.H., *The Liberty Ships*, Lloyds of London Press, New York, 1970.

Seary, V.P., *The Romance of the Maritime Provinces*, W.J. Gage and Co. Ltd Toronto, 1931.

Snow, Edward Rowe, *Secrets of the North Atlantic Islands*, Doss, Mead and Company, New York, 1950.

Soucoup, Dan, *Edwardian Halifax,* Nimbus Publishing Ltd., Halifax, 1998.

Stephens, David E., *Lighthouses of Nova Scotia*, Lancelot Press, Hantsport, Nova Scotia, 1973.

Stephens, David E., *W.D. Lawrence, The Man and the Ship*, Lancelot Press, Hantsport, N.S., 1994.

Sweeney, Susie and Gail Anne McNeil, *Disasters at Sea*, Copyright Tony Cranston, 1986.

Tolson, Elsie Churchill, *The Captain, the Colonel and Me*, Fort Sackville Press, Bedford, N.S. , 1979.

Van der Vat, Dan, *The Atlantic Campaign*, Harper & Row, New York, 1988.

Vienneau, Azor, *The Bottle Collector,* Petheric Press 1969.

Wright, Barry, *Embossed Soda Water Bottles of Nova Scotia*, Stuart Graphics and Printing, 1991.

Zinck, Jack, *Shipwrecks of Nova Scotia*, Lancelot Press, Hantsport, 1977.

Discover McNab's Island, Friends of McNab's Island Society, Halifax, 1995.

Halifax, Nova Scotia and its Attractions, Howard and Kutsche, Publishers, c. 1904.

Halifax *Mail-Star*, April 15, 1989.

Halifax Waterfront Urban Design Criteria, General Urban Systems Corp., Halifax, 1975.

Nova Scotian, March, 7, 1987.

The Angus L. MacDonald Bridge, Snider & D'Eon, Halifax, 1954.

The Halifax Herald, March 2, 3, 1906; July 7, 21, 22, 23, 1943.

The Halifax Herald, March and April, 1905.

The Making of the Viking, pamphlet, Newfoundland Historic Parks Association.

The Master Plan for the City of Halifax, Civic Planning Commission, Nov. 16, 1945.

The Morning Chronicle, March and April, 1905.

Report of Investigation Into The Cause Of The Wreck Of The Steamship "Atlantic." Halifax, N.S., April 18th, 1873.